100 MATHS LESSONS

conditions

INGS – READ CAREFULLY BEFORE USING

accompanying material belongs to Scholastic Limited. All

ompanying materials, the software may not be copied,
d, or exported in whole or in part or in any manner or form
nauthorised use or activities are prohibited and may give

he context for which it was intended in *100 Maths Lessons*
or purchasing institution that has purchased the book and
rs only and not for users from any lending service. Any
ght and that of other rights holders.

oduction. However, we recommend that you run virus-
olastic Ltd cannot accept any responsibility for any loss,
at may occur as a result of using either the CD-ROM or the
data held on it.

IF YOU ACCEPT THE ABOVE CONDITIONS YOU MAY PROCEED TO USE THE CD-ROM.

Recommended system requirements:

- Windows: XP (Service Pack 3), Vista (Service Pack 2), Windows 7 or Windows 8 with 2.33GHz processor
- Mac: OS 10.6 to 10.8 with Intel Core™ Duo processor
- 1GB RAM (recommended)
- 1024 x 768 Screen resolution
- CD-ROM drive (24x speed recommended)
- 16-bit sound card
- Adobe Reader (version 9 recommended for Mac users)
- Broadband internet connections (for installation and updates)

For all technical support queries, please phone Scholastic Customer Services on 0845 6039091.

SCHOLASTIC

Book End, Range Road, Witney, Oxfordshire, OX29 0YD
www.scholastic.co.uk

© 2014, Scholastic Ltd

23456789 4567890123

British Library Cataloguing-in-Publication Data
A catalogue record for this book is available from the
British Library.

ISBN 978-1407-127722-9
Printed by Bell & Bain Ltd, Glasgow

Due to the nature of the web we cannot guarantee the
content or links of any site mentioned. We strongly
recommend that teachers check websites before using
them in the classroom.

Author
Caroline Clissold

Series Editor
Ann Montague-Smith

Editorial team
Emily Jefferson, Jenny Wilcox, Lucy Tritton and
Margaret Eaton

Cover Design
Andrea Lewis

Design Team
Sarah Garbett, Shelley Best and Andrea Lewis

CD-ROM development
Hannah Barnett, Phil Crothers, MWA Technologies
Private Ltd

Typesetting and illustrations
Ricky Capanni, International Book Management

MIX
Paper from
responsible sources
FSC® C007785

Contents

Introduction

About the series

The *100 Maths Lessons* series is designed to meet the requirements of the 2014 National Curriculum, Mathematics Programme of Study. There are six books in the series for Years 1–6, and each book contains lesson plans, resources and ideas matched to the new curriculum. These six titles – along with the accompanying *100 Maths Planning Guide* – have been carefully structured to ensure that a progressive and appropriate school curriculum can be planned and taught throughout the primary years.

About the 2014 Curriculum

The curriculum documentation for Mathematics provides a yearly programme for Years 1 to 6 (ages 5 to 11).

The new curriculum goes further than the previous version with times tables to 12 x 12 by Year 4, an early introduction to long division and an increasingly complex understanding of fractions and decimals. The new curriculum also has a strong focus on varied and frequent practice of the fundamentals of maths – mastery of number facts and times tables should be developed throughout the primary phase.

There is a renewed emphasis on reasoning mathematically and solving problems with particular emphasis on multi-step problems and problems in the context of measurement, money and time. The main coverage of the use and application of mathematics however can be found in the aims of the curriculum:

> *The National Curriculum for Mathematics aims to ensure that all pupils:*
> - *become fluent in the fundamentals of mathematics, including through varied and frequent practice with increasingly complex problems over time, so that pupils have conceptual understanding and are able to recall and apply their knowledge rapidly and accurately to problems*
> - *reason mathematically by following a line of enquiry, conjecturing relationships and generalisations, and developing an argument, justification or proof using mathematical language*
> - *can solve problems by applying their mathematics to a variety of routine and non-routine problems with increasing sophistication, including breaking down problems into a series of simpler steps and persevering in seeking solutions.*

Terminology

The curriculum terminology has changed; the main terms used are:
- **Domains:** The main areas of mathematical study, such as Number and Geometry.
- **Topics:** These are identified in each weekly planning grid and drill the domains down into 'Place value', 'Addition and subtraction' and so on.
- **Curriculum objectives:** These are the statutory programme of study statements or objectives.

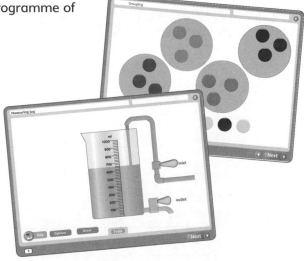

■SCHOLASTIC

About the book

This book is divided by term and week with a summary heading giving an indication of the week's work. Each week follows the same structure:

Weekly overview

At the start of each week you will find a summary of what is covered, which includes:

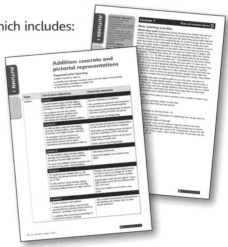

- **Expected prior learning:** What the children are expected to know before starting the work in the chapter.
- **Weekly planning grid:** A lesson-by-lesson breakdown of the coverage of each week – by 'topic', 'curriculum objectives' and 'expected outcomes'.
- **Oral and mental starters:** Suggested activities that might be used from the bank of starters that follow each half-term's lessons.
- **Overview of progression:** A brief explanation of the expected progress that children should make through each week's work.
- **Watch out for:** Possible mathematical misconceptions with ideas for addressing them.
- **Creative context:** How the week's work could link to other 2014 curriculum areas.
- **Vocabulary:** Key vocabulary to introduce or consolidate. (Words in bold also appear in the glossary, see CD-ROM notes on page 7.)
- **Preparation/You will need:** A full list of resources required from book and CD, as well as any general class resources requiring preparation. (A full resource list is given on page 256.)
- **Further practice:** Ideas for consolidating learning using additional resources or practical activities.

Lessons

Each half term contains six weeks' work. Each week contains five lessons. Each lesson includes the following:

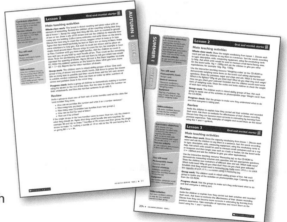

- **Curriculum objectives:** A list of the relevant objectives from the Programme of Study.
- **Success criteria:** Expected outcomes for the lesson written as 'can do' statements.
- **You will need:** List of required resources.
- **Whole-class work:** Ideas for working together as a class.
- **Group/Paired/Independent work:** Teaching notes for paired, groups or independent work.
- **Differentiation:** Ideas to support children who are not sufficiently fluent with concepts or to challenge children to apply their understanding (see 2014 National Curriculum aims for further information on the approach to differentiation).
- **Progress check:** 'Mini-plenaries' to enable teachers to check progress throughout the lesson.
- **Review:** Opportunity to reflect on children's learning, and address any misconceptions.

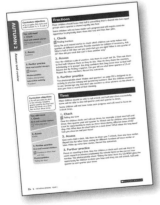

Assess and review

At the end of each half term are activities designed to assess children's understanding or mastery of key curriculum objectives. These can be conducted during the half-term's lessons or at the end, in an 'assess and review week'.

There are four curriculum objectives covered in each half–term. Each section includes ideas to:

- Check progress using appropriate starter activities.
- Assess children's learning using a mix of activities, problems and puzzles.
- Provide further practice activities to consolidate their understanding.

Oral and mental starter activities

In each half term a bank of oral and mental starters is provided. These can be used flexibly to address particular requirements, though suggestions are made within each weekly overview as to which starters might be used across a week's lessons. Each starter includes modelled teacher questions to probe children's ability to recall facts, rehearse strategies or apply learning.

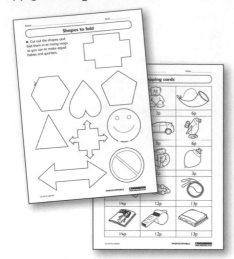

Photocopiable pages

At the end of each chapter, you will find a bank of photocopiable pages linked to the 'Assess and review' section. These sheets offer an 'I can...' statement at the bottom to allow self-assessment of pupil progress towards a particular curriculum objective. Ask the children to colour in the traffic lights next to each statement green, amber or red to reflect their confidence with the objective. There is also space for comments. Additional sheets, linked to the lessons, can be found on the CD-ROM (see page 7 for further information).

Equipment list

This provides an overview of all of the classroom resources required to teach each year's lessons. The resources are broken down by mathematics topic.

Vocabulary list

This provides a list of all key vocabulary to introduce or consolidate over the course of the year. Words appearing in bold type also appear in the glossary and can be found on the CD-ROM (see page 7 for further information).

▲▮SCHOLASTIC

About the CD-ROM

The CD-ROM contains:

- Printable versions of the photocopiable sheets from the book and additional photocopiable sheets as referenced in the lesson plans.
- Interactive activities for children to complete or to use on the whiteboard.
- Interactive teaching resources such as 'Number grids' and 'Pattern squares', designed to support whole–class teaching.
- Printable versions of the lesson plans and the oral and mental starters.
- Digital versions of the lesson plans with the relevant resources linked to them.

Getting started

- Put the CD-ROM into your CD-ROM drive.
  - For Windows users, the install wizard should autorun, if it fails to do so then navigate to your CD-ROM drive. Then follow the installation process.
  - For Mac users, copy the disk image file to your hard drive. After it has finished copying, double-click it to mount the disk image. Navigate to the mounted disk image and run the installer. After installation the disk image can be unmounted and the DMG can be deleted from the hard drive.
- To complete the installation of the program, you need to open the program and click 'Update' in the pop-up. **NB** This CD-ROM is web-enabled and the content needs to be downloaded from the internet to your hard-drive to populate the CD-ROM with the relevant resources. A web connection is only required on first use, after which you will be able to use the CD–ROM without any connection. If at any point any content is updated you will receive a pop-up message upon start–up when you are next connected to the web. You will then have the option to update the content as required.

Navigating the CD-ROM

There are two options to navigate the CD-ROM, either as a Child or as a Teacher.

Child

- Click on the 'Child' button on the first menu screen. In the second menu click on the relevant year group (please note only the books installed on the machine or network will be accessible. You can also rename year groups to match your school's naming conventions via Teacher > Settings > Rename Books area.)
- A list of interactive activities will be displayed; children need to locate the correct class or year group and click 'Go' to launch.
- There is the opportunity to print or save a PDF of the results of each activity on completion.

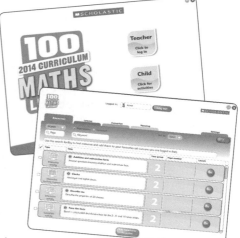

Teacher

- Click on the 'Teacher' button on the first menu screen and you will be taken to a menu showing which of the *100 Maths Lessons* titles you have purchased. From here, you can also access the credits and 'Getting started' information
- To enter the product, click 'Next' in the bottom right of the screen.
- You can then enter a password (the password is: login).
- On first use:
  - Enter as a Guest by clicking on the 'Guest' button.
  - If desired, create a profile for yourself by adding your name to the list of users. Profiles allow you to save favourites and to specify which year group(s) you wish to be able to view.
  - Go to 'Settings' to create a profile for yourself – click 'Add user' and enter your name. Then choose the year groups you wish to have access to (you can return to this screen to change this at any time). Click on 'Login' at the top of the screen to re-enter the CD-ROM with your new profile.
- On subsequent uses you can then select your name from the drop-down list.
- The 'Guest' option will always be available if you, or a colleague, prefer to use this.
- When you have set up your profile, you can then save activities or lessons in 'Favourites'.

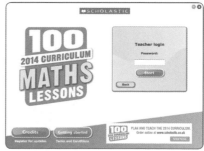

For more information about how to use the CD-ROM, please refer to the 'Help' file which can be found in the teacher area of the CD-ROM. It is displayed as a red button with a question mark inside, on the right-hand side of the screen just underneath the 'Settings' tab.

Number and place value: two-digit numbers

Expected prior learning

Children should be able to:

- count forwards or backwards in ones from any given number
- identify and represent numbers using concrete objects and pictorial representations including a number line
- read and write numbers from 1 to 20 in digits and words.

Topic	Curriculum objectives	Expected outcomes
Number and place value	**Lesson 1**	
	To count in steps of 2, 3, and 5 from 0, and in tens from any number, forward and backward. To identify, represent and estimate numbers using different representations, including the number line.	Count in steps of two, five and ten. Count objects in twos, fives and tens using objects and drawings.
	Lesson 2	
	To recognise the place value of each digit in a two-digit number (tens, ones).	Explain place value of each digit and partition into tens and ones.
	Lesson 3	
	To compare and order numbers from 0 up to 100; use <, > and = signs.	Order numbers on a number line from 0 to 50. Compare numbers using < and > signs.
	Lesson 4	
	To read and write numbers to at least 100 in numerals and in words.	Read and write numbers to 100 in numerals. Read and write numbers to 20 in words.
	Lesson 5	
	To use place value and number facts to solve problems.	Use place value to solve simple oral problems.

Preparation

Lesson 1: copy and laminate number cards to 50 enough for small group use; prepare groups of these cards for use with pairs of children ensuring that there is a mix of numbers in each, e.g. five of each 10, 20, 30, 40 and 50 number cards

Lesson 2: copy and laminate partitioning cards for tens and ones, enough for pairs of children; place up to 150 straws into a container, one container for each group

Lesson 3: make bundles of 46 and 72 straws tied with elastic bands

Lesson 5: prepare some additional simple problems to ask the class

Copy and laminate digit cards so that there are enough for one set per child and number cards to 50 enough for small group use

You will need

Photocopiable sheets
'Signs and symbols (1)'

General resources
'Number words'; 'Arrow cards'; '0–100 number cards'; 'Hundred square'; interactive teaching resource 'Number line'

Equipment
Interlocking cubes; straws; elastic bands; partitioning cards; individual whiteboards

Further practice

Photocopiable sheets
'Signs and symbols (2)'

Oral and mental starters suggested for week 1

See bank of starters on page 44. Oral and mental starters are also on the CD-ROM.

1 Ordering and writing two-digit numbers

2 Counting in tens

3 Partitioning

4 What's my value?

Overview of progression

During this week the children will extend their knowledge of counting from counting in ones to steps of two, five and ten. They will partition numbers into tens and ones and explain the place value of each number. They will extend their knowledge of reading and writing numbers to 100 in numerals and consolidate writing the numbers from 1 to 20 in words. Fluency in counting and understanding place value are pre-requisites for the work covered in the next few weeks on addition, subtraction, multiplication and division.

Watch out for

Some children may still be at the stage of counting in ones. Provide them with a numbered number line 0–20 so that they can use their finger to physically count in jumps of two. If they need help counting in fives, provide clock faces with 5-minute intervals written to 60 and for counting in tens, a 100 square.

Creative context

Encourage the children to say and make up number rhymes for counting in two, five and ten. Ask the children to spot numbers in the environment and make lists of these to share in class, such as house numbers, bus numbers, numbers on birthday cards.

Vocabulary

continue, count in fives, count in tens, count in twos, **multiple of**, one-digit number, partitioning, place, **place value**, predict, represents, sequence, stands for, 'teens' number, tens digit, two-digit number

Curriculum objectives
● To count in steps of 2, 3, and 5 from 0, and in tens from any number, forward and backward.
● To identify, represent and estimate numbers using different representations.

Success criteria
● I can count in steps of two, and ten forwards and backwards.
● I can count up to 50 objects in twos and tens and represent them using drawings.

You will need
General resources
'0–100 number cards'
Equipment
Interlocking cubes; individual whiteboards

Differentiation
Less confident learners
Give children number cards 10–20.
More confident learners
Ask the children to consider which is the most efficient way to count objects and why. Encourage them to think of times when counting groups of ten may work (large quantities) and occasions when counting in twos might be best (small quantities, below 10 or 20).

Main teaching activities

Whole-class work: Explain that this lesson is about counting. Ask the children what they think you mean by counting. They may suggest counting numbers in order or counting objects. Agree that both are correct but that today they will focus on counting objects in an efficient way. Put a pile of 20 interlocking cubes on the table. Invite a volunteer to count the cubes individually. *Do you think there is a quicker way of doing this?* If necessary, remind them of the starter activity when they counted in twos. Together count the cubes in twos. As you do, place two cubes at a time in separate groups. Invite children to lock each set of cubes together and stand them on the table as small towers. Check to ensure that there are still 20 cubes by pointing at the pairs and counting: *2, 4, 6, 8, 10, 12, 14, 16, 18, 20.* Say: *If we forget how many there are we can count again in twos which will be quicker than counting in ones.*

Repeat for other numbers of cubes. Each time ask the children to look at the cubes and estimate how many they think there are first and to write their estimate on their whiteboards. Once they have counted ask them to compare with their estimates.

Group work: Ask the children to work in pairs within groups of about four. Using their set of number cards, one pair hands a card to the other pair and vice versa. They then count out the appropriate interlocking cubes. They count in twos, placing two cubes together on each count. If they have an odd number the final cube stays on its own. Once they have counted out their cubes to make the number, the other pair checks by counting the small 'towers' in twos. They draw the total in their own way and write it as a number in figures.

Progress check: Invite groups to show the class what they have been doing. Ask the class to check by counting in twos.

Group work: Repeat the initial activity but, this time, ask the children to count out groups of ten and group them in 'towers'. Any that don't make ten are left on the table to count separately onto the final tens number. Again they draw the result in their own way and write the total number in figures.

Review

Together consider a pile of around 50 cubes.

- *What is the most efficient method of counting this pile of cubes?*
- *Let's count them in twos and then in tens. Which is better?*

Establish that for a higher quantity counting in groups of tens might be more efficient as if someone loses count they can count in the piles of tens instead of beginning at 1.

Curriculum objectives
• To recognise the place value of each digit in a two-digit number (tens, ones).

Success criteria
• I can explain the place value of each digit in a two-digit number up to 50.
• I can partition numbers into tens and ones.

You will need

Equipment
Straws; small elastic bands; partitioning cards

Differentiation
If the less confident learners find the activity sheet difficult to understand, let the more confident children in the mixed-ability groups explain what they have to do.

Lesson 2   Oral and mental starter 2

Main teaching activities

Whole-class work: This lesson is about counting and place value with an element of estimating. Remind the children of the counting activity that they did in lesson 1. Recap the ways that they did this, such as counted in groups of two or ten. Show a pile of 83 straws and ask the children to estimate how many you are holding. Collect some estimates and write these on the board. Discuss the best way to count the straws, suggest either in twos or in tens. Agree that tens would probably be best as there are so many of them. Invite some volunteers to help you. Ask each to count ten straws and to place an elastic band around them. Discuss ways to count the ten, for example in twos or fives. Continue until you have eight bundles. Ask the children to count in tens with you as you hold up each bundle of ten. Then count on the remaining three. Show the partitioning cards and ask them to tell you which two would represent the quantity of straws. Agree 80 and 3. Put them together to make 83. Write this addition sentence on the board to show what you have done: 80 + 3 = 83. Repeat this for other numbers of straws.

Group work: The children work in mixed-ability groups of four. Give each group a tray of straws and some elastic bands. Ask them to group the straws into as many tens as possible and then record these and the left over straws in suitable number sentences. Then ask them to make up other numbers of straws and partition these in the same way.

Progress check: Invite a group of children to demonstrate making a number using the straws to the rest of the class. Ask the class to write the number on their whiteboards, and then the number sentence to go with it.

Review

Invite a group to share one of their sets of straw bundles and tell the class the total number they have.

- *How can we partition this number and write it as a number sentence?*
- *How many tens are there?*
- *How many ones?* [Combine two bundles from two groups.]
- *How can we find the total of these?*
- *How can it be written?*

If the single straws in the two bundles come to more than ten, ask the children what they should do. Agree that they could bundle the tens together, for example 36 and 48, to make 7 bundles of 70 straws and then group the single straws to make 14, making a bundle of 10 to add to the 70 and leaving the 4, so giving 80 + 4 = 84.

Curriculum objectives
• To compare and order numbers from 0 up to 100; use <, > and = signs.

Success criteria
• I can order numbers on a number line from 0 to 50.
• I can compare numbers using < and > signs.

You will need

Photocopiable sheets
'Which number goes where?'

General resources
Interactive teaching resource 'Number line'

Equipment
Straw bundles; elastic bands

Differentiation

Less confident learners
Ask children to make teens numbers. The start and end numbers of their number lines should be 10 and 20.

More confident learners
Ask children to make up an additional two numbers to go in between those initially positioned.

Curriculum objectives
• To compare and order numbers from 0 up to 100; use <, > and = signs.
• To read and write numbers to at least 100 in numerals and in words.

Success criteria
• I can read and write numbers to 100 in numerals.
• I can read and write numbers to 20 in words.

You will need

Photocopiable sheets
'Signs and symbols (1)'

General resources
'Number words'

Equipment
Individual whiteboards

Differentiation

Less confident learners
Give the children the words for numbers up to 20.

More confident learners
Invite the children to make up two number statements for the = symbol.

Lesson 3 — Oral and mental starter 3

Main teaching activities

Whole-class work: Show bundles of 46 and 72 straws. Together count the tens bundles and single straws. The children write the two numbers on their whiteboards and partition them, such as 46 = 40 + 6. Show the interactive teaching resource 'Number line' on the CD-ROM and invite a volunteer to position the numbers onto it as accurately as they can. Discuss which is the smallest and how they know. Draw these symbols on the board: <, >. Emphasise that these show whether a number is greater or less than another. Write 4 < ? on the board and ask them to give you some numbers that could replace the question mark. Repeat for 4 > ? Ask the children to write two number sentences for 46 and 72 using these symbols (46 < 72, 72 > 46). Repeat with other two-digit numbers.

Independent work: Distribute photocopiable page 'Which number goes where?' from the CD-ROM and demonstrate the example shown. Ask children to use the numbers they made when carrying out the activity and use them to write < and > number sentences.

Progress check: Ask individuals to share their numbers with the class. Ask: *Which is the greatest number? Which is the smallest? Who can write a number sentence using two of the numbers and >?*

Review

Ask: *What two symbols have you been working with? Give an example of how to use them.* Write this on the board: 34 < 30. *Is this correct? How can we make it correct without swapping the numbers or the symbol?* Agree that they could take something away from the first number or add something to the second, for example 34 − 10 < 30, 34 < 30 + 10. Explore other examples.

Lesson 4 — Oral and mental starter 1

Main teaching activities

Whole-class work: Write four numbers on the board up to 20, for example 8, 19, 4 and 15. Ask the children to tell you the order of these from smallest to largest, explaining how they know, for example that 19 is larger than 15 (the tens are the same so look at the ones, 9 is larger than 5, so 19 must be larger than 15). Ask them to make up some statements using these numbers and the < and > symbols on their whiteboards. Invite individuals to share their ideas. Write 19 = 15. *Is this correct? Why not?* Agree that it isn't because whatever is on one side of = must equal what is on the other. *How can we make this correct?* Take feedback of their ideas, for example 19 = 15 + 4, 19 + 1 = 15 + 5. Explore other examples. *How else can we write numbers?* (In words.) Ask the children to help you write some of the numbers used in words.

Independent work: Distribute photocopiable page 'Signs and symbols (1)' from the CD-ROM and explain what the children need to do. Ask the children to focus on making statements using the <, > and = signs. Give some examples.

Progress check: Invite volunteers to share some of the statements they have made using the <, > and = symbols. Ask the rest of the class to say whether they are correct.

Review

Invite children to share the statements they made up using the equals sign.
- *16 = 7: how can we make this correct?*
- *What about this: 3 = 12?*

Curriculum objectives
● To use place value and number facts to solve problems.

Success criteria
● I can solve word problems using place value.

You will need

Equipment
Individual whiteboards

Differentiation

Less confident learners
Ask an adult to work with the group to help them to invent their word problem and to find the answer.

More confident learners
Challenge the children to invent four word problems.

Lesson 5   Oral and mental starter 4

Main teaching activities

Whole-class work: Explain that in this lesson you will be giving the children some problems to solve. Begin with this example: *Sam scored 25 points in the game, Saffir scored 27. Who scored more points?* Invite the children to decide the relevant information and what they need to do with it to solve the problem. Agree they need to decide which of the numbers is greater. Discuss what is meant by *more* in this context. *How do you know which number is more?* Agree that they need to examine the place value of each to be sure: both have two tens so they need to look at the ones. 7 is higher than 4 so 27 is more.

Repeat for other problems using two and three two-digit numbers such as: *Paul had 78p, Lauren had 64p and Stephen had 68p. Who has the least money?* It is important to discuss the vocabulary of more and less and most and least to ensure the children have a good understanding of these words (most and least is used to compare more than two things).

Paired work: Ask the children to work in pairs. They invent two word problems one that involves more/most and one that involves less/least. They then write them on their whiteboards for other pairs to solve. Ask each pair to discuss their answers and their reasoning.

Progress check: Invite volunteers to read out their word problems and ask the rest of the class to solve them explaining exactly how they know the number is either more/most or less/least.

● *What are you thinking about when you answer these problems?*
Agree children need to think about place value.

Review

Invite pairs of children to share one of their word problems for others to solve. Extend their thinking by asking how they think that they can use place value and partitioning to help them solve a problem such as *Tommy has 35 sweets and Tamira has 22. How many do they have altogether?* Take feedback from their thinking. Agree that they could partition both numbers and add the tens first then the ones. Tell the children that they will be working on this in future lessons.

Addition: concrete and pictorial representations

Expected prior learning

Children should be able to:

● identify and represent numbers using concrete objects and pictorial representations including a number line
● find totals by counting on.

Topic	Curriculum objectives	Expected outcomes
Addition	**Lesson 1**	
	To add numbers using concrete objects, pictorial representations, and mentally, including: a two-digit number and ones. To recognise and use the inverse relationship between addition and subtraction and use this to check calculations and solve missing number problems.	Use the vocabulary of addition. Use concrete and pictorial representations to add amounts and numbers together. Find totals by combining groups of objects and then counting on from one group. Check answers by taking away.
	Lesson 2	
	To add numbers using concrete objects, pictorial representations, and mentally, including: a two-digit number and tens. To recognise and use the inverse relationship between addition and subtraction and use this to check calculations and solve missing number problems.	Use concrete and pictorial representations to add amounts and numbers together. Find totals by combining groups of objects and then counting on from one group. Represent counting on from one group in ones using a number line. Check answers by taking away.
	Lesson 3	
	To add numbers using concrete objects, pictorial representations, and mentally, including: two two-digit numbers. To show that addition of two numbers can be done in any order (commutative).	Add using partitioning. Show that addition can be done in any order.
	Lesson 4	
	To recall and use addition facts to 20 fluently, and derives and use related facts up to 100. To add numbers using concrete objects, pictorial representations, and mentally, including: adding three one-digit numbers.	Partition the second and/or third number in order to get to a multiple of 10 then add the remaining part of that number. Explain place value of each digit in a two-digit number up to 50 and partition into tens and ones. Show that addition can be done in any order.
	Lesson 5	
	To solve problems with addition: ● using concrete objects and pictorial representations, including those involving numbers, quantities and measures ● applying their increasing knowledge of mental and written methods.	Use concrete and pictorial representations, partitioning and number lines to solve simple problems.

Preparation

Lesson 1: prepare up to 30 interlocking cubes in one small container per pair of children

Lesson 2: copy 'Hundred square', one per child

Lesson 4: copy and laminate 'Find the way! gameboard' for pairs of children

Lesson 5: prepare problems to ask the children similar to those in the main teaching activity

You will need

Photocopiable sheets
'Lots of numbers'

General resources
'Number lines 0–20'; 'Number lines 0–30'; 'Find the way! gameboard'; 'Hundred square'; 'Blank number lines'; interactive teaching resource 'Number square'

Equipment
Interlocking cubes; individual whiteboards; counting apparatus; counters

Further practice

Give children 'Blank number lines' and set them to a range of additions within 20 to answer using the number lines to check their answers

Oral and mental starters for week 2

See bank of starters on pages 44 to 45. Oral and mental starters are also on the CD-ROM.

5 One more, one less

2 Counting in tens

6 Counting in tens and ones

7 Number pairs to ten

8 Doubling and halving

Overview of progression

During this week children will extend their knowledge of addition. They will begin by using concrete and pictorial representations to add amounts and numbers together by combining groups and counting on. They will link this to number lines. They will explore how to find totals by partitioning. They will rehearse and use number facts to 10 to find totals. They will also use the mental calculation strategy of bridging 10. They will begin to check answers by using the inverse operation. They will use the strategies considered during the week to solve simple problems in the context of money that involve adding pairs or two-digit numbers to 50 and three single digits.

Watch out for

Some children may still have limited strategies for solving addition. A key strategy for solving addition is partitioning so provide these children with partitioning cards and concrete apparatus such as straws or base 10 apparatus so that they can visually see the tens and ones that make up a number.

Creative context

Encourage the children to make up problems involving addition using familiar scenarios.

Vocabulary

add, addition, altogether, **bridging ten**, inverse operation, make, more, partitioning, plus, sum, **tens boundary,** total

Curriculum objectives

● To add using concrete objects, pictorial representations, and mentally, including: a two-digit number and ones.
● To recognise and use the inverse relationship between addition and subtraction and use this to check calculations and solve missing number problems.

Success criteria

● I can talk about addition.
● I can add numbers together by counting on.

You will need

General resources

'Blank number lines'; 'Number lines 0–20'; 'Number lines 0–30'

Equipment

Interlocking cubes; individual whiteboards; A4 blank card or paper

Differentiation

Less confident learners

Give children up to 20 cubes and 'Number lines 0–20' from the CD-ROM to count on to find the total.

More confident learners

Give children 50 cubes. They draw their own number lines.

Lesson 1

Main teaching activities

Whole-class work: Explain that during the lesson the children will add two groups of objects by counting on from one group and then show this on a number line. Ask the children to give you the words they know which describe addition. Ensure those in the vocabulary list are covered. As you discuss these write the words on A4 card/paper to display and refer to during the week. Show the cubes. Invite a volunteer to count out 15 cubes and another to count out four. Write both numbers on the board. *How can we work out how many there are altogether?* Agree that they can count on 4 from the 15 objects. Do this together. Establish that there are 19 cubes altogether. Write the number sentence 15 + 4 = 19. Discuss other ways that they could do this and focus on the number line. Draw a number line 1–20 unlabelled on the board. Mark 0 and 15. Count on in ones for four jumps until you reach 19. *How can we check that we are correct?* Establish that they could take away the amount they added on to get the first number. Do this with the cubes and also counting back along the number line. Repeat for other numbers of cubes. Each time ask the children to count on from one group and then together show what this looks like on a number line and check by taking away the number they added.

Paired work: Give pairs of children piles of up to 30 cubes. Ask them to make two piles: one pile should contain a number above ten and the other a number below ten. They find the total by counting one group and then count on the other. They write the number sentence. Next, they draw this on a blank number line to show what they have done. Encourage them to check their answer by counting back along their number line.

Progress check: Invite pairs to share examples of the numbers of cubes they are counting.

● *How can you add these using a number line?*
● *How can you check that you are correct?*

Review

Write this calculation on the board: 66 + 8.

● *If Suzie had 66p and her friend gave her another 8p, how can we work out how much she has now?*
● *Could we count out 66p and then 8p?*

Agree that they could work out the answer using this method, but there would be lots of pennies. Focus on adding by using a number line as in their activity. Mark 66 on a number line, count on 8. If appropriate, discuss the fact that they could split 8 into 4 and 4, add 4 to 66 to make 70 and then add the remaining 4 to give 74.

Curriculum objectives

- To add using concrete objects, pictorial representations, and mentally, including: a two-digit number and tens.
- To recognise and use the inverse relationship between addition and subtraction and use this to check calculations and missing number problems.

Success criteria

- I can add two-digit numbers and tens.
- I can check my answer by taking away.

You will need

General resources

'Hundred square'; interactive teaching resource 'Number square'

Differentiation

Less confident learners

Children work with numbers to 20 and focus on adding 10.

More confident learners

Children add different numbers of tens, such as 30, 70.

Lesson 2   Oral and mental starter 2

Main teaching activities

Whole-class work: Display the interactive teaching resource 'Number square' on the CD-ROM. Invite a volunteer to highlight 34. Next count on 10 from 34 and highlight 44. Repeat this so that you have four different starting numbers highlighted and also the four that are 10 more. Ask the children what they notice about the numbers that have been highlighted. Agree that the number that is 10 more is underneath the starting number and that they can add 10 by moving down a row on a 100 square like this. Discuss what is the same and what is different between each pair (tens different, ones the same). Repeat this a few times and then do this for adding different numbers of tens (20, 30).

Independent work: Give each child photocopiable page 'Hundred square' from the CD-ROM. They pick a two-digit number and colour the square that it is in. Next they add ten, colour that square, and write a number sentence to show what they have done, such as 32 + 10 = 42. Ask children to add 20 and 30 onto their two-digit numbers.

Progress check:

- *What is 10 added onto 24?*
- *What is 20 added onto 69?*
- *How do you know?*

Review

Invite children to share the work they did. Write some two-digit numbers on the board, for example 34, 56, 78.

- *I added 10 onto a number and got 34/56/78. What was my number?*
- *How do you know?*
- *What does that tell us about adding and taking away?*

Curriculum objectives

- To add using concrete objects, pictorial representations, and mentally, including: two two-digit numbers.
- To show that addition can be done in any order (commutative).

Success criteria

- I can add using partitioning.
- I can show that addition can be done in any order.

You will need

General resources

'0–100 number cards'

Equipment

Individual whiteboards

Differentiation

Less confident learners

Ask children to work with numbers to 50.

More confident learners

Ask children to add two-digit numbers that total more than 100.

Lesson 3   Oral and mental starter 6

Main teaching activities

Whole-class work: Tell the children that they will be adding pairs of two-digit numbers by partitioning. Ask them what partitioning is. Establish that it is splitting a number into tens and ones. Write some two-digit numbers on the board and ask the children to partition them on their whiteboards. Write this calculation on the board: 34 + 25. Ask the children to think about how they could add these by partitioning. Agree that they could add the tens first and then the ones: 30 + 20 = 50, 4 + 5 = 9, 50 + 9 = 59. Ask the children what they think the answer to 25 + 34 would be. Test this out by partitioning: 20 + 30 = 50, 5 + 4 = 9, 50 + 9 = 59. Agree that it doesn't matter which way round an addition is done the answer will be the same. Repeat this for other pairs of numbers including those that have ones numbers that total more than 10, such as 48 + 27 = 60 + 15 = 75.

Independent work: Give the children a selection of numbers to add by partitioning. They could make two-digit numbers using digit cards or use appropriate number cards.

Progress check: Ask volunteers to demonstrate some of their calculations with the class. *How can we check that the answer is correct?*

Review

Discuss the strategy used for addition that the children have used in this lesson. Compare this with the other methods used during the week: number line and 100 square and ask the children if these can be used for adding two two-digit numbers. Agree that they can and together work through answering 34 + 17 using all three ways.

Lesson 4   Oral and mental starter 7

Main teaching activities

Whole-class work: Write this on the board: 7 + 3 + 8 and remind the children of the starter activity. *How can we add these numbers together?* Agree that they can add the two numbers that make ten and then the third number. Practise doing this. The children use their whiteboards for any jottings and answers. Move onto numbers that need to be partitioned in order to make a 10, for example. 6 + 5 + 8: 6 + 4 + 1 + 8 = 10 + 9 = 19. Now try some with a two-digit number and two single ones, for example, 23 + 8 + 4: 23 + 7 + 1 + 4 = 30 + 5 = 35. *Can we check by adding these numbers in a different order?* Agree that they can because it doesn't matter which way we add numbers the answer will be the same.

Paired work: Demonstrate the Find the way! game, which the children can use to practise this strategy. Explain that the aim is to get through the maze by adding lines of three digits together, two of which must total ten. They record their additions and draw lines connecting the numbers they use. Encourage them to check their answers by adding in a different order.

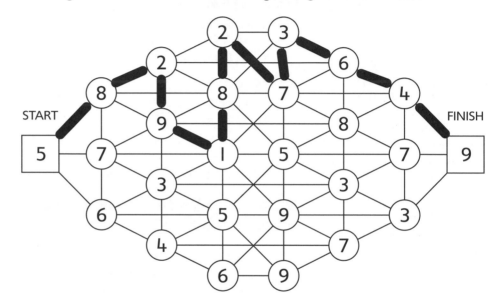

Progress check: Invite volunteers to share how they have added some of their numbers together.

● *How can we check that these are correct?*

Review

Display 'Find the way! gameboard' and invite children to show how they made it through the maze. Write a 1 in front of some of the numbers to make teens numbers.

● *Can we still use this strategy to add to these teens numbers?*

Agree that they can, for example 18 + 3 + 7 = 18 + 10 = 28. Play the game together adding to teens numbers.

Lesson 5

Curriculum objectives
● To solve problems with addition: using concrete objects and pictorial representations, including those involving numbers, quantities and measures; applying their increasing knowledge of mental and written methods.

Success criteria
● I can solve word problems using mental calculations including partitioning.

You will need
Photocopiable sheets
'Lots of numbers'

General resource
'Hundred square'; 'Number lines'

Equipment
Counting equipment; counters

Differentiation
Less confident learners
Some children may need a 'Hundred square' or 'Number lines 0–100' to help them.

More confident learners
Some children may want to choose five numbers to add together using two different methods.

Main teaching activities

Whole-class work: Explain that in this lesson you will be giving the children some problems to solve. *Michelle had five red, five blue, eight yellow and ten green counters. How many counters does she have altogether?* Ask the children to discuss with a partner how to find the answer. Take feedback and invite a volunteer to demonstrate how they would do this practically with coloured counters. Encourage them to think of ways other than counting the numbers separately, for example double 5 (10), double again (10 + 10) and add 8.

How can we check that we are correct? Agree that they could add the numbers in a different order or use a different strategy, for example, add three lots of 10 and take away 2.

How can we record this as a number sentence? Invite someone to demonstrate, for example 5 + 5 + 8 + 10 = 28. Discuss the meaning of the equals sign. Establish whatever is on one side is equal to whatever is on the other. Ask other problems similar to Michelle's that include the bridging ten strategy covered in lesson 4.

Ask this problem: *Scott has saved £15. Samir has saved £18. How much money do they have altogether?* Ask the children to discuss how they could solve this. Agree that they could partition. Invite a volunteer to demonstrate this. Ask similar problems.

Independent work: Distribute photocopiable page 'Lots of numbers' from the CD-ROM and work through the example together. Children use the numbers to create an addition calculation, check by adding in a different way and then invent a word problem to go with each calculation.

Progress check: Invite volunteers to read out one of their word problems and ask the rest of the class to solve them explaining their strategy.
- *Is there another way to add the numbers?*
- *How could we check this is the correct answer?*

Review

Invite volunteers to read out some of the problems they made up during the activity. Invite other children to write the numbers needed for the solutions on the board and demonstrate how these could be added. Invite another volunteer to suggest a method for checking. Finish the lesson by asking problems, such as: *Sunita had 12 dolls, Seema had eight, Hannah five and Natalie four. How many dolls did they have altogether?*

Subtraction: concrete and pictorial representation

Expected prior learning

Children should be able to:

- identify and represent numbers using concrete objects and pictorial representations including a number line
- take away a smaller amount from a larger one.

Topic	Curriculum objectives	Expected outcomes
Subtraction	**Lesson 1**	
	To subtract numbers using concrete objects, pictorial representations, and mentally, including: a two-digit number and ones.	Use the vocabulary of subtraction.
		Use concrete and pictorial representations to subtract amounts and numbers.
	To recognise and use the inverse relationship between addition and subtraction and use this to check calculations and solve missing number problems.	Know that subtraction is not commutative.
		Check answers by adding.
	Lesson 2	
	To subtract numbers using concrete objects, pictorial representations, and mentally, including: a two-digit number and ones.	Use concrete and pictorial representations to subtract amounts and numbers (link to taking away on a number line).
	To recall and use subtraction facts to 20 fluently, and derive and use related facts up to 100.	Use number facts and partitioning to subtract.
		Know that subtraction is not commutative.
		Check answers by adding.
	Lesson 3	
	To subtract numbers using concrete objects, pictorial representations, and mentally, including: a two-digit number and tens.	Know that subtraction is not commutative.
		Check answers by adding.
	To recognise and use the inverse relationship between addition and subtraction and use this to check calculations and solve missing number problems.	
	Lesson 4	
	To subtract numbers using concrete objects, pictorial representations, and mentally, including: a two-digit numbers.	Finding the difference by counting on.
		Check answers by adding.
	To recognise and use the inverse relationship between addition and subtraction and use this to check calculations and solve missing number problems.	
	Lesson 5	
	To solve problems with subtraction:	Use concrete and pictorial representations, partitioning and number lines to solve simple problems.
	• using concrete objects and pictorial representations, including those involving numbers, quantities and measures	
	• applying their increasing knowledge of mental and written methods.	

Preparation

Lesson 2: copy, laminate and cut out the shopping cards on photocopiable page 'Shopping cards' one set for each pair of children

Lesson 4: copy, laminate and cut out the dog food cards on photocopiable page 'Ivor Dog's dog and puppy food' one set per pair

Lesson 5: prepare problems to ask the children similar to the examples in the lesson

You will need

Photocopiable sheets

'What's in the box?'; 'Shopping cards'; 'Ivor Dog's dog and puppy food'; 'Add and subtract (1)'

General resources

'Blank number lines'; 'Number lines 0–20'; 'Number lines 0–30'; '0–100 number cards'; interactive teaching resource 'Number square'

Equipment

Interlocking cubes; individual whiteboards; straws (singles and in bundles of ten); coloured counters; 1p coins; counting apparatus

Further practice

Give children 'Blank number lines' from the CD-ROM and set them a range of subtractions within 20 to answer using the number lines to check their answers.

Oral and mental starters for week 3

See bank of starters on pages 44 to 45. Oral and mental starters are also on the CD-ROM.

9 Inversion loops

7 Number pairs to ten

5 One more, one less

8 Doubling and halving

10 Making numbers

Overview of progression

During this week children will extend their knowledge of subtraction. They will begin by using concrete and pictorial representations to subtract amounts and numbers from other amounts and numbers. They will link this to counting back along a number line. They will rehearse and use number facts to ten to enable them to subtract by bridging ten. They will begin to check answers by using the inverse operation. They will use the strategies considered during the week to solve simple problems in the context of money that involve subtracting pairs of two-digit numbers to 50.

Watch out for

Some children may have limited strategies for subtraction. Key strategies for subtraction during this unit are counting back and bridging ten so provide opportunities for these children to use numbered number lines and concrete apparatus.

Creative context

Encourage the children to make up problems involving subtraction using familiar scenarios. You could provide food packaging for the children to explore and compare the numbers they find.

Vocabulary

bridging ten, find the difference, how many more, minus, subtract, subtraction, take away, **tens boundary**

Curriculum objectives

● To subtract numbers using concrete objects, pictorial representations, and mentally, including: a two-digit number and ones.
● To recognise and use the inverse relationship between addition and subtraction and use this to check calculations and solve missing number problems.

Success criteria

● I can talk about subtraction.
● I can take away a single number from a two-digit number.

You will need

Photocopiable sheets

'What's in the box?'

General resources

'Blank number lines'; 'Number lines 0–20'

Equipment

Interlocking cubes; counters; individual whiteboards

Differentiation

Less confident learners

Adapt the photocopiable sheet 'What's in the box?' so that children work with single-digit numbers only.

More confident learners

Adapt the photocopiable sheet 'What's in the box?' so that children work with two-digit numbers above 20 and single-digit numbers.

Lesson 1 — Oral and mental starter 9

Main teaching activities

Whole-class work: Explain that during this lesson the children will take away single-digit from two-digit numbers using apparatus and then show this on a number line. Begin by asking the children to give you the words they know that describe subtraction. Ensure those in the vocabulary list are covered. As you discuss these write them on paper to display and refer to during the week. Show the cubes. Invite a volunteer to count out 18 cubes and another to take away six. *How can we write this as a number sentence?* Agree: $18 - 6 = 12$. Demonstrate this on the number line. Draw a numbered line on the board, circle 18 and then draw six jumps back in ones. *How can we check that we are correct?* Establish that they could add the amount they took away to see if they get back to 18. Do this with the cubes and also counting forward along the number line. Demonstrate this as an inversion loop:

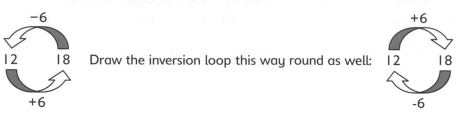

Discuss what is the same and what is different about these models. Establish that they both show the inverse properties of addition and subtraction but in a different order.

Repeat for other numbers of cubes. Each time ask the children to take away a quantity then together show what this looks like on a number line and check by adding and show the inversion loop.

Independent work: Tell the children that they will practise using inversion loops. Distribute photocopiable page 'What's in the box?' from the CD-ROM and model the example, pointing out that the questions on the sheet are similar to the second model you drew on the board. Then let the children complete the sheet. Provide the children with counters or cubes to help them if they need this support.

Progress check: Invite pairs to share examples of their work.

- *Can you explain how you found the missing number?*
- *Is there another way you could have done this?*

Review

Write this calculation on the board: $15 - 8$.

- *If Bobby had £15 and spent £8, how can we work out how much he has left?*
- *How can we work this out on a number line?*
- *What inversion loop can we draw to help us check?*

Agree that they could count back £8 from £15 on a number line to give £7 and then add £8 to the £7 to see if they get back to £15.

Curriculum objectives
● To subtract numbers using concrete objects, pictorial representations, and mentally, including: a two-digit number and ones.
● To use subtraction facts to 20, and use related facts up to 100.

Success criteria
● I can use number facts to help me take away.
● I can check my answer by adding.

You will need
Photocopiable sheets
'Shopping cards'
Equipment
1p coins

Differentiation
Less confident learners
Children work with just 15p and take one amount away each time.
More confident learners
Give children higher starting amounts, for example, 75p, £1.

Lesson 2   Oral and mental starter 7

Main teaching activities

Whole-class work: Set this problem: *Saima had 35p she gave 8p to a friend. How much did she have left?* Write the calculation 35p – 8p on the board. Ask the children how they could work out the answer using their number facts. Agree that they could partition 8p into 5p and 3p, then take away 5p to make 30p and then count back the remaining 3p to leave 27p. Demonstrate this using 1p coins. Repeat with similar examples.

Paired work: Give each pair a copy of photocopiable page 'Shopping cards' from the CD-ROM. Tell them that they have 50p to spend. They take it in turns to pick a shopping card and take the amount from their 50p. They record the number sentence to show how much they have left. On their next turn they take the new amount away from what they had left. Encourage them to use partitioning strategies as in the lesson. They continue until they can't afford anything else. They can repeat the activity with 50p or give them a greater starting amount.

Progress check: Invite pairs to share some of the amounts they have taken away and ask the class to tell them how much they had left.
- *How can we take 7p away from 22p?*
- *How can we check?*

Review
Ask a volunteer to give you an amount of pence between 50p and £1. Write it on the board. Ask other volunteers to pick shopping cards and to take these away from the starting amount as in the activity. For each, discuss methods for taking these away including partitioning numbers using number facts.

Curriculum objectives
● To subtract numbers using concrete objects, pictorial representations, and mentally, including: two-digit numbers and tens.
● To use the inverse relationship between addition and subtraction to check calculations and solve missing number problems.

Success criteria
● I can subtract ten from a two-digit number.
● I can check by adding.

You will need
General resources
Interactive teaching resource 'Number square'; 'Hundred square'

Differentiation
Less confident learners
Ask children to subtract ten from numbers to 20.
More confident learners
Ask children to subtract different multiples of ten.

Lesson 3   Oral and mental starter 5

Main teaching activities

Whole-class work: Remind the children of week 2, lesson 2 when they looked at a 100 square to help them add ten to a number. Display the interactive teaching resource 'Number square'. Invite a volunteer to highlight 29. Next count back ten from 29 and highlight 19. Repeat this so that you have different starting numbers and those that are ten less highlighted. Ask the children what they notice about the numbers that have been highlighted. Agree that the number that is ten less is above the starting number and that they can subtract ten by moving up a row on a 100 square like this. Discuss what is the same and what is different between each pair (tens different, ones the same). Repeat a few times and then subtract different numbers of tens, such as 20, 30.

Independent work: Give each child photocopiable page 'Hundred square from the CD-ROM. They pick a two-digit number and colour the square that it is in. Next they subtract ten and colour that square. Finally they write a number sentence to show what they have done, such as 27 – 10 = 17.

Progress check: Ask volunteers to demonstrate some of their calculations with the class.
- *How can we check that the answer is correct?*
Agree that they can add.

Review
Call out two-digit numbers and ask the children to take 10, 20 and 30 away from these numbers. Discuss how they can subtract 10 from 134. Agree that the hundreds and ones numbers stay the same, they simply focus on the tens: 124. Repeat with other examples.

Curriculum objectives

● To subtract numbers using concrete objects, pictorial representations, and mentally, including: two-digit numbers.
● To recognise and use the inverse relationship between addition and subtraction and use this to check calculations and solve missing number problems.

Success criteria

● I can find the difference by counting on.
● I can check by adding.

You will need

Photocopiable sheets

'Ivor Dog's dog and puppy food'

General resources

'Number lines 0–20'; 'Number lines 0–30'

Equipment

Counting apparatus

Differentiation

Less confident learners

Edit the cards so that the children work with numbers to 20 and provide number lines for them to use.

More confident learners

Edit the cards so that the costs are between 50p and 99p.

Lesson 4

Main teaching activities

Whole-class work: Set this problem: *Carly had 24 sweets, she gave away 19. How many did she have left?* Discuss how the children could find the answer to this. Agree that they could take 19 away from 24. Establish that they could also find the difference by counting on. Draw a rectangle on the board with 24 written inside it. Tell the children that this represents the 24 sweets Carly had. Underneath draw one with 19 in it to represent the sweets she gave away.

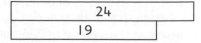

Explain that they need to find the value of the space between the two. Agree they could count back in ones from 24 to 19 or on from 19 to 24. Do both. Which do the children prefer? Next, demonstrate using a number line like this showing how the line from 0 to 19 is scrawled through and then counting up to 24 which equals 5:

$$24 - 19 = 5$$

Paired work: Give each pair a set of cards from photocopiable page 'Ivor Dog's dog and puppy food' from the CD-ROM. The children take it in turns to pick two. They both find the difference by counting on. They draw a number line to show their work.

Progress check: Invite pairs to share some of the differences that they found and to explain how they found their answers.
● *What is the difference between 45p and 36p?*
● *How do you know?*
● *How can we check?*

Review

Ask the children to give you two amounts of dog food. Write these on the board. Invite a volunteer to demonstrate how to find the difference.
● *How can we check this is the correct answer? Is there another way to check?*
Write $72 - 34$ on the board. Draw the rectangles and number line as in the lesson. Together work out how this could be answered: add 6 to make 40, add 30 to make 70 then add 2, giving a difference of 38.

■SCHOLASTIC

Curriculum objectives
● To solve problems with subtraction: using concrete objects and pictorial representations, including those involving numbers, quantities and measures and applying their increasing knowledge of mental and written methods.

Success criteria
● I can solve word problems involving subtraction.

You will need
Photocopiable sheets
'Add and subtract (1)'
General resources
'Hundred square'

Differentiation
Less confident learners
Provide children with a 'Hundred square' or a 'Number lines 0–100' when they do the activity.

More confident learners
Children choose five numbers to subtract using two different methods.

Lesson 5
Oral and mental starter 10

Main teaching activities

Whole-class work: Explain that in this lesson you will be giving the children some problems to solve. *Ben made 25 biscuits, he gave 12 away. How many did he have left?* Discuss possible strategies for finding the answer. Draw out these strategies: partition 12 into 10 and 2; count on from 12 to 25. Work through each method. Give the children photocopiable page 'Hundred square' from the CD-ROM to take away 10 and 2. For counting on demonstrate with the

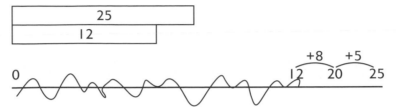

rectangles and number lines as in lesson 4:

Demonstrate checking using the inverse operation using the inversion loop: add the answer to the second number (12 + 13 = 25), for example:

Repeat with similar problems. *Scott saved £15. Samir saved £18. How much more money did Samir save?* Ask the children to discuss how they could solve this. Agree that they could partition and take 10 away then 5 from 18. Invite a volunteer to demonstrate this. Agree that they could also count on from the smallest number. Invite a volunteer to demonstrate. Discuss which they think is the best method to use. Agree counting on because the numbers are close together. Ask similar problems.

Independent work: Distribute photocopiable page 'Add and subtract (1)' from the CD-ROM and explain what the children need to do, demonstrating with an example. Be aware that the children have not covered negative numbers previously. When they have finished, ask them to choose some of the numbers they made to make up subtraction problems for the class to solve in the review session.

Progress check: Invite volunteers to read out some of the calculations they made using the numbers from the grid.

- *Is there another way to add/subtract the numbers?*
- *How could we check this is the correct answer?*
- *Can you make up a problem using these two numbers?*

Review

Invite volunteers to ask some of the problems they made up during their activity. Invite other children to write the numbers needed for the solution on the board and demonstrate how these could be added. Invite another volunteer to suggest a method for checking. Finish the lesson by asking problems, such as those in the main activity.

Multiplication and division: repeated addition and subtraction

Expected prior learning

Children should be able to:

- count in twos, fives and tens
- know that doubling is two lots of the same number.

Topic	Curriculum objectives	Expected outcomes
Multiplication and division	**Lesson 1**	
	To recall and use multiplication and division facts for the 2, 5 and 10 multiplication tables, including recognising odd and even numbers. To calculate mathematical statements for multiplication and division within the multiplication tables and write them using the multiplication (×), division (÷) and equals (=) signs.	Know tables facts for the two-, five- and ten-times tables. Recognise odd and even numbers. Use the symbols for multiplication and division.
	Lesson 2	
	To calculate mathematical statements for multiplication and division within the multiplication tables and write them using the multiplication (×), division (÷) and equals (=) signs. To show that multiplication of two numbers can be done in any order (commutative).	Understand multiplication as repeated addition. Understand that it doesn't matter which way round a multiplication calculation is solved, the answer will be the same.
	Lesson 3	
	To calculate mathematical statements for multiplication and division within the multiplication tables and write them using the multiplication (×), division (÷) and equals (=) signs.	Understand division as repeated addition. Know that division and multiplication are inverse operations.
	Lesson 4	
	To calculate mathematical statements for multiplication and division within the multiplication tables and write them using the multiplication (×), division (÷) and equals (=) signs. To show that multiplication of two numbers can be done in any order (commutative).	Understand multiplication as repeated addition and division as repeated subtraction. Check answers by multiplying or dividing. Link repeated addition and subtraction to arrays.
	Lesson 5	
	To solve problems involving multiplication and division, using materials, arrays, repeated addition, mental methods and multiplication and division facts, including problems in contexts.	Use concrete and pictorial representations to solve simple problems.

Preparation

Lesson 1: prepare containers of up to 50 interlocking cubes for the activity

Lesson 3: prepare containers of 20 interlocking cubes for the activity

Lesson 5: prepare problems to ask the children similar to the examples in the lesson

You will need

Photocopiable sheets

'Array for maths! (1)'; 'Make me a problem'

General resources

'0–100 number cards' (0–9 cards)

Equipment

Counters; counting apparatus; cuboids or candy bars; individual whiteboards; interlocking cubes; number lines to 20; plastic bags (or similar); sugar paper; teddy bears; toy cars

Further practice

Photocopiable sheets

'Array for maths! (2)'

Oral and mental starters for week 4

See bank of starters on page 45. Oral and mental starters are also on the CD-ROM.

11 Counting in twos, fives and tens

9 Inversion loops

8 Doubling and halving

10 Making numbers

Overview of progression

During this week children will extend their knowledge of multiplication and division. They will begin by using concrete and pictorial representations to reinforce two-, five- and ten-times table facts. They will develop the idea that multiplication is repeated addition and division is repeated subtraction. They will check answers by using the inverse operation and learn that multiplication is commutative. They will use the strategies considered during the week to solve simple problems in a familiar context that involve multiplication and division.

Watch out for

Some children may add two numbers together instead of multiplying them and subtract two numbers instead of dividing them. You could give them symbol cards to refer to, for example write 2×3 with $2 + 2 + 2$ underneath. Ask them questions involving each of the four operations. They show you the symbol card that indicates the operation needed.

Creative context

Encourage the children to make up counting rhymes for the two-, five- and ten-times tables.

Vocabulary

array, column, divide, divided by, equal groups of, groups of, lots of, multiplied by, **multiple of,** multiply, repeated addition, repeated subtraction, row, times

Curriculum objectives

● To recall and use multiplication and division facts for the 2, 5 and 10 multiplication tables, including recognising odd and even numbers.
● To calculate mathematical statements for multiplication and division within the multiplication tables and write them using the multiplication (×), division (÷) and equals (=) signs.

Success criteria

● I know my two-, five- and ten-times tables.
● I can recognise odd and even numbers.

You will need

Equipment

Interlocking cubes; counters; individual whiteboards; sugar paper

Differentiation

Less confident learners

Give children 20 cubes and ask them to find out which numbers are odd and which are even.

More confident learners

Once children have practised finding odd and even numbers, ask them to predict which numbers above 50 will be odd and which will be even and to think about why this is.

Lesson 1 — Oral and mental starter ⏱

Main teaching activities

Whole-class work: Explain that during the next few lessons the children will be thinking about multiplication and division. Begin by finding out how much they already know, including the vocabulary that would be used to describe multiplication and division. Write the words they tell you on a large piece of sugar paper so that you can display it for the children to refer to during the week. Add any words that are in the vocabulary list that they don't say. Together, focus on each word on your list sharing ideas as to what they mean. For some of the words invite volunteers to draw pictures on the board to illustrate the meanings.

Give pairs of children 24 interlocking cubes. Ask them to make towers of two cubes and then line them up. Ask the children to count out seven groups. Ask how many cubes there are (14). Discuss how this can be written as a multiplication ($7 \times 2 = 14$) and invite a volunteer to write this on the board. Repeat for four groups of two. Next ask the children to recite their times tables facts to 12×2 pointing at the appropriate number of groups of cubes as they do.

Ask pairs of children to take one of the towers of two cubes between them. *Is 2 an odd or an even number?* If they are not sure tell them that an even number can be equally shared between two. They separate their cubes and hold one cube each. Agree that it is even, they both have one cube. *Are all multiples of 2 even?* Try 4. Ask pairs of children to put two groups of two cubes together as a tower and then separate them into two equal piles. Repeat for three groups (six cubes) etc. up to 12 groups (24 cubes). Agree all these numbers are even. Write the even numbers up to 24 on the board and point out the sequence of even ones digits: 2, 4, 6, 8, 0 showing that all multiples of two must be even.

Repeat this with 60 cubes for the five-times table and, working in a group of four, 120 for the 10 times table. Pairs of children group different numbers of fives and tens and share into two equal groups to establish whether they are odd or even numbers. In this way they will see that five and some of its multiples are odd and some even and that all multiples of ten are even.

Paired work: Give pairs of children a container of interlocking cubes. They count out groups of cubes and find out whether the number they have is an odd number or an even one by sharing them into two groups. They record their findings in their own way.

Progress check: Invite pairs to tell you some of the numbers they have made.
- *Do you think this is an odd number or an even one?*
- *How can we find out?*

Review

Ask the more confident learners to give examples of the numbers above 50 that they worked with.
- *Who thinks this is an odd number? Why?*
- *How can we tell that a number is odd or even?*

Agree that any number that is a multiple of two is even and the others are odd. Finish the lesson by calling out two- and three-digit numbers. If they are odd the children stand up, if they are even the children clap once.

Curriculum objectives
- To calculate mathematical statements for multiplication and division within the multiplication tables.
- To show that multiplication of two numbers can be done in any order (commutative).

Success criteria
- I can solve a multiplication using repeated addition.
- I can multiply numbers in any order.

You will need

General resources
'0–100 number cards'

Equipment
Five small plastic bags

Differentiation

Less confident learners
Provide objects for these children to use for repeated addition.

More confident learners
Ask children to make statements about multiples of two, five and ten.

Lesson 2 — Oral and mental starter 11

Main teaching activities

Whole-class work: *Cherish has five bags. In each bag there are two sweets. How many sweets does she have altogether?* Ask the children to talk to a partner about how they would find the answer. Demonstrate by asking five children to each hold a bag. Give each child two cuboids ('sweets') to put in the bag. Together, count in twos five times. Demonstrate on the board by drawing five biscuits in three bags and below write $2 + 2 + 2 + 2 + 2$ (repeated addition). Underneath this draw the following diagram:

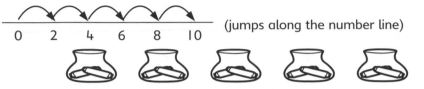

(jumps along the number line)

How could we write this as a number sentence? Agree 2×5 means five lots of two or two five times. Write 2×5 on the board. *If we multiply two lots of five do you think the answer will be the same? Why?* Agree it will, linking to addition.

Independent work: Ask the children to pick a digit card and multiply the number by two. They show this as repeated addition and using a number line.

Progress check: Invite individuals to demonstrate how they worked out 2×4 by drawing and repeated addition. *How else can we multiply 2 and 4 to give 8?*

Review

Take feedback from the activity by inviting children of different confidence levels to share the problems they made up. Invite others to demonstrate how they can be solved using repeated addition. Ask the rest of the class to work out the answers.

Curriculum objectives
- To calculate mathematical statements for multiplication and division within the multiplication tables and write them using the multiplication (x), division (÷) and equals (=) signs.

Success criteria
- I can solve a division using repeated subtraction.
- I can check my answer using repeated addition.

You will need

Equipment
Interlocking cubes; counters

Differentiation

Less confident learners
Ask children to focus on taking groups of two away from up to ten cubes.

More confident learners
Ask children to take away multiples of two, five and ten.

Lesson 3 — Oral and mental starter 9

Main teaching activities

Whole-class work: Ask the children for the opposite operation to addition. Draw an arrow diagram (inversion loop) on the board. Agree subtraction is the opposite. Remind them that they can use subtraction to check an addition and vice versa. Say: *If multiplication is repeated addition, what do you think division is?* Demonstrate this example using interlocking cubes: five lots of two is $2 + 2 + 2 + 2 + 2 = 10$, so $10 ÷ 2$ must be $10 − 2 − 2 − 2 − 2 − 2 = 0$. Demonstrate repeated subtraction on a number line. Say: *Liam has 15 biscuits to put into bags of five. How many bags will he need?* Demonstrate this with 15 counters, giving five counters to volunteers. Agree that he will need three bags. Demonstrate by drawing five biscuits in three bags and below write $15 − 5 − 5 − 5$. Underneath this draw the following diagram:

(jumps along the number line)

How can we write this as a number sentence? Repeat with other examples.

Paired work: Give pairs of children a container of cubes. They count groups of even numbers of cubes and divide by two. They record their work as a drawing and a repeated subtraction and then write the division sentence.

Progress check: Ask volunteers to demonstrate their work. *How can we check that the answer is correct?* Agree that they can add the groups together.

Review

Take feedback from the children's activity, writing some of their number sentences on the board ($14 ÷ 2 = 7$). Then ask the children to tell you the multiplication number sentences that go with them ($2 \times 7 = 14$).

Curriculum objectives

● To calculate mathematical statements for multiplication and division within the multiplication tables and write them using the multiplication (x), division (÷) and equals (=) signs.
● To show that multiplication of two numbers can be done in any order (commutative).

Success criteria

● I can make arrays to show multiplication and division.
● I can check my answer by multiplying or dividing.

You will need

Photocopiable sheets

'Array for maths! (1)'

Equipment

Counters, individual whiteboards, interlocking cubes, sugar paper, toy cars

Differentiation

Less confident learners

Edit the cards so that the children work with numbers to 20 and provide number lines for the children to use.

More confident learners

Edit the cards so that the costs are between 50p and 99p.

Lesson 4 — Oral and mental starter 8

Main teaching activities

Whole-class work: Set this problem: *Sammy had three boxes. In each box there were five toy cars. How many toy cars did he have altogether?* Discuss what operation the children would need to do to find the answer to this. Agree multiplication. Invite three children to represent three boxes. Give each child five toy cars. As a class, count five three times. Represent this in the ways described in lesson 2 and write the number sentence $5 \times 3 = 15$. Ask the children to do this on their whiteboards. Discuss how to check by doing the inverse operation and demonstrate this on the board. Set the cars out so that there are three columns of five cars. Tell the children that you have made an array. Draw this on a large piece of sugar paper using circles to represent cars:

Explain how this shows five things three times which is 15 or $5 \times 3 = 15$ and $15 \div 3 = 5$.

Then turn the paper to show:

Explain that this now shows $3 \times 5 = 15$ and $15 \div 5 = 3$.

Repeat in exactly the same way for other numbers of cars and boxes.

Paired work: Tell the children that they will be working in pairs to interpret arrays. Show them photocopiable page 'Array for maths! (1)' from the CD-ROM and demonstrate how to draw the two arrays for each question. Also demonstrate how to write the divisions for each array. The children should write the appropriate division beside the different arrays.

Progress check: Invite pairs to demonstrate one of their arrays. Ask the class to say what they think the multiplication and the division number sentences are. *What does this tell us about multiplication and division?*

Review

Recap the main concepts that the children have been thinking about during the lesson. Take an example from their activity and demonstrate how this can be shown as a drawing, an array, on a number line and as a number sentence.

Curriculum objectives

● To solve problems involving multiplication and division, using materials, arrays, repeated addition, mental methods and multiplication and division facts, including problems in contexts.

Success criteria

● I can solve simple problems involving multiplication and division.

You will need

Photocopiable sheets

'Make me a problem'

Equipment

Counting bears; individual whiteboards

Differentiation

Less confident learners

Adapt the photocopiable sheet 'Make me a problem' so children multiply and divide by two only. If writing is a problem for children, ask them to say their problems to you or to a teaching assistant so you can write them down for them.

More confident learners

Edit the photocopiable sheet 'Make me a problem' so that the children are working with numbers more suited to their attainment.

Lesson 5
Oral and mental starter 10

Main teaching activities

Whole-class work: Recap the work that the children have covered over the previous four lessons with examples set in problem contexts, for example; *Summer has three teddy bears, her friend has five times as many. How many teddies does her friend have?* Set out 15 counting bears in an array and ask the children to draw this on their whiteboards and group them in threes by drawing loops. Show this as a repeated addition on a number line and ask the children how this would be written as a number sentence ($3 \times 5 = 15$). Next discuss how they could check this and demonstrate on the number line using repeated subtraction. Ask them to write the division number sentence on their whiteboards ($15 \div 3 = 5$). Repeat for other examples.

Write two numbers and a multiplication symbol on the board. Ask the children to make up a problem using these and then to solve it. Repeat a few times with divisions included as well. Ask the children to explain how they solved each problem and how they could check that they were correct.

Independent work: Distribute photocopiable page 'Make me a problem' from the CD-ROM and explain that they need to make up their own problems for the class to answer in the review session. Demonstrate using the example from the sheet.

Progress check: Invite volunteers to read out one of the problems they made up.

- *What number sentence could we write for this problem?*
- *How could we find the answer?*
- *How could we check this is the correct answer?*

Review

Invite volunteers to ask some of the problems they made up during their activity. Invite other children to demonstrate using pictures and number lines how these could be solved. Together agree on the answers. Invite another volunteer to suggest a method for checking. Finish the lesson by asking problems, such as those in the main activity.

Geometry: properties of 3D and 2D shape

Expected prior learning

Children should be able to:

- identify and describe the 3D shapes: sphere, cone, cylinder, cube, cuboid
- identify and describe the 2D shapes: circle, triangle, square, rectangle.

Topic	Curriculum objectives	Expected outcomes
Geometry: properties of shapes	**Lesson 1**	
	To identify and describe the properties of 3D shapes, including the number of edges, vertices and faces.	Identify and describe the properties of spheres, cones, cylinders, cubes, cuboids. Use knowledge of shape names and properties to sort, for example, which will roll.
	Lesson 2	
	To identify 2D shapes on the surface of 3D shapes [for example, a circle on a cylinder and a triangle on a pyramid].	Identify and name the 2D shapes on the surface of 3D shapes. Identify 3D and 2D shapes in the environment.
	Lesson 3	
	To identify and describe the properties of 2D shapes, including the number of sides and line symmetry in a vertical line.	Identify and describe the properties of circles, squares, rectangles, pentagons and hexagons.
	Lesson 4	
	To identify and describe the properties of 3D shapes, including the number of edges, vertices and faces. To identify 2D shapes on the surface of 3D shapes [for example, a circle on a cylinder and a triangle on a pyramid].	Sort 3D and 2D shapes according to their properties. Make 3D shapes from their 2D faces.
	Lesson 5	
	To compare and sort common 2D and 3D shapes and everyday objects.	Use shapes to solve different types problems that involve reasoning.

Preparation

Lesson 1: prepare sets of the following shapes so there are enough for groups of four: sphere, cone, cylinder, cube, cuboid, pyramid

Lesson 2: make a collection of the following 3D shapes to put in different places in the classroom: spheres, cones, cylinders, cubes, cuboids and pyramids

Lesson 3: photocopy, laminate and cut out the shapes on 'Templates for irregular shapes', and 'Templates for regular shapes'. Make an A3 copy of '2D shape vocabulary'

Lesson 4: ensure that you have paper copies of 'Templates for irregular shapes' and 'Templates for regular shapes' for the children to sort

Lesson 5: prepare problems similar to those in the lesson

You will need

Photocopiable sheets

'What shape could it be?'; '3D shapes'

General resources

'2D shapes'; 'Templates for regular shapes'; 'Templates for irregular shapes'; '3D shape vocabulary'; '2D shape vocabulary'

Equipment

3D shapes: spheres, cones, cylinders, cubes, cuboids, square-based pyramids, triangular prism; 3D objects classroom objects that are shaped like a: sphere, cone, cylinder, cube, cuboid, square-based pyramid; individual whiteboards; feely bag; Plasticine®

Further practice

Interactive activity 'Describe me' offers further practice identifying properties of shapes including line symmetry

Oral and mental starters for week 5

See bank of starters on pages 44 to 45. Oral and mental starters are also on the CD-ROM.

1 Ordering and writing two-digit numbers

2 Counting in tens

3 Partitioning

12 Number sequences

4 What's my value?

Overview of progression

During this week children will extend their knowledge of 3D and 2D shape. They will begin by identifying familiar 3D shapes. They will describe their properties in terms of faces, edges and vertices. They will identify the properties of the 2D shapes that make up the faces of 3D shapes. They will identify other 2D shapes and explore their properties including symmetry. From their explorations of 3D shapes and their 2D faces, they will begin to visualise how these can be made. They will also explore the shapes that they can see in the environment.

Watch out for

Some children may find it difficult to visualise shapes. Provide these children with real shapes for the activities and interlocking shapes so that they can explore how 3D shapes are made.

Creative context

Encourage the children to use their knowledge of shape in art and topic work, for example in designing patterns and model making.

Vocabulary

circle, cone, corner, cube, cuboid, cylinder, edge, face, hexagon, octagon, pentagon, pyramid, quadrilateral, rectangle, side, sphere, square, symmetry, triangle, **vertex**

Curriculum objectives
- To identify and describe the properties of 3D shapes including the number of edges, vertices and faces.

Success criteria
- I can name 3D shapes.
- I can describe 3D shapes.

You will need
Photocopiable sheets
'3D shapes'

General resources
'3D shape vocabulary'

Equipment
3D shapes: spheres, cones, cylinders, cubes, cuboids, square-based pyramids; a feely bag; plasticine®

Differentiation
Arrange the class in mixed-ability groups so that children can support each other in making the different shapes.

Lesson 1   Oral and mental starter 1

Main teaching activities

Whole-class work: Show the children a sphere, cone, cylinder, cube, cuboid and square-based pyramid. Ask them to tell you what types of shape these are. Establish that they are three dimensional or 3D shapes. Explain that they have three dimensions: a height, width and length. Point to these dimensions on the cube as you say them. Do the same for the other shapes.

Hold up the sphere again and ask the children to name it and to tell you its properties. Agree that it has a curved surface, it has no edges because you need two faces or a face and a curved surface to create an edge and it has no vertices because you need edges to create a vertex. Repeat this for the other shapes. For each shape with a face, ask the children to tell you the name of the 2D shape that makes it. Show photocopiable page '3D shape vocabulary' from the CD-ROM and ask volunteers to match the words with the 3D shapes.

Independent work: Follow the instructions and discussion prompts on photocopiable page '3D shapes' and demonstrate as you go along, guiding the children through the instructions. After the cube, ask the children to flatten it a little to make a cuboid. It is important, for continuity, to follow the instructions in order: the discussion of each 3D shape and the 2D shapes of the faces should follow on naturally from the previous one.

Progress check: Ask: *What are the properties of a sphere? What in real life is this shape? How did you turn your sphere into a cube? How did you turn your cube into a cuboid?*

Review
Invite a child to feel a 3D shape in a feely bag and describe it to the rest of the class. Encourage them to use all the properties that were discussed in the lesson.

Curriculum objectives
- To identify 2D shapes on the surface of 3D shapes.

Success criteria
- I can name the faces on a 3D shape.

You will need
Photocopiable sheets
'What shape could it be?'

Equipment
3D shapes: 3D objects placed around the classroom

Differentiation
Less confident learners
Give children 3D shapes to look at to help them visualise.

More confident learners
Show children a picture of a triangular prism. They visualise which shapes the faces of this could be and add this to the appropriate part of the activity sheet.

Lesson 2   Oral and mental starter 2

Main teaching activities

Whole-class work: Show some 3D shapes (sphere, cone cylinder, cube, and so on) and ask the children to draw the shapes of the faces. *How many different-shaped faces do the shapes have?* Ask the children to look around the classroom for the 3D objects. Can they find them all? Invite individuals to collect them up and place them together. The children name them and describe their properties. As a class sort all the shapes into groups of the same name.

Independent work: Distribute photocopiable page 'What shape could it be?' from the CD-ROM and demonstrate what the children need to do.

Progress check: Invite individuals to share what shapes they think the circle might be part of. Ask: *How do you know it might be a sphere? ...cylinder? ...cone?*

Review
Take feedback from the activity by inviting learners of different confidence levels to share with you what 3D shape each 2D shape might be from and to give an explanation as to why.

Lesson 3
Oral and mental starter 3

Main teaching activities

Whole-class work: Explain that today the children will focus on 2D shapes. To make the link with 3D shapes, display a cone, cylinder, cube, cuboid and square-based pyramid and discuss the 2D shapes of their faces. Describe the properties of the 2D faces in terms of number of sides, corners and lines of symmetry. You may need to remind the children of the property of symmetry as one half being the same as the other. Talk about these shapes, asking the children to name them and describe their properties including symmetry. Explain that regular shapes all have sides of equal length and corners of the same size and irregular shapes don't. Call out some shape names and ask the children to draw them on their whiteboards.

Paired work: Ask the children to complete photocopiable page '2D shapes' from the CD-ROM. Demonstrate and explain what they are doing as they work.

Progress check: Invite volunteers to show the shapes they have made. Ask: *What irregular shape have you made? How do you know it is irregular? What is the name of your shape? How do you know?*

Review

Display photocopiable page '2D shape vocabulary'. Ask the children to look at their shape and drawing. Call out shape names and properties and ask the children to stand if their shape has the name or property.

Lesson 4
Oral and mental starter 12

Main teaching activities

Whole-class work: Show the 3D shapes in turn and ask the children to identify their properties in terms of number and shape of faces, number of edges and vertices. Discuss the shapes of the faces and any lines of symmetry that they can see. Ask the children to look around the classroom and out of the windows and see if they can see these shapes around them.

Ask the children to try to sketch each shape as a 2D representation on their whiteboards. They give their whiteboard to a partner who attempts to identify them. Discuss how you can sort the 3D shapes into two groups. Try out their ideas and draw a table on the board to illustrate their suggestions.

Vertices	No vertices
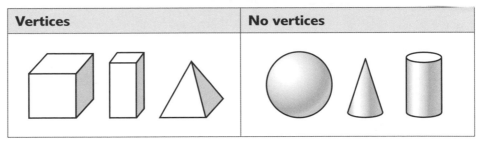	

Repeat this so that several ways of sorting are included. Ask the children to think of a way to sort the 2D shapes of the faces into a table.

Paired work: Give the children a selection of shapes from the general resources listed and tell them they will be sorting them into two groups. Give them a piece of A3 paper. They fold it in half and label their sorting headings at the top. They then sketch their shapes in the appropriate place.

Progress check: Invite pairs to share how they sorted their shapes. Ask: *What headings did you use? Why did you put those shapes there?*

Review

Recap the 3D and 2D shapes that have been covered during the lesson. Ask the children to describe the properties of each.

Curriculum objectives
● To compare and sort common 2D and 3D shapes and everyday objects.

Success criteria
● I can solve simple problems involving shape.

You will need
General resources
'Templates for irregular shapes'; 'Templates for regular shapes'

Equipment
3D shapes: cone, cylinder, cube, cuboid, square-based pyramid, triangular prism; individual whiteboards

Differentiation
Less confident learners
Children find just one line of symmetry on the 2D shapes in the paired work.

More confident learners
Children find as many lines of symmetry on the 2D shapes as they can in the paired work.

Lesson 5
Oral and mental starter 4

Main teaching activities

Whole-class work: Recap the work that the children have covered over the previous four lessons. Hold the different 3D shapes up and ask the children to name and describe their properties. Ask more confident children to identify the triangular prism. Repeat for 2D shapes. Ensure they identify whether these shapes have symmetry or not.

Ask: *Yukesh has a collection of 3D shapes. He has noticed that they all have at least one triangular face. What shapes could he have?* Give the children a cone, cylinder, cube, cuboid, square-based pyramid, triangular prism. They examine them in order to find out what shapes Yukesh could have. Agree triangular prisms and square-based pyramids. Repeat for other shaped faces. Ask similar problems for 2D shapes, such as: *Olivia has a collection of 2D shapes. She has noticed that all her shapes have four sides. What shapes could she have?* Again, ask the children to think about the possible shapes. They draw them on their whiteboards. *What is the name for shapes with four sides?* (Quadrilateral.)

Paired work: Give pairs copies of the general resources. They identify which shapes have symmetry. They record by drawing the shapes on paper and drawing on the line (or lines) of symmetry. They then make up a problem of their own.

Progress check: Invite volunteers to show some of the shapes that have symmetry.
- *How do you know this shape is symmetrical?*
- *Can you draw it on the board with one of its lines of symmetry?*

Review
Draw some 2D symmetrical shapes on the board. Ask the children to draw the lines of symmetry of the shapes. Invite volunteers to ask some of the problems they made up during their activity. Invite other children to solve them.

Measures and money

Expected prior learning

Children should be able to:

- compare, describe and measure simple lengths, masses (weights) and capacities
- recognise and know the value of our coins and notes.

Topic	Curriculum objectives	Expected outcomes
Measurement	**Lesson 1**	
	To choose and use appropriate standard units to estimate and measure length/height in any direction (m/cm); mass (kg/g); temperature (°C); volume and capacity (litres/ml) to the nearest appropriate unit, using rulers, scales, thermometers and measuring vessels. To compare and order lengths, mass, volume/capacity and record the results using >, < and =.	Use standard units of measurement. Use the appropriate language and abbreviations. Compare using >, <, = and order lengths. Read scales to the nearest sensible division.
	Lesson 2	
	To choose and use appropriate standard units to estimate and measure length/height in any direction (m/cm); mass (kg/g); temperature (°C); volume and capacity (litres/ml) to the nearest appropriate unit using rulers, scales, thermometers and measuring vessels. To compare and order lengths, mass, volume/capacity and record the results using >, < and =.	Use standard units of measurement. Use the appropriate language and abbreviations. Compare using >, <, = and order masses. Read scales to the nearest sensible division.
	Lesson 3	
	To choose and use appropriate standard units to estimate and measure length/height in any direction (m/cm); mass (kg/g); temperature (°C); volume and capacity (litres/ml) to the nearest appropriate unit using rulers, scales, thermometers and measuring vessels. To compare and order lengths, mass, volume/capacity and record the results using >, < and =.	Use standard units of measurement. Use the appropriate language and abbreviations. Compare using >, <, = and order capacities and volumes. Read scales to the nearest sensible division.
	Lesson 4	
	To recognise and use the symbols for pounds (£) and pence (p); combine amounts to make a particular value. To find different combinations of coins that equal the same amounts of money.	Increase fluency in counting and recognising coins. Use the symbols £ and p accurately and say amounts of money confidently.
	Lesson 5	
	To solve simple problems in a practical context involving addition and subtraction of money of the same unit, including giving change.	Use money to solve different types of problems that involve length and finding totals and change.

Preparation

Lesson 1: enlarge the cards from photocopiable page 'Measures vocabulary (1) and (2)' to A3. Prepare strips of paper that are longer than 1m but shorter than 2m

Lesson 2: ensure that the vocabulary words from lesson 1 are available for the children to see

Lesson 3: make a collection of different-sized plastic beakers or cups for use in the activity

Lesson 4: prepare containers with a selection of different coins: 1p, 2p, 5p, 10p, 20p, 50p, £1 and £2

Lesson 5: prepare problems similar to those in the lesson

You will need

Photocopiable sheets

'Lots of coins'; 'Money problems'; 'Measures activities'

General resources

'Measures vocabulary (1) and (2)'; interactive teaching resource 'Measuring jug'; interactive teaching resource 'Money'

Equipment

30cm rulers; metre stick marked in 10cm intervals; strip of paper between 1m to 2m in length; bucket balance; dial scales; kg weights; 100g weights; ½l, 1l and 2l bottles of water; cup; bucket; saucepan; A3 paper; scissors; glue; containers of 1p, 2p, 5p, 10p, 20p, 50p, £1 and £2 coins; measuring jugs; pictures of different types of scales, such as ruler, measuring jug

Further practice

Give further practical experience of using measuring equipment such as rulers, tape measures, scales, measuring jugs

Oral and mental starters for week 6

See bank of starters on pages 44 to 45. Oral and mental starters are also on the CD-ROM.

1	Ordering and writing two-digit numbers
6	Counting in tens and ones
11	Counting in twos, fives and tens
13	Order, order
12	Number sequences

Overview of progression

During this week children will extend their knowledge of measures. They will estimate and measure lengths, masses, capacities and volumes and look at the units used to describe them and their abbreviations. They will also explore money; identifying the notes and coins used in our monetary system and use these to pay and give change. They will solve problems involving money and length.

> ### Watch out for
> Some children may find it difficult to read scales. Provide them with rulers or pictures of measuring jugs and weighing scales and use these as number lines. Ask the children to put their fingers on certain numbers and count on and back different amounts.

Creative context

Encourage the children to use their knowledge of measures in DT activities, especially when making things and cooking.

Vocabulary

capacity, centimetre, empty, full, gram, heavy, kilogram, length, light, litre, long, mass, measure, measuring jug, metre, millilitre, short, volume, weigh

Curriculum objectives

● To choose and use appropriate standard units to estimate and measure length/height in any direction (m/cm); mass (kg/g); temperature (°C); volume and capacity (litres/ml) to the nearest appropriate unit using rulers, scales, thermometers and measuring vessels.
● To compare and order lengths, mass, volume/capacity and record the results using >, < and =.

Success criteria

● I can measure in centimetres and metres.
● I can compare and order lengths.

You will need

Photocopiable sheets

'Measures activities'

General resources

'Measures vocabulary'

Equipment

Large piece of sugar paper; metre stick marked in 10cm intervals; 30cm ruler; a strip of paper between 1m and 2m in length; scissors

Differentiation

Organise the class in mixed-ability pairs or groups.

Less confident learners

Check that they are fully focused on the task and are contributing to the work being done.

Lesson I

Oral and mental starter I

Main teaching activities

Whole-class work: Tell the children that this week they will be thinking about measures. Ask: *What do you think is meant by 'measures'? Tell me any words that indicate what is being measured?*

If not, ask them what they think is meant by length (how long/short/wide/narrow something is), mass (how heavy something is), capacity (how much a container holds) and volume (how much liquid is in a container).

Hold up the cards from photocopiable page 'Measures vocabulary' from the CD-ROM one at a time and ask the children to tell you which type of measure they describe. Stick them onto the sugar paper in three columns, one headed length, the second mass, the third capacity and volume.

Say that for the rest of this lesson they will be estimating and measuring length. Ask: *In what units do we measure length?* Expect them to be able to tell you metres and centimetres. They may also say, feet, inches and miles as these imperial units are often still used.

Hold up a metre stick and ask: *What in this room do you think is about 1 metre long?* For each of the children's suggestions, invite them to take the metre stick and check by holding it alongside the items. Repeat this for a 30cm ruler.

Show the 10cm section of the metre stick and ask them to draw a line that they think will be the same length. Next ask them to use their rulers to see how close they were. Now ask them to draw a line shorter and then longer than 10cm. They check with their ruler and write number sentences to describe their lines, for example 2cm < 10cm, 13cm > 10cm. Repeat this a few times.

Group work: Ask the children to work in groups of four or five with a metre stick. Give each child a copy of the length activities from photocopiable page 'Measures activities' from the CD-ROM. Ask the children to work together in their groups to carry out the different activities. They make jottings on the back of their sheet where they need to record or make a list.

Progress check: Ask: *How would you estimate whether this is longer or shorter than a metre? How can you check?*

Review

Invite children from each group to give feedback on what they have done. Ask: *Did you estimate which were longer/shorter than a metre? Did you make a good guess? How close were your actual measurements?* Hide the metre stick and show the strip of paper. Ask a pair of children to cut the paper so that they have a strip about a metre long. Ask the other children: *Do you think they have made a good estimate?* Invite another pair to measure it with the metre stick. Discuss how making good estimates will improve with practice.

Curriculum objectives

● To choose and use appropriate standard units to estimate and measure mass.
● To compare and order different masses.

Success criteria

● I can estimate and measure in kilograms and grams.

You will need

Photocopiable sheets

'Measures activities'

Equipment

Vocabulary poster from lesson 1; 1kg weights; 100g weights; bucket balance; dial scales

Differentiation

Less confident learners

Check that the children are taking an active part.

More confident learners

Check that children are not dominating the activity.

Lesson 2   Oral and mental starter 6

Main teaching activities

Whole-class work: Recap the different measures using the vocabulary poster made in lesson 1 and ask the children to identify those that refer to weight. Tell the children that today they will focus on estimating and measuring weight or mass. Pass the kilogram weights around the class so that everyone can feel how heavy 1kg is. Put one weight in a bucket on the balance and invite children to choose different objects and estimate whether they are going to be heavier or lighter than 1kg. They check by placing each in the other bucket. Ask: *What is your estimate? How can you check by looking at the balance?*

Explain that the kilogram weight is too heavy to measure the weight of lighter items accurately, so grams are used. Repeat the above activity with a 100g weight.

Group work: Give groups photocopiable page 'Measures activities' from the CD-ROM and ask them to work through the weight section. They record their work in a simple table. Repeat for other weights, such as 100g, 200g, 500g.

Progress check: Ask: *How would you estimate whether this is heavier or lighter than 100g? How can you check?*

Once they have estimated whether the items are heavier or lighter than for example.100g, ask them to place the items in order from lightest to heaviest.

Review

Take feedback from the activity by inviting learners of different confidence levels to share what they found out. Ask questions such as: *How many grams are there in 1kg?*

Curriculum objectives

● To choose and use appropriate standard units to estimate and measure; volume and capacity.
● To compare and order volume/capacity and record the results.

Success criteria

● I can estimate and measure in litres and millilitres.

You will need

General resources

Interactive teaching resource 'Measuring jug'

Equipment

Vocabulary poster from lesson 1; 1l bottle; 2l bottle; saucepan; bucket; teaspoon; plastic beakers/cups; measuring jug

Differentiation

Less confident learners

Check that the children are taking an active part.

More confident learners

Check that children are not dominating the activity.

Lesson 3   Oral and mental starter 11

Main teaching activities

Whole-class work: Recap the different measures using the poster made in Lesson 1 and ask the children to identify those that refer to capacity and volume. Explain and demonstrate that capacity is the amount of liquid a container will hold and volume is the amount of liquid in a container. Show a litre jug half full of water to demonstrate this: *This jug has a capacity of a litre and the volume of water in it is half a litre.* Show different-sized containers, such as a 1l bottle, a 2l bottle, a 5ml teaspoon. Agree that there are 1000ml in a litre. Show the scale on a measuring jug and then the interactive teaching resource 'Measuring jug' on the CD-ROM. Ask questions about the scale likening it to a number line. Point to different intervals and ask the children to tell you the volume. Show the saucepan and ask everyone to estimate its capacity, then test this out using the measuring jug. Repeat for the bucket and cup.

Group work: Provide each group with a plastic beaker or cup, a measuring jug and water. The children should estimate how many beakers will make a litre and then try it out, comparing their estimate with the real amount. They repeat with different-sized cups or beakers and record their results in a simple table.

Progress check: Ask: *How would you estimate how many beakers will make a litre? How can you check?*

Once they have estimated and measured, ask the children to place the containers in order from most to least.

Review

Fill a measuring jug with water to 500ml. Ask the children to read the scale. Explain that the jug will hold more so this isn't the capacity. The amount of water in the jug is the volume.

Curriculum objectives
● To combine amounts to make a particular value.
● To find different combinations of coins that equal the same amounts of money of the same unit, including giving change.

Success criteria
● I can show you what coins we use and say how much each coin is worth.

You will need
Photocopiable sheets
'Lots of coins'

General resources
Interactive teaching resource 'Money'

Equipment
Containers; coins: 1p, 2p, 5p, 10p, 20p, 50, £1, £2

Differentiation
Less confident learners
Give children 20 1p coins to exchange.

More confident learners
Give children 50 1p coins to exchange.

Lesson 4
Oral and mental starter 13

Main teaching activities

Whole-class work: Ask: *What can you tell me about money?* Give the children a minute to discuss and take feedback. Show the coins on the interactive teaching resource 'Money'. Ask children to identify each one. Talk about their sizes, shapes and values. Give eight volunteers one of the coins: 1p, 2p, 5p, 10p, 20p, 50p, £1 and £2. Ask the class to order them from least to most value.

Show a 1p coin and ask how many would be the same as a 2p coin. Invite a child to count out two 1p coins and exchange them for a 2p coin. Repeat this for all the coins. Give pairs of children a pile of 1p coins. Ask them to count how many they have, grouping them in piles of ten. *What can we exchange the piles of ten 1p coins for?* Agree a 10p coin. *What about any that might be left?* Agree a 5p, 2p, 1p. Children write down in pence the amount of coins they have and draw the coins they have exchanged them for.

Paired work: Give pairs of children a container of 1p coins and some 2p, 5p and 10p coins and photocopiable page 'Lots of coins' from the CD-ROM. Demonstrate what they have to do.

Progress check: Invite pairs to share how they exchanged their coins.
- *How many pennies would you exchange for a 5p coin?*

Review
Recap the lesson, asking questions such: *How many 1p coins would I need to exchange two 2p coins?*

Curriculum objectives
● To solve problems involving addition and subtraction of money of the same unit, including giving change.

Success criteria
● I can add money to find totals.
● I can find out how much change to give.

You will need
Photocopiable sheets
'Money problems'

Equipment
Containers; coins

Differentiation
Less confident learners
Adapt the price list on the photocopiable sheet so that the children work with 10p, 20p and 30p. Give them 1p and 10p coins to work with.

More confident learners
Adapt the price list on the photocopiable sheet so that the children are working with more complicated amounts.

Lesson 5
Oral and mental starter 12

Main teaching activities

Whole-class work: *Tanya wants to sell her teddy bear for 30p. Sally gave her the exact amount. What coins could she have given Tanya? Discuss this with your partner.* Take feedback encouraging different ways, for example 30 1p coins; three 10p coins; six 5p coins; ten 1p coins and two 10p coins. Use real coins. Invite volunteers to show those that Sally could have used and how they know they are correct. Repeat for similar scenarios: *Suzie bought one of Tanya's dolls for 45p. Suzie gave her 50p. How much does Tanya need to give her back? Talk to your partner about this.* Take feedback. Draw a number line from 0 to 50p. Mark 45p and highlight the amount between 45p and 50p. Count on in ones and agree that she needs 5p. Ask: *How much in total did Tanya make from these two sales? Talk to your partner about what you need to do.* Invite volunteers to describe how they could do this. Aim for adding three tens to the 45p. Demonstrate this on a number line. Discuss which coins Tanya might have had. Repeat for similar scenarios.

Paired work: Distribute photocopiable page 'Money problems' from the CD-ROM and explain what the children need to do.

Progress check: Ask questions such as these:
- *If I bought two cola drinks, how much would that cost?*
- *What coins could I use to pay?*

Review
Take feedback from photocopiable page 'Money problems'. Ask the children to share the problems that they made up.

Curriculum objectives
- To recognise the place value of each digit in a two-digit number (tens, ones).
- To compare and order numbers from 0 up to 100; use <, > and = signs.

You will need
I. Check
Oral and mental starters
3 Partitioning
13 Order, order

2. Assess
Bundles of ten straws and single straws; 'Arrow cards'; '0–100 number cards'

3. Further practice
Oral and mental starters
6 Counting in tens and ones
4 What's my value?

Photocopiable sheets
'Place value and ordering'; 'Signs and symbols (2)'

Curriculum objectives
- To add and subtract using concrete objects, pictorial representations, and mentally, including: a two-digit number and ones.

You will need
I. Check
Oral and mental starters
5 One more, one less
9 Inversion loops

2. Assess
'0–100 number cards'

3. Further practice
Oral and mental starters
12 Number sequences
10 Making numbers

Photocopiable sheets
'Adding single-digits to two-digit numbers'

Place value of two-digit numbers

Most children should be able to understand the value of tens and ones numbers. Some children will not have made such progress and will need practice using practical apparatus such as bundles of ten straws and single straws, matching these to arrow cards.

I. Check
3 Partitioning
13 Order, order

Encourage the children to recall the answers by keeping the pace sharp. Observe which children are confident and which need further practice. Extend to three-digit numbers to 200 for more confident children. *What does the 3 in 36 represent? What about the 6? How do you know? How can you partition 36? Is there another way?* Repeat for other numbers and then ask the children to order all the numbers discussed from smallest to largest.

2. Assess

The children pick a number card. They match the card with the correct number of tens bundles and single straws and make the number using the arrow cards. Repeat for three different numbers, then order the three numbers from smallest to greatest. Ask them to write number sentences using the symbols < and >. Watch out for children who do this confidently and those that struggle to find the correct arrow cards. Record the outcomes.

3. Further practice

Photocopiable page 46 'Place value and ordering' provides practice in partitioning and recombining and ordering numbers. Children work on this independently. For less confident learners provide the amounts given in real straw bundles and singles.

Adding single-digit and two-digit numbers

Children choose their own method which could be combining groups of objects and counting them all or counting on from one group. Most children should be able to add a single-digit number to a two-digit number by counting on from the largest number using their fingers or a number line. Some children will not have made such progress and will require number lines to assist them.

I. Check
5 One more, one less
9 Inversion loops

Using OMS 'One more, one less', check children can now say the number that is one more than another number using fingers to help. Using the OMS activity 'Inversion loops' ask children to explain how they can check to make sure a number is one more than the starting number. *What number is two more than 21? How did you work that out? How can you check you are right?*

2. Assess

Ask the children to pick a two-digit card and a one-digit card. When they have, they add the single-digit number to the two-digit number. Observe how they do this. For the more confident, encourage them to use one of the mental calculation strategies. Less confident children may need a numbered number line. Record the outcomes.

3. Further practice

With photocopiable page 47 'Adding single-digits to two-digit numbers' most children will count on from the larger number using their fingers or a mental calculation strategy. Some children will need concrete apparatus.

You will need
I. Check
Oral and mental starters

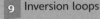

5 | One more, one less

9 | Inversion loops

2. Assess
Counters; '0–100 number cards'

3. Further practice
Oral and mental starters

14 | Forwards and backwards

7 | Number pairs to ten

8 | Doubling and halving

Photocopiable sheets
'Taking away'

Subtraction of single-digit from two-digit numbers

Most children should be able to take a single-digit number from a two-digit number by counting back from the larger number using their fingers or a number line or by using a mental calculation strategy such as bridging ten. Some children will not have made such progress and will require number lines or concrete apparatus such as counters to assist them.

I. Check

5 | One more, one less

9 | Inversion loops

Using the oral and mental starter 'One more, one less', check children can now say the number that is one less than another number using fingers to help. Using the OMS starter 'Inversion loops' ask children to explain how they can check to make sure a number is one less than the starting number. *What number is I less than 20? How do you know? How can you check you are right?*

2. Assess

Give the children a handful of at least 15 counters. Ask them to count how many there are. They pick a number card 1–9 and take that number of counters away. They then write a number sentence to show what they have done. Encourage more confident children to use one of the mental calculation strategies that they practised and then check using addition. Record the outcomes.

3. Further practice

On photocopiable page 48 'Taking away' the children choose a two-digit number and pick a number card 1–9 and perform a subtraction. Expect most children to count back from the larger number using their fingers or a mental calculation strategy. Some children will need concrete apparatus.

You will need
I. Check
Oral and mental starter

11 | Counting in twos, fives and tens

2. Assess
Counters; 'Number line 0–20'

3. Further practice
Oral and mental starters

8 | Doubling and halving

15 | Multiples

Photocopiables sheets
'Repeated addition and repeated subtraction'

Multiplication and division

This activity assesses the children's understanding of multiplication as repeated addition and division as repeated subtraction and multiplication and division as inverse operations. Most children will successfully make arrays and write number sentences with numbers to 20. Some children will not have made such progress and will require smaller arrays to describe.

I. Check

11 | Counting in twos, fives and tens

Ask questions that involve division as you carry out the activity. Look out for children who can do this confidently. For those children who cannot, give further practice using fingers. *What is 2 × 6? How did you work that out? What is 15 ÷ 5? Show me how you can use your fingers to work this out.*

2. Assess

Give each child 12 counters. Ask them to make an array of three lots of four rows and to explain the two repeated addition number sentences that they can make. Next ask children to show you the two ways in which the array can be grouped and explain the two repeated subtraction number sentences that they can make. Children draw these on a number line using loops from one number to the next. Record the outcomes.

3. Further practice

On photocopiable page 'Repeated addition and repeated subtraction' from the CD-ROM children interpret arrays as repeated addition and repeated subtraction.

Oral and mental starters

Number and place value

1 Ordering and writing two-digit numbers

Using a set of number cards 1–9, invite three children to pick one each. Stick or write them on the board. Ask the children to write all the two-digit numbers they can find from the cards. For example, 2, 6 and 9: 26, 29, 62, 69, 92, 96. Ask them to read each one to a partner. Take feedback, writing the numbers they say on the board. Next ask them to write the numbers in order from smallest to greatest on their whiteboards and then to circle the even numbers and underline the odd numbers. Recap the place value of each number.

Extension

You could ask the children to write the numbers as words.

2 Counting in tens

Tell the children that they will rehearse counting in tens. Provide 'Hundred square' from the CD-ROM for the children to use initially. Call out a number e.g. four. Ask them to count in tens to 94. Repeat with other numbers. Call out a number, for example 97. Ask the children to count back in tens to seven.

Extension

Encourage the children to think about the pattern as they count, for example tens increase or decrease, ones stay the same.

3 Partitioning

Ask the children to give you a two-digit number. Pick five and write them on the board. Give the children two minutes to partition each number in as many different ways as possible. Take feedback, ensuring you have all possible ways that have a multiple of ten and another number, for example 67: 60 + 7, 50 + 17. Repeat a few times.

4 What's my value?

Write 54 on the board. Ask the children what each digit is worth. Ask them to write some number sentences on their whiteboards to show how the number is made. Take feedback and write the number sentences they suggest on the board. Aim for: 50 + 4 = 54, 40 + 14 = 54, 30 + 24 = 54, 20 + 34 = 54, 10 + 44 = 54. Repeat for other numbers such as 27, 68 and 33. Write a two-digit multiple of ten on the board and ask the children what the zero represents: (place holder for the ones number). Ask the children to write down what the number would be without the place holder. Repeat with a few more of these numbers.

Extension

Over time, repeat this for three-digit numbers. For example, 104. Each time ask what the number would be without the place holder: 14.

5 One more, one less

Explain that when you say a number, you would like the children to write the number that is one more on their whiteboards. When you say *Show me*, the children should hold up their whiteboards to show you their written number. Begin with numbers to 20. Repeat, but ask the children to show you the number that is one less.

Extension

Over time extend this to numbers to 100.

6 Counting in tens and ones

Tell the children that they will practise counting in tens and ones. Give them a 'Hundred square' to use and then a starting number, for example ten. Hold up one finger then ten fingers. When you hold up one finger the learners count on in ones. When you hold up ten they count in tens, for example 10, 11, 21, 31, 32. Repeat this for different starting numbers going forwards and backwards.

Extension
Children who can do this confidently using a 100 square could do this without, visualising the 100 square in their heads instead.

11 Counting in twos, fives and tens

Explain that the children will practise counting in steps of two, five and ten. Show the counting stick. Explain that at one end is 0 and at the other is 20. Ask the children to tell you what steps they will count in to get from 0 to 20. Agree twos and count backwards and forwards in these steps. Put your finger on different intervals. *What number goes here? How many lots of two is that?* Repeat for counting in fives and tens.

12 Number sequences

Write this sequence of numbers on the board: 12, 14, 16, 18 and ask the children to write the next five numbers on their whiteboards. Ask them to tell you about the sequence: all even, increases in steps of two, two-digit numbers. Repeat with this sequence: 21, 19, 17, 15 (decreases in steps of two, all odd numbers). Write up some more, varying them so that they increase and decrease in steps of three, four, five and ten. Ask the children to make a sequence of their own and to write it on their whiteboard. They should then pass it to a partner to complete. Take feedback, inviting a few of the children to write their sequences on the board for the class to continue. For each, ask them to tell you about the sequence.

13 Order, order

Invite five children to pick a number card from a pile you have in front of you. Ask the class to order the children from lowest number to highest. Ask everyone to draw a number line on their whiteboards and to plot the numbers where they think they should go. Check with them by drawing an empty number line on the board. Discuss and plot on helpful marker numbers: 50, 25 and 75. Write < on the board and ask the children to write two numbers either side of it. Repeat for >. Repeat this whole procedure a few times with different sets of five numbers.

14 Forwards and backwards

Tell the children that they will practise counting forwards and backwards in ones. Give a starting number for example 12. The children count in ones from 12 to 30 and then back to 12. Repeat with other starting numbers. Occasionally, ask the children to count backwards first and then forwards to get back to the starting number.

Addition and subtraction

7 Number pairs to ten

Give the children a set of 0–9 digit cards from '0–100 number cards'. Call out numbers to ten. As you do they show you the card with the number that goes with yours to total ten, for example you say three, they show seven. After practising with digit cards, use a set and turn them over one at a time and show them to the children. They call out the number that goes with it to make ten, for example you show one, they call out nine. Time them to see how quickly they can do this.

Repeat but this time call out a number that they take away from ten. The children show you the number that is left, for example you call out six, children say four.

Extension
Extend this to pairs for all numbers to 10 and then 20.

Oral and mental starters 8, 9 and 10 continue on the CD-ROM.

Place value and ordering

■ Look at the straws. Work out how many there are.

Here is an example:

How many bundles of ten?   1   How many singles?   4

How many altogether? 14

Write this as a number sentence: 10 + 4 = 14

How many bundles of ten? _____   How many singles? _____

How many altogether? _____

Write this as a number sentence:

How many bundles of ten? _____   How many singles? _____

How many altogether? _____

Write this as a number sentence:

How many bundles of ten? _____   How many singles? _____

How many altogether? _____

Write this as a number sentence: _____

■ Now order all the numbers from smallest to largest:

_____

I can order numbers.

How did you do?

PHOTOCOPIABLE

Adding single-digits to two-digit numbers

- Add these numbers together.
- Show how you did it in your own way.

Here is an example:

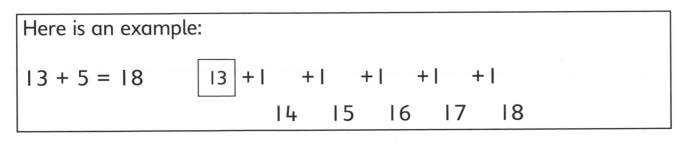

13 + 5 = 18   [13] + 1   + 1   + 1   + 1   + 1
                      14   15   16   17   18

1. 12 + 4 =

2. 15 + 6 =

3. 13 + 7 =

4. 21 + 5 =

5. 24 + 8 =

6. 36 + 3 =

7. 32 + 9 =

8. 47 + 6 =

I can add a single-digit to a two-digit number.

How did you do?

Taking away

24   18   23   32

- You will need 1–9 digit cards for this activity.
- Choose a two-digit number from one of the numbers above.
- Pick a digit card and take this away from the number you chose.
- Draw or write how you worked out the answer.

Here is an example:

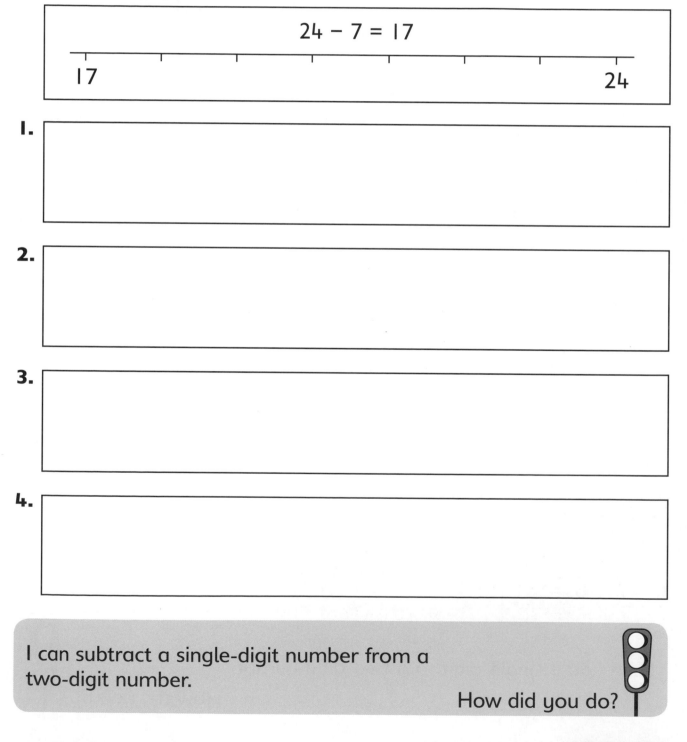

$$24 - 7 = 17$$

17   24

1.

2.

3.

4.

I can subtract a single-digit number from a two-digit number.

How did you do?

Number and place value: comparing, ordering and place value

Expected prior learning

Children should be able to:

- count forwards or backwards in steps of two, five and ten
- partition two-digit numbers into tens and ones
- read and write numbers from 1 to 50 in digits and from 1 to 20 in words.

Topic	Curriculum objectives	Expected outcomes
Number and place value	**Lesson 1**	
	To count in steps of 2, 3, and 5 from 0, and in tens from any number, forward and backward. To read and write numbers to at least 100 in numerals and in words.	Count in steps of two, five and ten. Estimate and count objects in twos, fives and tens. Read and write numbers to 100 in numerals.
	Lesson 2	
	To recognise the place value of each digit in a two-digit number (tens, ones). To read and write numbers to at least 100 in numerals and in words.	Explain place value of each digit and partition into tens and ones. Read and write two-digit numbers in numerals and those to 30 in words.
	Lesson 3	
	To compare and order numbers from 0 up to 100; use <, > and = signs.	Order numbers on a number line from 0–100. Compare numbers using < and > signs. Round numbers to the nearest ten.
	Lesson 4	
	To identify, represent and estimate numbers using different representations, including the number line. To read and write numbers to at least 100 in numerals and words.	Read and write numbers to 100 in numerals. Read and write numbers to 30 in words.
	Lesson 5	
	To use place value and number facts to solve problems.	Use place value to solve simple oral problems.

Preparation

Lesson 1: prepare containers containing mainly the same colour counter with a few of another colour

Lesson 2: enlarge the arrow cards to A3, cut out and laminate

Lesson 3: prepare '0–100 number lines' in marked intervals of ten for those that need them

Lesson 4: copy, laminate and cut out photocopiable page 'Place-value circles' in squares or circles depending on the time you have (either will work well)

Lesson 5: prepare some additional simple problems to ask the class

Copy and laminate number cards so that there are enough for one set per child and number cards to 50 enough for small group use

You will need

Photocopiable sheets
'Number pair problems'

General resources
'Arrow cards'; 'Place-value circles'; '0–100 number lines'; '0–100 number cards'; 'Up the mountain'; 'Up the mountain gameboard'; interactive activity 'The name game'

Equipment
Coloured counters; individual whiteboards; straws; elastic bands; 1p and 10p coins; dice

Further practice

Interactive activity 'The name game' offers further practice in identifying numbers to 30 in numerals and words, and extends to numbers to 100 (screens 2 and 3)

Oral and mental starters for week 1

See bank of starters on pages 85 to 86. Oral and mental starters are also on the CD-ROM.

 Counting

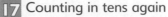 Counting in tens again

18 Number pairs

19 Odd and even numbers

Overview of progression

During the week the children will consolidate their knowledge of counting in steps of two, five and ten. They will continue to compare and order numbers. They will partition numbers into tens and ones and explain the place value of each number. They will extend their knowledge of reading and writing numbers to 100 in numerals and consolidate writing the numbers from 1 to 30 in words and above. They will practise number pairs to ten and use this to solve problems.

Watch out for

Some children may still not fully understand partitioning. For those that do not give them bundles of ten straws, up to nine single ones and arrow cards. They group some of the bundles together and take a few single straws. They then find the correct arrow cards to show the number.

Creative context

Ask the children to look at birthday cards and in shopping catalogues to find numbers. They could cut these out to make number posters.

Vocabulary

continue, count in twos, count in fives, count in tens, **multiple of**, nearest ten, one-digit number, **partitioning**, place, **place value**, predict, represents, round, sequence, stands for, tens digit, 'teens' number, two-digit number

■SCHOLASTIC

Curriculum objectives

- To count in steps of 2, 3, and 5 from 0, and in tens from any number, forward and backward.
- To read and write numbers to 100 in numerals.

Success criteria

- I can count in steps of two, five and ten forwards and backwards.
- I can count up to 50 objects in twos and tens and represent them using drawings.

You will need

General resources

'0–100 number cards'

Equipment

Different coloured counters

Differentiation

Less confident learners

Give the children smaller numbers, for example two sets of number cards 1–5.

More confident learners

Ask them to count their counters in twos and fives. Encourage them to decide which is the most efficient method to use.

Lesson 1   Oral and mental starter 16

Main teaching activities

Whole-class work: Explain that this lesson is about counting. Give pairs of children between 20 and 100 counters of one colour depending on their confidence. They estimate how many they have. Ask: *How could you count them?* Agree in groups of ten. Provide pairs with a few counters of a second colour. They count out a group of ten counters and swap this for one of the other colour. Emphasise that the new counter represents ten. They repeat until they have exchanged all of them. Discuss how to count the counters that are left, for example in fives and twos. Finally, children compare the actual amount with their estimate.

Ask pairs to explain how many counters they have, for example six 'tens' counters which is 60 and three 'ones' counters, totalling 63. Children write a number sentence, for example $60 + 3 = 63$. Focus on the = sign and reinforce that it is a sign of equality therefore the number sentence could also be: $63 = 60 + 3$. Draw a number line from 0–100. Invite pairs to write their numbers where they think they belong. Repeat for other numbers of counters.

Paired work: Ask the children to work with a partner. They take it in turns to drop handfuls of counters on the table. They estimate how many they think there are. They then check by counting and grouping them in tens.

Progress check: Invite pairs to show the class what they have been doing.

- *How many counters do you think there are?*
- *How can we check?*

Review

Take feedback from the activity. Invite the children to share the total number of counters they had in total and write the number sentence to show how many groups of ten and how many single counters. Write some two-digit numbers on the board and ask the children to write number sentences, for example $30 + 6 = 36$. Draw a number line on the board and invite children to plot their numbers on it.

Curriculum objectives

- To recognise the place value of each digit in a two-digit number (tens, ones).
- To read and write numbers to at least 100 in numerals.

Success criteria

- I can partition numbers into tens and ones.
- I can read and write numbers to 100 in numerals.

You will need

General resources

'Arrow cards'; 'Up the mountain'; 'Up the mountain gameboard'

Differentiation

Organise the children into mixed-ability groups for this activity so the more confident can support the less confident.

Lesson 2   Oral and mental starter 17

Main teaching activities

Whole-class work: Tell the children that they will be revising how to make numbers over ten by combining tens and ones. Show one of each of the arrow cards, such as 30 and 8. Ask: *What number can we make if we put these two together?* Agree 38 and put the cards together to show the children. Repeat using different tens and ones cards. Invite two children to come to the front of the class and pick a tens number and a ones number respectively. The class read each card and then say what the number will be when the cards are combined. Ask the two children to demonstrate.

Hold up a tens and a ones card and ask the children to write down the number sentence to show what number will be made when the cards are combined.

Group work: Model the instructions for the 'Up the mountain' game then let the children play in groups.

Progress check: Invite a group of children to demonstrate how they are playing the game and check that everyone is playing correctly.

Review

Invite four or five children to each select a tens and a ones card, combine them and say what their new number is and write it on the board. Ask the class to order these from the lowest number to the highest. Ask: *How do you know this is the right order? Which number gives you the clue?* Repeat with different children.

Curriculum objectives
● To compare and order numbers from 0 up to 100; use <, > and = signs.

Success criteria
● I can order numbers on a number line from 0 to 100.
● I can compare numbers using < and > signs.
● I can round numbers to the nearest ten.

You will need

General resources
'Number lines 0–100'; '0–100 number cards'

Equipment
Individual whiteboards

Differentiation

Less confident learners
Give children number lines with the intervals of ten already marked on.

More confident learners
Encourage children to make three-digit numbers as well as two-digit numbers.

Lesson 3
Oral and mental starter 18

Main teaching activities

Whole-class work: Explain that today the children will be concentrating on writing, ordering, comparing and rounding numbers. Write the digits 3, 5 and 8 on the board and ask the children to write on their whiteboards all the two-digit numbers that they can using these digits: 35, 53, 38, 83, 58, 85.

Draw a number line on the board and ask the children to tell you which 'marker' numbers would be helpful to mark on first so that the numbers they made can be plotted more accurately, such as. 50, 25, 75. They should do this on their whiteboards too. They then plot the numbers they made onto it. Invite children to plot the numbers on the class line. For each ask the class if they agree. Ask questions about each number:

● *Is 35 odd or even? How do you know?*
● *What would we see if we took five away from 35? (30) What is that zero?*

Remind the children that the zero is the place holder, holding the place for the ones, without it the number would be 3. Write the signs < and > on the board and ask the children to tell you what they mean. Demonstrate with a number sentence, 35 < 53. Ask the children to make some up using the numbers on the line.

Discuss rounding to the nearest ten, explaining that this is a useful skill when estimating. Explain to the children when a number ends in 1-4 round down to 0; if a number ends in 5-9 round up to the next ten. Ask the children to round the numbers on the line, 53 would be 50. Repeat with another set of numbers. Discuss what happens when a number ends in 5. Agree that it is rounded up to the next ten for example 45 would be rounded to 50.

Independent work: Give children number cards 1–9. They pick four and make as many two-digit numbers as they can. They draw a number line from 0–100 and plot the numbers onto it. They then make up some < and > number sentences using the numbers they have made. They then round the numbers to the nearest ten.

Progress check: Ask individuals to share the numbers that they made with the class.

● *How can we write a number sentence to show that 45 is smaller than 54?*
● *What is 45 rounded to the nearest ten? What about 54?*

Review

Draw a number line on the board and ask 12 children to plot one of their numbers onto it. Ask everyone to make < and > number sentences on their whiteboards and to explain them to a partner. Focus on rounding and ask: *What are the 12 numbers rounded to the nearest ten?* They write the new numbers and show you.

Curriculum objectives

- To identify, represent and estimate numbers using different representations, including the number line.
- To read and write numbers to at least 100 in numerals and in words.

Success criteria

- I can show numbers in different ways.
- I can read and write numbers to 100 in numerals.
- I can read and write numbers to 30 in words.

You will need

General resources

'Place-value circles'; interactive activity 'The name game'

Equipment

Straws; elastic bands; 1p and 10p coins; dice

Differentiation

Organise the children into mixed-ability pairs for the activity.

Less confident learners

Consolidate understanding of numbers to 30 using interactive activity 'The name game' (screen 1).

More confident learners

Extend understanding to numbers to 100 using interactive activity 'The name game' (screens 2 and 3).

Lesson 4   Oral and mental starter 18

Main teaching activities

Whole-class work: Explain to the children that during this lesson they will explore different ways to show numbers and also different ways to partition them. Remind them of the work they did with straws in week 1 of the first term. Give out piles of straws and elastic bands to pairs of children. Ask them to work with their partner to show you 36 using the straws. You might need to remind them to make bundles of ten straws. When they have done this invite pairs to say what they have in front of them, for example three bundles of ten straws and six singles. Encourage each pair to show their straws in this way: one child holds the three bundles and the other the six single straws. Write this on the board: $36 = 30 + 6$. Ask: *How else can we partition 36?* If they need some help suggest that the child holding the bundles of ten gives one of them to their partner. *What will our number sentence be this time?* Agree $36 = 20 + 16$. Discuss the other way to partition: $36 = 10 + 26$.

Draw a number line from 0–100 on the board. Remind them that to help plot numbers more accurately 50, 25 and 75 are helpful markers. Invite children to position these three numbers on to it and then 36 onto it. *How else can we write 36?* Agree, in words. Ask the children to help you write 36 in words.

Give pairs of children 1p and 10p coins. Ask them to count out 48 pennies and then count out groups of ten and substitute for a 10p coin. Repeat the above activity with the straws for the coins, include other ways to partition. Plot 48 on the number line and write it in words.

Show the children the place-value circles cut out from photocopiable page 'Place-value circles' from the CD-ROM and ask them how they could make 67 using these. Establish that they can take six 'tens' circles and seven 'ones'. Write $67 = 60 + 7$. Discuss other ways to partition and ask volunteers to write these on the board ($50 + 17$, $40 + 27$ and so on).

Paired work: Tell the children that they will play a place-value circle game. Give each pair ten 'tens' circles and 30 'ones' circles. Explain the instructions: *Take it in turns to throw the dice and collect that number of 'ones' circles. Keep doing this. Each time you collect ten 'ones' circles, exchange them for a 'tens' circle. The winner is the first one to get 50 or more 'tens' circles.* Let children play this a few times.

Progress check: Invite volunteers to share the number they have, for example two 'tens' and five 'ones' which is 25 altogether.

- *How many 'ones' circles do you need to exchange for a 'tens'?*

Review

Play the game as a class. You could divide the class into two groups for this or make it a teacher versus class game. At certain points, stop and count how many each of you or the groups have and plot these on the number line. Invite children to write these numbers in words on the board.

Curriculum objectives
● To use place value and number facts to solve problems.
Success criteria
● I can solve word problems using place value and number facts.

You will need
Photocopiable sheets
'Number pair problems'

Differentiation
Less confident learners
Adapt the photocopiable sheet 'Number pair problems' so that children are working with single-digit numbers only. Provide counters so that they can partition the second number.
More confident learners
Once children have completed the photocopiable sheet 'Number pair problems', ask similar problems but with a teens number to be added.

Lesson 5   Oral and mental starter 19

Main teaching activities
Whole-class work: Remind the children of the starter activities from lessons 3 and 4. Recap the number pairs for all numbers to ten. Explain that in this lesson they will be solving problems and that knowing number pairs to ten will help them. Begin with this example: *Ellie made six cakes, her friend made eight. How many did they make altogether? Talk to your partner about how you could solve this.* Take feedback and agree that they need to add 6 and 8. Establish that they could use their number pair facts: partition 8 into 4 and 4, then add 4 to 6 to make 10 and then add the remaining 4 to make 14. Write this as a number sentence: $6 + 4 + 4 = 10 + 4 = 14$.

Write some calculations on the board so that the children can practise this strategy: $7 + 9$, $8 + 5$, $4 + 8$. Invite children to explain how they worked out the answers using number pair facts. Once they have practised, ask this problem involving a two-digit and a one-digit number: *Bobby had 25p, his sister gave him another 7p. How much did he have altogether?* Agree that 7p can be partitioned into 5p and 2p, 5p can be added onto 25p to make 30p and then the final 2p can be added. Write this as a number sentence: $25p + 5p = 30p$ $30p + 2p = 32p$. Ask: *James had 36 football cards. John had five more. How many football cards did John have?* Work through this in the same way as the previous problem. Repeat with similar scenarios.

Independent work: Distribute photocopiable page 'Number pair problems' from the CD-ROM. Explain that the children need to solve the problems using the strategy covered above. Once they have completed the activity sheet, they invent some of their own problems to ask the class in the review.

Progress check: Invite volunteers to explain how they answered the questions they have done so far and to show the appropriate number sentence. Ask the rest of the class if they agree.

● *How could you partition 9 to add it to 17?*
● *What would the number sentence be?*

Review
Invite children to share one of their word problems for others to solve. Finish the lesson by asking the children a few more problems as in the main activity. Ensure you include problems for the more confident children. Say: *Olivia counted 26 people in the shop. India counted 16 more. How many did India count?*

Addition and subtraction

Expected prior learning

Children should be able to:

- identify and represent numbers using concrete objects and pictorial representations including a number line
- find totals by counting on.

Topic	Curriculum objectives	Expected outcomes
Addition and subtraction	**Lessons 1 and 2**	
	To solve problems with addition and subtraction using concrete objects and pictorial representations. To recognise and use the inverse relationship between addition and subtraction and use this to check calculations and solve missing number problems. To show that addition of two numbers can be done in any order (commutative) and subtraction of one number from another cannot.	Use the vocabulary of addition and subtraction. Use concrete and pictorial representations and number facts to add and subtract. Check answers using the inverse operation. Understand that addition is commutative, subtraction is not.
	Lesson 3	
	To add and subtract numbers using concrete objects, pictorial representations, and mentally, including: a two-digit number and tens; two two-digit numbers. To show that addition of two numbers can be done in any order (commutative) and subtraction of one number from another cannot.	Solve addition and subtraction problems within the context of number and money. Add and subtract by partitioning. Show that addition can be done in any order but subtraction cannot. Check answers using the inverse operation.
	Lesson 4	
	To add and subtract using concrete objects, pictorial representations, and mentally, including: a two-digit number and ones; two two-digit numbers.	Solve addition and subtraction problems within the context of number and money. Add and subtract by bridging ten.
	Lesson 5	
	To solve problems with addition and subtraction: • using concrete objects and pictorial representations, including those involving numbers, quantities and measures • applying their increasing knowledge of mental and written methods.	Use mental calculation to solve simple addition and subtraction problems within the context of money.

Preparation

Lesson 1: have available a large piece of sugar paper for the vocabulary poster

Lesson 3: prepare an enlarged copy of the 'Lost in space gameboard' for the review session

You will need

Photocopiable sheets
'Add and subtract (2)'; 'Bridge that ten'; 'Lost in space gameboard'; 'Lost in space recording sheet'

General resources
'0–100 number cards'; interactive activity 'In my head'

Equipment
Interlocking cubes; individual whiteboards; counting apparatus; sugar paper; 100 squares

Further practice

Offer further practice of adding and subtracting a single digit and two digit number using 'Add and subtract template' or interactive activity 'In my head'.

Oral and mental starters for week 2

See bank of starters on pages 85 to 86. Oral and mental starters are also on the CD-ROM.

20 Adding 11

21 Adding nine

22 Adding and subtracting

23 Bridging ten

24 The equals sign

Overview of progression

During this week children will use mental calculation strategies for addition and subtraction. These strategies include using number facts, adding/subtracting 9 and 11 by adding/subtracting ten and adjusting, bridging ten and partitioning. They will be encouraged to use concrete apparatus, 100 squares and number lines. They will check answers using the inverse operation and begin to understand that addition is commutative and subtraction is not. Throughout they will be solving simple problems within the context of number and money. They will also use the strategies considered during the week to solve simple problems in the context of time.

Watch out for

Some children may be continuing to add and subtract in ones. They need to develop their understanding of partitioning to enable them to add and subtract more efficiently. During the week focus on this strategy for addition with these children. Work with them for some of the time demonstrating with concrete apparatus and arrow cards to help deepen their understanding.

Creative context

Encourage the children to make up problems involving addition and subtraction using familiar scenarios.

Vocabulary

add, addition, altogether, **bridging ten**, difference, **inverse operation,** make, more, **partitioning**, plus, subtract, sum, take away, **tens boundary**, total

Curriculum objectives
- To solve problems with addition and subtraction using concrete objects and pictorial representations.
- To recognise and use the inverse relationship between addition and subtraction and use this to check calculations and solve missing number problems.
- To show that addition can be done in any order and subtraction cannot.

Success criteria
- I can solve simple problems by adding and subtracting.
- I can show you that it does not matter which way we add numbers together.
- I can show you that it does matter which way we subtract numbers.

You will need
Photocopiable sheets
'Add and subtract (2)'
Equipment
Interlocking cubes; individual whiteboards; sugar paper

Differentiation
Less confident learners
Adapt photocopiable page 'Add and subtract template' so that the children are working with numbers to ten.
More confident learners
Adapt photocopiable page 'Add and subtract template' so that the children are working with numbers to 49.

Lesson 1   Oral and mental starter 20

Main teaching activities

Whole-class work: Explain that during this lesson the children will add and subtract using their knowledge of number facts to ten. They will do this using objects and number lines. They will also be investigating whether it matters in which order we add and subtract numbers. Ask: *What does add mean?* As they explain, encourage the children to tell you all the words they can think of. Repeat for subtraction. Ensure those in the vocabulary list are covered. Write these on sugar paper to display and refer to during the week.

Write on the board 18 and 6. Invite a child to count out a pile of 18 cubes and then 6 cubes. Ask: *How could we add these two amounts together?* Agree that you could, for example, put the cubes together and count them all from one; add to the group of 18 and count on from there; or use their number facts and add 2 to 18 to make 20 and then add the other 4. Ask: *What addition number sentence could we make?* Agree 18 + 6 = 24. Demonstrate this on a number line. *Could we do this the other way around?* Agree that you can, that adding 18 on from 6, adding 4 of the 18 to make 10 and then adding the other 14 would also make 24. Ask: *What addition number sentence could we make this time?* Agree 6 + 18 = 24. Again, show this on a number line. Emphasise that whichever way you add the two numbers the answer will be the same.

Now focus on subtraction. Show 18 cubes. Invite a volunteer to take away 6 cubes and tell you how many are left. Write this as a number sentence: 18 − 6 = 12 and demonstrate on a number line: in the middle write 0, and from there the numbers 1 to 18. Circle the 18 and count back 6. Now show 6 cubes and ask the children what will happen if they try to take 18 away. Establish that they can't because there are not enough cubes. Demonstrate this on a number line.

Explain that our numbers go on forever and that on the other side of zero these numbers are mirrored but are negative. Write −1 to −18 on the other side of zero. Discuss where they might see negative numbers (temperatures in winter are a good example). Circle 6 and count back 18. Agree that they are at −12. Do this to emphasise that it does matter how you take away numbers as the answer will be different. There is no need to teach negative numbers at this stage but it is important that the children begin to understand that subtraction is not commutative and why.

Group work: Explain that the children are going to prove that it doesn't matter which way they add, but it does matter which way they subtract. Give each child a copy of photocopiable page 'Add and subtract (2)' from the CD-ROM and talk through the activity with each group.

Progress check: Invite groups to share an example of the numbers they picked and the number sentences they made.
- *Are the answers the same when you add?*
- *Are the answers the same when you subtract?*

Review
Write these numbers on the board: 27, 8.
- *How can we add these numbers together? Is there another way?*
- *Who can write two number sentences on the board to show the possible additions? Will the answers be the same?*
- *What two number sentences can we write to show the possible subtractions?*
- *Will the answers be the same?*
- *What does this tell us about addition and subtraction?*

Ask the children to think of an occasion when it does not matter which way round two numbers are subtracted. If they cannot answer, prompt them by writing the same number twice on the board, for example 3 − 3 =.

Curriculum objectives

● To add and subtract using concrete objects and pictorial representations.
● To recognise and use the inverse relationship between addition and subtraction.
● To show that addition can be done in any order and subtraction cannot.

Success criteria

● I can add and subtract a two-digit number and a single one.
● I can check my answer by taking away.

You will need

General resources

'0–100 number cards';
'Hundred square'

Equipment

Individual whiteboards

Differentiation

Less confident learners

Work with numbers to 20.

More confident learners

Work with numbers beyond 50.

Lesson 2
Oral and mental starter 21

Main teaching activities

Whole-class work: Explain that the children will be thinking about the strategy of adding a multiple of ten and adjusting. Set this problem: *Sanjit had 56p, his brother gave him 9p more. How much does Sanjit have now? Talk to your partner about how you would find the answer.* Take feedback and agree that they could add 10p and then take 1p away, giving 65p. Demonstrate this on a number line. Repeat for similar money problems that involve adding 9p and 11p. Give each child a 'Hundred square' to help them work the problems out. For each problem encourage the children to show on their whiteboards how they can check using subtraction.

Ask: *Samira had £26, she gave £9 to charity. How much did she have left?* Agree that they could take away £10 and then, because they have taken away £1 too many they add £1. Demonstrate this on a number line. Repeat with similar money problems and check answers by addition.

Independent work: Give each child some number cards 0–50. They pick one and add 9 and then 11, then they subtract 9 and 11. Each time they check using the inverse operation. Once they have done this, they make up a problem for each calculation.

Progress check: Invite children to share how they added and subtracted 9 and 11 to their numbers. Ask the rest of the class if they agree that they have used the appropriate strategy correctly. Ask: *How can we check that their answer is correct?*

Review

Invite children to share the problems they made up and ask the class to answer them.

Curriculum objectives

● To add and subtract using pictorial representations: a two-digit number and tens; two two-digit numbers.
● To show that addition can be done in any order and subtraction cannot.

Success criteria

● I can add and subtract by partitioning.
● I can show that addition can be done in any order but subtraction cannot.

You will need

Photocopiable sheets

'Lost in space gameboard';
'Lost in space recording sheet'

General resources

'0–100 number cards'

Differentiation

When playing the 'Lost in space' game, it may be helpful to pair less confident children with more confident children or with an adult.

Lesson 3
Oral and mental starter 22

Main teaching activities

Whole-class work: Recap the strategy of partitioning into tens and ones and recombining. Go through a few examples of addition and subtraction where the second number is a multiple of ten, for example 36 + 20, 45 − 30. For each, partition the first number and add or subtract the numbers of tens, for example 30 + 20 + 6 = 56. Move onto numbers such as 35 + 14, 56 − 24. Use this as an opportunity to reinforce the fact the children can add numbers in any order and the answer will be the same but this doesn't apply for subtraction. Discuss what happens when the ones digits total ten or more as in 34 + 27. This makes 30 + 20 + 4 + 7 = 50 + 11. Point out that 11 is 10 and 1, so you can add 50 and 10 and then add 1 to make 61. Repeat this a few times. Discuss how they can check their answers. Aim towards adding in a different order.

Group work: Distribute photocopiable pages 'Lost in space gameboard' and 'Lost in space recording sheet' from the CD-ROM. They play independently but in groups of four. Model the game. Each group will need a set of number cards 0–50 and paper for recording. They take turns to pick two number cards to add as in the lesson by partitioning into tens and ones, then move the number of ones that the answer shows, for example if the answer is 65, move five spaces.

Progress check: Ask volunteers to demonstrate some of their calculations with the class. Ask: *How can we check that the answer is correct?*

Review

Divide the class into three teams and play the game on an enlarged copy of the 'Lost in space gameboard'. Choose individuals to assess by asking them to demonstrate their additions on the board for their team.

Curriculum objectives
● To add and subtract using concrete objects, pictorial representations, and mentally, including: a two-digit number and ones; two two-digit numbers.

Success criteria
● I can add by bridging ten.
● I can subtract by bridging ten.

You will need

Photocopiable sheets
'Bridge that ten'

General resources
'0–100 number cards'; interactive activity 'In my head'

Equipment
Counting apparatus; individual whiteboards

Differentiation

Less confident learners
Children use number cards 11–20 when playing the game 'Bridging ten'.

More confident learners
Children play the game 'Bridging ten' with two pairs of two-digit numbers.

Lesson 4   Oral and mental starter 23

Main teaching activities

Whole-class work: Write on the board: 37 + 6. Ask: *Timmy has 37 shells, he found 6 more at the beach. How many does he have now? How can we solve this? Talk to your partner.* Take feedback and focus on an efficient method for this calculation (bridging ten). Discuss the different ways to partition 6, for example, 1 + 5, 2 + 4, 3 + 3. Ask: *Which of these will help us add 6 to 37?* Agree partitioning 6 into 3 + 3, you can then add 3 to 37 to make 40 and then add the remaining 3 to give 43 shells. Repeat with similar problems.

Set this problem: *Frankie had 23 toy cars. He gave 7 to his friend. How many did he have left? How can we solve this?* Agree that the children could use the same strategy. Ask them to write down on their whiteboards all the ways to make 7, for example 1 + 6, 2 + 5, 3 + 4. *Which of these will help us take 7 from 23?* Establish that they can take 3 away from 23 to make 20 and then take the remaining 4 away to give 16 cars.

Move onto adding and subtracting pairs of two-digit numbers using this strategy. Ask: *Maggie had 46p, she was given another 28p. How much does she have now?* Ask the children to work out how to solve this on their whiteboards. Take feedback. Agree that they could add the 20p to 46p to make 66p and then partition 8p into 4p and 4p. They add 4p to make 70p and then the other 4p to give 74p. Repeat with similar examples.

Focus on subtraction in the same way. Ask: *Kieran had 82p, he spent 67p on sweets. How much did he have left?* Together subtract 60p from 82p to leave 22p, partition the remaining 7p into 2p and 5p. Subtract the 2p to give 20p and then the remaining 5p leaving 15p. Again repeat with similar examples.

Paired work: Distribute photocopiable page 'Bridge that ten' from the CD-ROM and demonstrate what the children need to do: pick a number card and a digit card. Either add or subtract the number on the digit card to or from the number on the number card. To do this, partition the number so that you can make a ten. The number that remains is the number of points you score. This is a game of strategy in that the children need to decide which operation will give the highest score. For example, if the numbers 21 and 5 are picked and you add there is no need to partition so there will be no score; if you subtract you partition the 5 into 4 and 1, take the 1 away which will leave 4 remaining which is your score.

Progress check: Invite pairs of children to share how they are getting on with the game. Are they playing it correctly?
● *How do you know whether to add or subtract the second number?*

Review

Play the game as a class. You could divide the class into two teams or you could play against the whole class. For each of the numbers picked invite someone to show how to add or subtract.

Finish the lesson by reviewing number pairs for different single-digit numbers, such as 5, 6, 7 and 8. For further practice, go through the interactive activity 'In my head' on the CD-ROM, with the class asking them to write answers on their whiteboards.

Curriculum objectives

● To solve problems with addition: using concrete objects and pictorial representations, including those involving numbers, quantities and measures; applying their increasing knowledge of mental and written methods.

Success criteria

● I can solve word problems using mental calculations.
● I can check my answers using a different strategy.

You will need

Equipment

Individual whiteboards

Differentiation

Less confident learners

Work with children during the pair activity to assess their understanding and lend assistance as required.

More confident learners

During the pair activity, once the children have made their problems, ask them to invent two more for using any other strategy they can think of, such as using number facts.

Lesson 5 — Oral and mental starter 24

Main teaching activities

Whole-class work: Explain that in this lesson you will be giving the children some problems to solve that involve adding and subtracting using the different strategies that they have been thinking about this week. *Tell me some of the different ways to add and subtract that we have been thinking about this week.* Take feedback and list those they say on the board: adding and subtracting 9 and 11 by adding; subtracting 10 and adjusting; partitioning and bridging ten. Write up a calculation that would be best answered using one of these strategies and ask the children to answer them on their whiteboards. Repeat for all the strategies. Now give a variety of problems and ask the children to solve them on their whiteboards using the strategy that they think is best. Here are some examples of possible problems:

Bertie had £26. He spent £9 on a book. How much did he have left?

Louis and Alfie scored points in the quiz for their team. Louis scored 45 and Alfie scored 37. How many points did they score altogether?

Tina received £23 from her gran and £11 from her aunt for her birthday. How much money did she get in total?

Carol baked 23 cakes. She gave 7 away. How may did she have left?

Ensure that you ask problems that encourage addition and subtraction using each strategy. After you have asked each problem, discuss the ways that the children answered them. Did they all use appropriate strategies? Also ask them how they can check they are correct. Encourage them to use the inverse operation or a different strategy.

Paired work: Ask the children to work with their partner to devise two problems for each strategy. One should be for addition and the other subtraction.

Progress check: Invite pairs to read out one of their word problems and ask the rest of the class to solve them explaining their strategy.

- *Which is the best strategy to use to solve this?*
- *How could you check? Is there another way?*

Review

Invite children to ask some of the problems they made up during their activity. Ask the class to answer these problems on their whiteboards. When they have solved each one invite volunteers to share the strategies they used. Do the class think these are appropriate?

Multiplication and division: repeated addition and subtraction

Expected prior learning

Children should be able to:

- count in twos, fives and tens
- know that multiplication is repeated addition
- know that division is repeated subtraction.

Topic	Curriculum objectives	Expected outcomes
Multiplication and division	**Lesson 1**	
	To recall and use multiplication and division facts for the 2, 5 and 10 multiplication tables, including recognising odd and even numbers.	Understand multiplication as repeated addition.
	To calculate mathematical statements for multiplication and division within the multiplication tables and write them using the multiplication (×), division (÷) and equals (=) signs.	Understand division as repeated subtraction. Understand the relationship between multiplication and division.
	Lesson 2	
	To calculate mathematical statements for multiplication and division within the multiplication tables and write them using the multiplication (×), division (÷) and equals (=) signs.	Understand the link between repeated addition and arrays.
	To show that multiplication of two numbers can be done in any order (commutative).	Understand that multiplication of two numbers can be done either way round.
	Lesson 3	
	To calculate mathematical statements for multiplication and division within the multiplication tables and write them using the multiplication (×), division (÷) and equals (=) signs.	Understand the link between repeated addition and repeated subtraction and arrays.
	To show that multiplication of two numbers can be done in any order (commutative).	Use tables facts to solve multiplication and division.
	Lesson 4	
	To calculate mathematical statements for multiplication and division within the multiplication tables and write them using the multiplication (×), division (÷) and equals (=) signs.	Understand division as grouping. Check answers by multiplying.
	Lesson 5	
	To solve problems involving multiplication and division, using materials, arrays, repeated addition, mental methods and multiplication and division facts, including problems in contexts.	Use concrete and pictorial representations to solve simple problems.

Preparation

Lesson 2: prepare containers of interlocking cubes for use in the main teaching and during the children's activity

Lesson 3: prepare containers of counters for use in the main teaching and during the children's activity

Lesson 4: familiarise yourself with the interactive teaching resource 'Grouping' and ensure you can find and manipulate the counters

Lesson 5: prepare problems to ask the children similar to the examples in the lesson

You will need

Photocopiable sheets
'Hooray arrays!'

General resources
Interactive teaching resource 'Grouping'; interactive teaching resource 'Number line'; '0–100 number cards'

Equipment
Nine pairs of socks; counters interlocking cubes; individual whiteboards

Further practice

The interactive teaching resource 'Grouping' can be used to model and practice repeated addition and subtraction.

Oral and mental starters for week 3

See bank of starters on pages 85 to 86. Oral and mental starters are also on the CD-ROM.

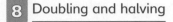 8 Doubling and halving

 25 Times tables facts

15 Multiples

Overview of progression

During this week children will extend their knowledge of multiplication and division. They will continue to develop the idea that multiplication is repeated addition and division is repeated subtraction using practical apparatus and number lines. They will check answers by using the inverse operation and learn that multiplication is commutative. They will link repeated addition and subtraction to arrays. They will begin to extend repeated subtraction into grouping. They will use the strategies considered during the week to solve simple problems in familiar contexts.

Watch out for

Some children may add two numbers together instead of multiplying and subtract two numbers instead of dividing. Work with them as a focus group as appropriate during the week.

Creative context

You could set up a class shop where the children can 'buy' two, five or ten of different items and work out total costs using multiplication.

Vocabulary

array, column, divide, divided by, equal groups of, grouping, groups of, inverse operation, lots of, multiple of, multiplied by, multiply, remainder, repeated addition, repeated subtraction, row, times

■ SCHOLASTIC

Curriculum objectives
- To calculate mathematical statements for multiplication and division within the multiplication tables and write them using the multiplication (×), division (÷) and equals (=) signs.

Success criteria
- I can answer a multiplication using repeated addition.
- I can answer a division using repeated subtraction.

You will need
Equipment

Nine pairs of socks; counters; interlocking cubes; individual whiteboards

Differentiation
Less confident learners

Children focus on finding different numbers of pairs of cubes.

More confident learners

After children have found groups of two, five and ten they could explore groups of three.

Lesson 1   Oral and mental starter 8

Main teaching activities

Whole-class work: Set this problem: *Charlie had nine pairs of socks. How many single socks did he have altogether? Remember that a pair is two. What mathematics do we need to know about to solve this?* Give the children a minute or so to think about this problem and to share their thoughts with a partner. Encourage them to think about the mathematics involved, how to find the answer and any vocabulary that they could use to describe what they might do. Take feedback, agreeing that the mathematics involved is multiplication and make a note of anything valuable that they say on the board.

Show the pairs of socks and invite a child to set them out in a row. Give each child a pile of counters and ask the class to set their counters out in twos in a row so that they have nine groups of two. *How could we show this on a number line?* Draw an empty number line beginning with zero on the board. Take one pair of socks and make a loop to represent this pair. Write two at the end of the loop and one at the top of the loop (one lot/group of two). Do this again, writing four at the end and two on the top. *We have taken two pairs of socks and represented them on this number line. How many socks are there?* Agree four. Repeat this for all the pairs of socks so that you have 18 at the end of the last loop and nine on the top. Ask the children to do this with their counters and draw the number line on their whiteboards. *What number sentence can we write to describe this?* Agree: $2 + 2 + 2 + 2 + 2 + 2 + 2 + 2 + 2 = 18$ and $2 \times 9 = 18$. Reinforce the fact that multiplication is repeated addition.

Next make a pile of 18 socks and ask: *Charlie has 18 socks and wants to know how many pairs he has. What mathematics does this involve?* Agree division. *How can we show this on a number line?* Give the children a few minutes to draw what they think on their whiteboards. Then demonstrate with the pile of 18 socks, and use the number line from the previous example. Begin at 18. Take two socks away from the pile and then draw, under the line, a loop from 18, back two to 16. Write 1 under the loop. Continue to do this until you have nine pairs. Did the children do this? *What number sentence can we write to describe this?* Agree: $18 - 2 - 2 - 2 - 2 - 2 - 2 - 2 - 2 - 2 = 0$ and $18 \div 2 = 9$. Reinforce the fact that division is repeated subtraction. Also remind the children that multiplication and division are inverse or opposite operations.

Repeat for similar scenarios that involve multiplying and dividing by two, five and ten.

Paired work: Give pairs of children a container of cubes. They count out even numbers and pair them together to make 'towers'. Once they have done this they draw number lines to show the repeated additions and subtractions they can make and write the appropriate number sentences as in the lesson. They then explore making groups of five and ten.

Progress check: Check that the children are doing what is expected by inviting pairs to share some of the number lines they have made. The class then work out, for each, the different number sentences that can be made.

Review

Take feedback from the paired work inviting children to write their number sentences on the board and asking other children to draw what these would look like on a number line.

Curriculum objectives

- To calculate mathematical statements for multiplication and division.
- To show that multiplication of two numbers can be done in any order (commutative).

Success criteria

- I can use arrays to solve multiplication problems.

You will need

Photocopiable sheets

'Hooray arrays!'

Equipment

Interlocking cubes or counters; individual whiteboards

Differentiation

Less confident learners

Adapt the photocopiable sheet so children multiply by two.

More confident learners

Ask children to make up their own calculations.

Lesson 2 — Oral and mental starter 25

Main teaching activities

Whole-class work: Say: *Peter had an egg box full of eggs. There were two rows of six eggs. How many eggs did he have altogether?* Ask the children to talk to a partner about how they would find the answer. Demonstrate practically by inviting a child to place some cubes in two rows of six. Together count the 'eggs' one at a time. Draw a picture of the array on the board:

Remind the children that this is an array. Ask: *How could we count the eggs without counting them one at a time?* Establish that they could add 6 twice. Agree that the number sentence to show this is $6 \times 2 = 12$. *Is there another way we could count them?* Agree counting in twos six times: $2 \times 6 = 12$. Agree that it doesn't matter which way you multiply, the answer will always be the same. Repeat with similar problems asking the children to draw the arrays on their whiteboards and to work out the two multiplication sentences for each.

Independent work: Distribute photocopiable page 'Hooray arrays!' from the CD-ROM and demonstrate what the children need to do.

Progress check: To check their understanding, ask the children:

- *What is an array? Can you explain in a different way? Can you give an example?*

Review

Take feedback from the activity. Invite children to demonstrate their arrays. Draw an array to demonstrate 3×5. Label the rows and columns and write a number sentence using the multiplication symbol.

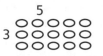 $3 \times 5 = 15$

Curriculum objectives

- To calculate mathematical statements for multiplication and division.

Success criteria

- I can solve a division using arrays.

You will need

Equipment

Counters; individual whiteboards

Differentiation

Less confident learners

Children make even numbers to 20.

More confident learners

Ask children to find and draw other arrays for the numbers of counters they pick.

Lesson 3 — Oral and mental starter 25

Main teaching activities

Whole-class work: Remind the children of the problem you set in lesson 2 relating to Peter's box of eggs. Ask the children what they did to find the answer. Draw the 12 eggs again on the board in an array (see lesson 2 above).

Invite a child to draw loops around the eggs to show there are two rows of six eggs. *How could we write this as a number sentence?* Agree $12 \div 2 = 6$. *Is there another number sentence?* Loop the eggs in two groups of six as a clue: $12 \div 6 = 2$. Repeat for other examples, asking the children to make arrays with counters and write the number sentences on their whiteboards.

Paired work: Give pairs of children a container of counters. They take groups of even numbers of counters and make arrays showing two columns or two rows. They record their work as a drawing and a number sentence.

Progress check: Ask volunteers to demonstrate an array that they have made and the number sentence to go with it.

Review

Take feedback from the children's activity, writing some of their number sentences on the board, such as $16 \div 2 = 8$. Then ask the children to explain how they could use multiplication tables to help them. Agree that they could count in twos to 16 and the number of twos counted would give the answer.

Curriculum objectives
● To calculate mathematical statements for multiplication and division within the multiplication tables and write them using the multiplication (×), division (÷) and equals (=) signs.

Success criteria
● I can divide by grouping.
● I can check my answer by multiplying.

You will need
General resources
Interactive teaching resources 'Number line' and 'Grouping'

Equipment
Interlocking cubes

Differentiation
Less confident learners
Give children different numbers of cubes to 20 and ask them to group each into twos, writing the number sentences.

More confident learners
Children group in threes as well as the other groupings and record their findings.

Lesson 4 — Oral and mental starter 15

Main teaching activities

Whole-class work: Recap on all that the children have learned so far about multiplication and division. Explain that today they will be focusing on division by grouping. Explain this as repeated subtraction as in lesson 1 but change the language to 'take away one group of...'. Using the interactive teaching resource 'Number line' on the CD-ROM, explain that you have 20 counters to be placed in bowls, two in each, and that you need to find out how many bowls you need. Use the tools to highlight the sets of two on the number line until you reach 20, then count the jumps and conclude that ten bowls are needed. Model this with crosses: (xx)(xx)(xx)(xx)(xx)(xx)(xx)(xx)(xx)(xx) Write the number sentence $20 \div 2 = 10$, reinforcing that this means ten groups of two fish have been taken away. Repeat for 26 counters and five bowls, modelling with crosses and writing the number sentence: $26 \div 5 = 5$ remainder 1. The interactive teaching resource 'Grouping' on the CD-ROM could also be used to model these number sentences. Discuss the one left over and what this means: an extra bowl. Repeat with similar scenarios. Discuss how children can check (multiplication or repeated addition).

Group work: Give small groups of children 50 interlocking cubes or similar and ask them to group these into twos, work out how many groups there are, record using crosses or other symbols and write the number sentence as in class. Ask them to repeat this for groups of five and then ten.

Progress check: Invite groups to demonstrate one of their groupings.
● *How can we check they are correct?*

Review
Take feedback from the activity, inviting children to come to the front of the class to demonstrate their work on the board, drawing symbols to represent their cubes. Together work out if they are correct by doing the reverse process (multiplication).

Curriculum objectives
● To solve problems involving multiplication and division, using materials, arrays, repeated addition, mental methods and multiplication and division facts, including problems in contexts.

Success criteria
● I can solve problems involving multiplication and division.

You will need
General resources
'0–100 number cards'
Equipment
Counting equipment

Differentiation
Less confident learners
Give children number cards 10–20. They just group in twos.

More confident learners
Children group in threes as well as twos, fives and tens and record their findings and problems.

Lesson 5 — Oral and mental starter 15

Main teaching activities

Whole-class work: Recap on what the children did in lesson 4, asking them to explain clearly what grouping is all about, how the answer to a grouping question can be checked by multiplication and what a remainder is. Set this problem: *Autumn has 23 dolls. She wants to put them in baskets, five in a basket. How many baskets will she need?* Invite someone to explain what they need to do to be able to answer the question. They should draw 23 crosses and group them in fives showing what this would look like on a number line. Another child writes the appropriate number sentence. Agree this would be 23 ÷ 5 = 4 remainder 3. *How many baskets does Autumn need?* Agree five: four for groups of five dolls and one extra for the three remaining. Repeat this for other scenarios.

Group work: Give children a pile of number cards 10–30. They pick a card and draw that number of crosses and also draw a number line from 0–30. They then group their crosses firstly in twos, then fives and tens. For each they make the jumps as you demonstrated and then write the appropriate number sentence. Finally, they make up a problem to go with each.

Progress check: Invite volunteers to read out one of the problems they made up.

- *What number sentence could we write for this problem?*
- *How could we find the answer?*
- *How could we check this is the correct answer?*

Review

Take feedback from the activity, inviting groups to come to the front of the class, share one of their problems and then demonstrate their groupings, number lines and sentences on the board. Together, work out if they are correct by doing the inverse process. Ask the class to make up alternative problems for each one demonstrated.

 ■SCHOLASTIC

Fractions of quantities, shapes and sets of objects

Expected prior learning

Children should be able to:

- know that one half is one of two equal parts
- know that one quarter is one of four equal parts.

Topic	Curriculum objectives	Expected outcomes
Fractions	**Lesson 1**	
	To recognise, find, name and write fractions ⅓, ¼, ²⁄₄ and ¾.	Understand that a fraction is part of a whole. Understand that the size of each half is the same even if it doesn't look the same.
	Lesson 2	
	To recognise, find, name and write fractions ⅓, ¼, ²⁄₄ and ¾.	Understand that a fraction is part of a whole. Understand that the size of each quarter is the same even if it doesn't look the same.
	Lesson 3	
	To recognise, find, name and write fractions ⅓, ¼, ²⁄₄ and ¾. To write simple fractions such as ½ of 6 = 3 and recognise the equivalence of ²⁄₄ and ½.	Understand the equivalence between halves and quarters. Know that the bottom number (denominator) of the fraction shows how many parts there are.
	Lesson 4	
	To recognise, find, name and write fractions ⅓, ¼, ²⁄₄ and ¾. To write simple fractions such as ½ of 6 = 3 and recognise the equivalence of ²⁄₄ and ½.	Find fractions of quantities, sets of objects and numbers. Position fractions on a number line and begin to count in halves and quarters.
	Lesson 5	
	To recognise, find, name and write fractions ⅓, ¼, ²⁄₄ and ¾. To write simple fractions such as ½ of 6 = 3 and recognise the equivalence of ²⁄₄ and ½.	Find fractions of quantities, sets of objects and numbers. Position fractions on a number line and begin to count in halves and quarters.

Preparation

Lesson 1: draw six 2×4 squares on squared paper one sheet for each child; make a sandwich that can be cut into quarters

Lesson 3: prepare three strips of paper for each child; each needs to be approximately 3cm wide and the length of the width of A4; familiarise yourself with the interactive activity 'Fractions'

Lesson 5: prepare containers of 10p and 1p coins and problems to ask the children similar to the examples in the lesson

You will need

Photocopiable sheets

'Feed Cedrick!'; 'Feed Cedrick spinners'

General resources

Interactive activity 'Fractions'

Equipment

Two apples; chocolate bar with 2×4 sections; sandwich; paper with large squares; A4 paper of two different colours; £1, 50p, 10p and 1p coins; individual whiteboards interlocking cubes; scissors; strips of paper 3cm wide; glue; counters; A3 paper

Further practice

Interactive activity 'Fractions' offers practice of recognising fractions of shapes, set of objects and quantities.

Oral and mental starters for week 4

See bank of starters on pages 85 to 86. Oral and mental starters are also on the CD-ROM.

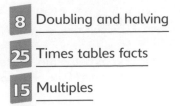

8	Doubling and halving
25	Times tables facts
15	Multiples
26	Finding fractions

Overview of progression

During this week children will extend their knowledge of fractions. They will begin by exploring the fact that halves are equal sizes even though they might not look the same. They will continue to develop this concept with quarters. They will use fraction strips to explore the equivalence between halves and quarters. They will begin to link finding fractions to sharing and use this knowledge to find fractions of sets of objects and small numbers. They will use their understanding gained during the week to solve simple problems in familiar contexts.

Watch out for

Children who think one quarter is bigger than one half because four is bigger than two. Give them plenty of practice at finding halves and quarters of the same amounts so that they can 'see' that a quarter is a smaller amount because it has been shared into more groups.

Creative context

You could set up a café in your role-play area, where the food could be sold in halves and quarters, such as cakes, sandwiches, pizzas. You could encourage the children to make up menus to show prices for these.

Vocabulary

equal parts, equivalent, four quarters, fraction, one half, one quarter, one whole, part, three quarters, two quarters

Curriculum objectives
● To recognise, find, name and write fractions ⅓, ¼, ¾ and ¾.

Success criteria
● I can explain that a fraction is part of a whole thing.
● I can find different ways to make a half.

You will need

Equipment
Chocolate bar with 2×4 sections; paper with large squares; sandwich

Differentiation

Less confident learners
Give children squared paper with the grids already drawn.

More confident learners
Ask children to work out how many quarters will be the same as a half and a whole.

Lesson 1
Oral and mental starter 8

Main teaching activities

Whole-class work: Set this problem: *Debbie is going to give half of her chocolate bar to her friend. How can she do this?* Write ½ on the board. Ask the children to tell you what they know about this. Take feedback, establishing that half is a fraction whereby something is shared into two equal parts. Show the chocolate bar and draw several representations as rectangles, marking the pieces, on the board. Agree she needs to share it equally into two and establish that the bottom number of the fraction gives that information. Demonstrate one way in which Debbie could share the bar into two equal pieces. *Who can show me how else she can give half to her friend?* Invite different children to share their ideas. They shade the chocolate bars on the board to show half. Give each child a piece of squared paper with six 2×4 rectangles marked onto it. Ask them to find different ways of making half. They shade one half each time. Take feedback, inviting volunteers to draw their ideas on the board. How many ways can they find altogether? Agree that half of their chocolate bars would be any four pieces, for example:

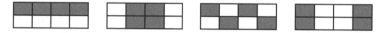

Set this problem: *Harry has a sandwich. He wants to cut it into quarters. How can he do this?* Write ¼ on the board. Ask the children to tell you what they know about this. Agree that the bottom number of the fraction is four and that this shows that the sandwich must be cut into four equal pieces. Show your sandwich and invite someone to describe how you could cut it. Do what they suggest. Do the rest of the class agree that these are quarters?

Independent work: Give the children a piece of paper with large squares. Ask them to draw 3×4 rectangular grids onto it to represent sandwiches and then shade all the different ways they can of showing a quarter.

Progress check: Check that the children are doing what is expected by inviting individuals to share some of the quarters they have made.

Review

Take feedback from the activity, inviting children to draw some of their ways to show one quarter on the board. Establish that each quarter will be four squares. Ask the more confident learners to say how many will be the same as a half and also a whole and to explain how they know. Write ¾ = ½ and ¾ = 1 to confirm what they tell you. Finish by asking: *Which fraction is bigger, half or quarter?* Agree half because if you cut a sandwich into two each piece would be bigger than if you cut it into four.

Curriculum objectives
● To recognise, find, name and write fractions ⅓, ¼, ¾ and ¾.

Success criteria
● I can explain that halves are equal amounts even if they don't look the same.

You will need

Equipment
A4 paper in two different colours; scissors; glue; two apples

Differentiation
This is a whole-class activity. It would be a good idea to pair the less confident learners with those that are more confident for peer support.

Lesson 2

Oral and mental starter 25

Main teaching activities

Whole-class work: Show two apples to the class. Say that you are going to cut one into half and the other into quarters. Ask: *Which would be the bigger part, the half or the quarter?* Take feedback and cut the apples as equally as you can to prove that the half is bigger. Demonstrate that two halves make a whole by putting the two halves together. Repeat for four quarters making a whole. Write the appropriate number sentences on the board: ½ + ½ = 1, ¼ + ¼ + ¼ + ¼ = 1. *How many quarters will be the same as a half?* Put two of the quarters together and write ¼ + ¼ = ½.

Ask: *Do halves have to look the same?* Listen to their thoughts on this. Inform the children that they have to be the same amount but don't necessarily have to look the same. Remind them of the different ways they halved the chocolate bar in lesson 1.

Show a piece of A4 paper. *How can I give you half of this paper?* Agree you could fold it down the middle and then tear it to make two equal halves. *Is there another way I could give you half?* Ask the children to talk to their partner about this. Establish that you could tear or cut the paper in different ways to give half. The important thing is that the two halves are the same amount. Demonstrate this idea through the following activity.

Demonstrate first. Give pairs of children three pieces of A4 paper, two of one colour and the third of another. They fold and tear the third piece of paper down the middle. They each hold half and place it beside the other whole piece of A4 paper. *What fraction of this piece of A4 is the small piece?* Agree half. Together, stick the small rectangle in the middle of the A4 paper:

Draw out the fact that the rectangle in the middle is half and therefore the amount around the outside must also be half even though it doesn't look the same. All cut around the outside of the small piece and hold what you have up beside the small piece. Agree that both pieces are half. Ask the children to prove this by cutting the longer piece into four equal strips and sticking them over the original small piece. The strips should cover the small piece proving that it is the same size and therefore the same fraction.

Progress check: To check their understanding, ask the children:
● *How many halves make a whole?*
● *Can you explain why the area around the outside of the small rectangle must be half?*

Review

Ask the children what the activity has shown them. Establish that fractions do not always look the same, what is important is that they are equal amounts.

■SCHOLASTIC

Curriculum objectives

- To recognise, find, name and write fractions $\frac{1}{3}$, $\frac{1}{4}$, $\frac{2}{4}$ and $\frac{3}{4}$.
- To recognise the equivalence of $\frac{2}{4}$ and $\frac{1}{2}$.

Success criteria

- I can show that two quarters are the same as a half.

You will need

General resources

Interactive activity 'Fractions'

Equipment

Strips of paper; individual whiteboards; A3 paper

Differentiation

Less confident learners

Provide children with prepared fraction strips.

More confident learners

Ask children to take a fourth strip and fold it three times making eighths. They make statements that include equivalences with these.

Lesson 3

Oral and mental starter 25

Main teaching activities

Whole-class work: Give each child three strips of paper. Ask them to write 1 in the middle of one of them. *This is the whole strip.* Ask them to take a second strip and to fold it in half. *How many parts do you think we will have when we open this up? What fraction do you think each part will be?* They label each part $\frac{1}{2}$ and place it under the whole strip. *How many halves are the same as the whole strip?* Agree two. Children take a third strip and fold it in half and then half again. Repeat the questions from above. They label each part a $\frac{1}{4}$ and place it under the one showing $\frac{1}{2}$. *How many quarters are the same as a whole? How many are the same as a half?* Ask the children to write these number sentences on their whiteboards: $\frac{1}{2} + \frac{1}{2} = 1$, $\frac{1}{4} + \frac{1}{4} + \frac{1}{4} + \frac{1}{4} = 1$, $\frac{1}{4} + \frac{1}{4} = \frac{1}{2}$, $\frac{1}{4} + \frac{1}{4} + \frac{1}{4} = \frac{3}{4}$. $\frac{1}{2} + \frac{1}{4} = \frac{3}{4}$. Reinforce using the interactive activity 'Fractions' on the CD-ROM.

Paired work: Give pairs of children a piece of A3 paper. They use the strips they made in the lesson to produce a fraction wall with the smallest fraction at the bottom. They then list some fraction equivalences and then make statements using <, > and =, for example $\frac{1}{2} > \frac{1}{4}$, $\frac{1}{2} < \frac{3}{4}$, $\frac{1}{4} + \frac{1}{4} + \frac{1}{4} = \frac{3}{4}$.

Progress check: Ask: *Which is the smallest fraction you have made? Can you tell me any equivalent fractions?*

Review

Ask the children to tell each other and then the class what they did. Take feedback from anyone who explored eighths. What fractions did they make?

Curriculum objectives

- To recognise, find, name and write fractions $\frac{1}{3}$, $\frac{1}{4}$, $\frac{2}{4}$ and $\frac{3}{4}$.
- To write simple fractions such as $\frac{1}{2}$ of 6 = 3 and recognise the equivalence of $\frac{2}{4}$ and $\frac{1}{2}$.

Success criteria

- I can find $\frac{1}{2}$ and $\frac{1}{4}$ of different numbers.

You will need

Photocopiable sheets

'Feed Cedrick!'; 'Feed Cedrick spinners'

Equipment

Interlocking cubes; individual whiteboards; counters

Differentiation

Less confident learners

Give them the spinners which show $\frac{1}{2}$ only.

More confident learners

Give them the spinners which show $\frac{1}{3}$, $\frac{2}{3}$, $\frac{1}{10}$, $\frac{7}{10}$, $\frac{3}{5}$, $\frac{1}{5}$.

Lesson 4

Oral and mental starter 15

Main teaching activities

Whole-class work: Discuss that to find half the children need to share between two. Give pairs a pile of cubes and ask them to use these to find half of different numbers, such as 10, 16, 22 by sharing into two groups. Ask them to write number sentences on their whiteboards to show their results, for example $\frac{1}{2}$ of 22 = 11. Next, ask them to find quarters of different numbers in the same way and write the appropriate number sentences. *What do you notice about finding halves and quarters of counters?* Agree that half the number of counters must be a multiple of two and quarters must be a multiple of four.

Paired work: Tell the children that they will be playing a game to help them practise halving and quartering numbers. Demonstrate the game 'Feed Cedrick!'. Ask them to think back to the fraction strip activity in lesson 3. When they folded the quarter strip they halved and halved again. They could use this strategy for finding a quarter of the number that they spin. The first child to collect 20 counters is the winner.

Progress check: Invite pairs to demonstrate how they found halves and quarters of the numbers they spin.

- *How can you find half?*
- *How can you find a quarter?*

Review

Ask some quick-fire questions. *What is half of eight?...a quarter of eight? ...half of 12? ...a quarter of 12?* Target appropriately, giving extra time to those children who need it. Ask the children to write their answers on their whiteboards. Assess their answers to identify those who are still unsure about work involving halves and quarters.

Curriculum objectives
● To recognise, find, name and write fractions ⅓, ¼, ¾ and ¾.
● To write simple fractions such as ½ of 6 = 3 and recognise the equivalence of ¾ and ½.

Success criteria
● I can find fractions of quantities, sets of objects and numbers.
● I can position fractions on a number line and begin to count in halves and quarters.

You will need
Equipment
£1.50p, 10p and 1p coins
General resources
Interactive activity 'Fractions'

Differentiation
Less confident learners
Give children 1p coins to the value of 20p. Ask them to focus on half and quarter initially.

More confident learners
Give children a range of coins and encourage them to make up amounts using the least number of coins, such as 24p: a 20p and two 2p coins. When they work out the fractions, they exchange the coins to those that share more easily.

Lesson 5
Oral and mental starter 26

Main teaching activities

Whole-class work: Recap on what the children have done during the week. Reinforce that the bottom number of the fraction (denominator) tells them how many to share into and that fractions are the same amount but may not necessarily look the same. Set this problem: *Alberto was offered half of £5 or three quarters of £4. He is saving for a toy and wants the most money. Which amount of money should he choose?* Give the children a few minutes to work out how they could find the answer. Take feedback and establish that they need to find half of £5 and three quarters of £4. Before they answer the problem, give pairs of children some £1 and 50p coins. Establish that two 50p coins will make 100p which is the same as £1. Call out different fractions of amounts to find, for example ½ of £1, ¼ of £2. Children hold up the coins to show their answers. If ¼ of £2 is 50p what is ¾ of £2? Ask the children to physically move three 50p coins (¼) and group them together and add them to make £1.50. Repeat for other quarter amounts. Return to the problem and ask them to solve it with their partner. Agree that ½ of £5 is £2.50 and ¾ of £4 is £3, so Alberto should take the latter amount. Repeat this for other scenarios.

Paired work: Give the children 10p and 1p coins. Ask them to count out different amounts of money. For each amount they work out what half, quarter and three quarters will be, for example, 44p (4×10p, 4×1p): ½ = 22p, ¼ = 11p, ¾ = 33p. If these can't be made they add or subtract coins until they can physically share them equally into two and four. They record their results as number sentences. For each they make up a problem.

Progress check: Invite volunteers to share examples of their work.
● *What is half of 12p? What is a quarter of 12p? What about three quarters?*
● *How could we find three quarters of 24p?*

Review

Take feedback from the activity, inviting pairs to share one of their problems. The class solves the problem using coins. If time is available, go through interactive activity 'Fractions' with the whole class as it offers practice of recognising all types of fractions covered in this week's work.

SCHOLASTIC

Geometry and measurement

Expected prior learning

Children should be able to:

- order and arrange combinations of objects and shapes in patterns and sequences
- describe position, directions and movements, including half, quarter and three quarter turns
- tell the time to the hour and half past the hour and draw the hands on a clock face to show these times.

Topic	Curriculum objectives	Expected outcomes
Geometry: position and direction	**Lesson 1**	
	To order and arrange combinations of mathematical objects in patterns and sequences.	Make patterns of shapes, including those in different orientations. Predict which shape will be the tenth, twelfth, and so on in a sequence.
	Lesson 2	
	To use mathematical vocabulary to describe position.	Use the appropriate vocabulary to describe the position of shapes.
	Lesson 3	
	To use mathematical vocabulary to describe position, direction and movement including movement in a straight line and distinguishing between rotation as a turn and in terms of right angles for quarter, half and three quarter turns (clockwise and anti-clockwise).	Use the appropriate vocabulary to describe the movement of objects.
Measurement	**Lesson 4**	
	To compare and sequence intervals of time.	Order days of the week and months of the year. Order different times during the day.
	Lesson 5	
	To know the number of minutes in an hour and the number of hours in a day. To tell and write the time to five minutes, including quarter past/to the hour and draw the hands on a clock face to show these times.	Tell and write o'clock, quarter past, half past and quarter to times. Draw these times on a clock face.

Preparation

Lesson 2: prepare position vocabulary cards (beside, between, underneath, next to) for each pair of children

Lesson 3: prepare movement vocabulary cards (clockwise, anti-clockwise, backwards, forwards) for each pair of children

Lesson 4: enlarge and cut out the words from photocopiable page 'Time vocabulary'

You will need

Photocopiable sheets
'Telling the time (1)'

General resources
'Time vocabulary'

Equipment
Individual whiteboards; counters; counting toys, such as bears; class analogue clock; individual small clocks; sugar paper

Further practice

Give children further practice of building patterns and sequences using sets of flat 2D shapes.

Oral and mental starters for week 5

See bank of starters on pages 85 to 86. Oral and mental starters are also on the CD-ROM.

18	Number pairs
23	Bridging ten
8	Doubling and halving
25	Times tables facts
26	Finding fractions

Overview of progression

During this week children will extend their knowledge of position, direction and movement. They will order and arrange shapes to create patterns. They will use these to work out which shape will come in later, unseen, stages of their sequence. They will explore the vocabulary of position and direction through practical activities. They will also extend their knowledge of time. They will find, write and draw o'clock, quarter to, half past and quarter to times on clocks. They will use their ability to do this to solve problems within the context of time. Time is an area that children often find difficult so it is important to practise this regularly every day, for example, reading the time at the start of the day and asking the children to tell you when it is lunch time.

Watch out for

Some children may not be able to tell o'clock and half past times. They will need to be secure in telling these times before progressing to quarter past and quarter to times. Provide children with clock faces and ask them to match them with different o'clock and half past times on the class clock during the day and to tell you the times they have made.

Creative context

Position, direction and motion could be included in PE activities. Playing games such as 'What's the time Mr Wolf?' are helpful for reinforcing the vocabulary used when telling the time.

Vocabulary

apart, April, analogue clock/watch, **anti-clockwise**, August, beside, between, centre, **clockwise,** corner, day, December, digital clock/watch, direction, edge, February, half past, half turn, hands, hour, January, journey, July, June, left, March, May, middle, minute, month, next to, November, o'clock, October, opposite, over, position, quarter past, quarter to, quarter turn, right, right angle, second, September, straight line, timer, today, tomorrow, turn, whole fortnight, week, weekend, year, yesterday

Curriculum objectives
● To order and arrange combinations of mathematical objects in patterns and sequences.

Success criteria
● I can make patterns with 2D shapes.
● I can tell you where a shape will appear in my pattern.

You will need

Equipment
Different-coloured counters; individual whiteboards; coloured pencils

Differentiation
The children work in mixed attainment pairs to give each other support.

Lesson 1   Oral and mental starter 18

Main teaching activities

Whole-class work: Tell the children that in this lesson they will be investigating shape patterns. To begin, recap the names and properties of the 2D shapes they looked at in autumn 1, week 5: circles, triangles, quadrilaterals including square and rectangle, pentagon, hexagon and octagon. Ask the children to draw irregular and regular versions on their whiteboards and to describe their properties in terms of sides, corners and lines of symmetry. Draw two squares on the board in these two orientations:

Ask the children to name them. Watch out for any that say the second is a diamond. Point out that it has the properties of a square so must be one. Recap 3D shape by asking the children which 2D shapes make up the faces of cubes, cuboids, square-based pyramids, and so on.

Draw this pattern on the board and ask the children to continue it for the next three shapes on their whiteboards:

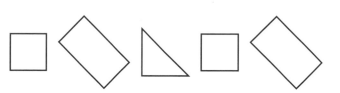

What will the tenth shape be? How do you know? Encourage the children to consider that the pattern is in groups of three shapes, so the tenth will be the first of a new group and therefore the square. Ask them to work out what shapes will be in other positions, such as, 15th, 19th, 21st and to explain how they know. Repeat for other sets of three or four shapes.

Paired work: Give pairs of children a container of different-coloured counters. Ask them to create repeating patterns using these. They set out the first six of their pattern and draw a representation on paper. They then work out what colour the 8th, 12th, 18th and 24th counters will be. They draw these and then check by continuing the pattern with their counters. They could make several different patterns if there is time.

Progress check: Check that the children are making repeating patterns by asking questions such as:
● *What shape will be eighth in your pattern?*
● *How do you know?*

Review

Take feedback by inviting pairs to share their patterns. The class works out which the 8th, 12th, 18th and 24th counters will be and the pair show them whether they are correct or not.

Curriculum objectives
● To use mathematical vocabulary to describe position.

Success criteria
● I can use words to describe different positions.

You will need
Equipment
3D shapes: spheres, cones, cylinders, cubes, cuboids, square-based pyramids; position vocabulary cards; counting toys, such as, bears

Differentiation
Organise the children into mixed attainment pairs. Check that the less confident learners have the opportunity to take part in the paired activity and that the more confident learners don't dominate.

Lesson 2   Oral and mental starter 23

Main teaching activities

Whole-class work: Explain that today the children are going to think about the position of objects. Give each child a 3D shape. Hold up each position vocabulary card in turn and ask the children with a particular shape to put it in a place that is appropriate to that word. For example, ask the children with a cube to put it somewhere that shows what is meant by the position word 'underneath'. Ask those children to explain what they did. Do this for each word.

Paired work: Give each pair three or four position vocabulary cards and a counting toy. They need to make up a story about their toy that includes the words on the cards, then practise acting it out. Explain that some of them will act out their stories to the class later.

Progress check: Spend a few minutes with pairs of children to make sure they understand the position words.

Review

Choose those children whom you wish to assess to act out their stories first. If there is time, invite others to share their stories.

Curriculum objectives
● To use mathematical vocabulary to describe direction and movement.

Success criteria
● I can describe the movement of objects.

You will need
Equipment
Counting toys, (for example bears); movement vocabulary cards

Differentiation
The children will be working in mixed attainment pairs. Check that the less confident learners have the opportunity to take part in the paired activity and that the more confident learners don't dominate.

Lesson 3   Oral and mental starter 8

Main teaching activities

Whole-class work: Recap with the children what they did in lesson 2, asking them to turn to a partner and together think of as many position words as they can. Say: *Today we are going to think about moving things around.* Ask them to think of words to do with this and record them on the board, for example backwards, forwards. Ask them to describe what they mean as a 'think, pair, share' activity.

Paired work: The children's task is similar to the last lesson, the difference being that they should use three or four direction cards to make up their story with their counting toy. Leave 'movement' out of the selection that you give to the children. After they have made up their story, encourage them to act it out.

Progress check: Spend a few minutes with pairs of children to make sure they understand the movement words.

Review

Choose pairs to act out their stories. After this, ask them to think of how they can also add some of the position words they thought of last time in their story. Give them a few minutes to think and take feedback. Ask them to tell each other one thing they have learned over the last two lessons and then share it with the class.

Curriculum objectives
● To compare and sequence intervals of time.
Success criteria
● I can order the days of the week.
● I can order the months of the year.

You will need
General resources
'Time vocabulary'
Equipment
Individual whiteboards; sugar paper

Differentiation
Less confident learners
Children focus on the units of time and days of the week for their poster.
More confident learners
Children add extra information to their posters, for example. how many minutes in an hour, hours in a day, days in a week.

Lesson 4
Oral and mental starter 25

Main teaching activities

Whole-class work: *What time words do you know?* The children share their thoughts with a partner and then the class: seconds, minutes, hours, days, weeks, months, years, days of the week, months of the year. Ask: *How many minutes in one/two/three hours? How many months in one/two/three years?* Use this to rehearse addition, doubling and multiplying. The children write their answers on their whiteboards and show you. Give seven children one each of the cards showing the days of the week. Ask them to order themselves. The class checks. Invite individuals to share things that they do at school or at home on each day of the week. Repeat this for the months of the year.

Set this problem: *Patti is six years old. She will be seven in three days' time. On what day will she be seven?* Discuss and solve it together. Repeat with questions for other days of the week and months of the year. Talk about different times during the day, such as watching television time, bed time, school time, and so on. Ask the children to order these from first to last.

Paired work: Give groups of children the cards from photocopiable page 'Time vocabulary' from the CD-ROM. They sort them according to their own criteria and make a vocabulary poster using sugar paper.

Progress check: As they make their posters groups ask questions such as: *What day comes after Thursday? How do you know? What is the fifth month of the year?*

Review
Take feedback. Invite groups to share how they sorted the words.

Curriculum objectives
● To tell and write the time to five minutes.
● To know the number of minutes in an hour and the number of hours in a day.
Success criteria
● I can read and draw o'clock and half past times and quarter past and quarter to times.

You will need
Photocopiable sheets
'Telling the time (1)'
Equipment
Analogue class clock; individual clocks

Differentiation
Less confident learners
Adapt the photocopiable sheet so that the children focus on o'clock and half past times.
More confident learners
Adapt the photocopiable sheet so that the children draw times such as 10 minutes past 3, 20 minutes to 6.

Lesson 5
Oral and mental starter 26

Main teaching activities

Whole-class work: Show the class an analogue clock. *What can you tell me about this?* Emphasise the following:

- long hand shows minutes, short hand hours
- minute hand takes 60 minutes (an hour) to go round the clock once
- hour hand takes an hour to move from one number to the next
- small intervals show the minutes, numbers show hours.

Give each child a clock. *Show me 6 o'clock. Say the time to your partner and write it on your whiteboard.* Repeat for other times including quarter past, half past and quarter to, such as half past 8.

Set this problem: *Mbemi was two hours late to the park. She was expected at 2 o'clock. What time did she arrive?* Demonstrate by counting on along a number line.

Check by counting back. Ask similar problems.

Independent work: Distribute photocopiable page 'Telling the time (1)' from the CD-ROM for children to complete.

Progress check: During the activity ask individuals questions such as. Ask: *How would half past 12 be shown on a clock? What about 4 o'clock? Quarter past 3?*

Review
Take feedback from the photocopiable sheet. Invite children to share the clocks they drew. Invite others to share the problems they made up and to demonstrate finding the difference between times using a number line.

Statistics

Expected prior learning

Children should be able to:

- answer a question by collecting and recording information in a list or table
- present outcomes using practical resources, pictures, block graphs or pictograms
- use diagrams to sort objects into groups according to given criteria.

Topic	Curriculum objectives	Expected outcomes
Statistics	**Lesson 1**	
	To interpret and construct simple pictograms, tally charts, block diagrams and simple tables.	Gathering information using a tally.
	To ask and answer simple questions by counting the number of objects in each category and sorting the categories by quantity.	Making and interpreting lists and tables.
	To ask and answer questions about totalling and comparing categorical data.	
	Lesson 2	
	To interpret and construct simple pictograms, tally charts, block diagrams and simple tables.	Gathering information using a tally.
	To ask and answer simple questions by counting the number of objects in each category and sorting the categories by quantity.	Turn lists and tallies into tables.
	To ask and answer questions about totalling and comparing categorical data.	Extract information from tables.
	Lesson 3	
	To interpret and construct simple pictograms, tally charts, block diagrams and simple tables.	Making and interpreting pictograms.
	To ask and answer simple questions by counting the number of objects in each category and sorting the categories by quantity.	
	To ask and answer questions about totalling and comparing categorical data.	
	Lesson 4	
	To interpret and construct simple pictograms, tally charts, block diagrams and simple tables.	Making and interpreting block graphs.
	To ask and answer simple questions by counting the number of objects in each category and sorting the categories by quantity.	
	To ask and answer questions about totalling and comparing categorical data.	
	Lesson 5	
	To interpret and construct simple pictograms, tally charts, block diagrams and simple tables.	Solve problems involving making and interpreting block graphs.
	To ask and answer simple questions by counting the number of objects in each category and sorting the categories by quantity.	
	To ask and answer questions about totalling and comparing categorical data.	

Preparation

Lesson 2: copy photocopiable pages 'Ways to organise data' for pairs of children to share

Lesson 4: copy photocopiable page 'Sports block graph', one of each per child

You will need

Photocopiable sheets

'Tables'; 'Pictograms'; 'Popular sports'; 'Block graphs'; 'Sports block graph'

General resources

'Ways to organise data'

Equipment

Individual whiteboards; large pieces of sugar paper; interlocking cubes (white, pink, yellow and brown)

Further practice

Interactive activity 'Sorting it out' can be used to practice to interpret data and construct block diagrams.

Oral and mental starters for week 6

See bank of starters on pages 85 to 86. Oral and mental starters are also on the CD-ROM.

16 Counting

22 Adding and subtracting

26 Finding fractions

27 Telling the time

Overview of progression

During this week children will focus on collecting, organising, presenting and analysing data in lists, tables, pictograms and block diagrams. The children will do this by being given problems to solve. They will be encouraged to evaluate the different methods of presenting information with regard to their suitability in each case. This is the first time that children will encounter this area of mathematics in the National Curriculum. However, sorting into lists and tables is part of other areas of mathematics such as shape, so it is likely that they will have some prior knowledge of this even though it is not specifically called data handling.

Watch out for

Some children may find it difficult to collect, record and interpret information in lists and simple tables. Making and interpreting lists and tables are the early stages in data handling so it is important that the children are able to do this. Provide opportunities to practise in other area of mathematics such as shape and also during the day outside of the maths lesson, for example. ask them to make a list of children who have packed lunches.

Creative context

Data handling is an important aspect of science work. Look for opportunities to link work done in science to the mathematics covered in this area.

Vocabulary

block graph, count, label, list, most/least common/popular, pictogram, represent, sort, set, table

Lesson 1 — Oral and mental starter 16

Main teaching activities

Whole-class work: *What do you think is meant by data handling?* Establish that it is to do with solving a problem by collecting, representing and interpreting information. Tell the children that presentation of information is through pictures and diagrams so that it can be seen clearly. *What words can you think of to do with data handling? Talk to your partner.* Agree and list on the board the following words: sort, set, represent, table, block graph, list, pictogram, count, label, most/least common/popular. Discuss the meaning of each.

Tell the children that today they will be thinking about lists and tables. Ask them to make a list of as many different types of fruit as they can in a minute on their whiteboards. They share their lists, you write all the fruit mentioned on the board in one list. Ensure banana is there. *I think the most popular fruit in this class is going to be banana. How can we find out if I am correct?* Take feedback and agree to take a vote. Call out the fruits listed on the board. The children put their hands up for the fruit that is their favourite. Make a tally beside each fruit. Explain to the children that each line represents one, and the fifth item is shown by putting a line through the first four.

Ask the children to tell you how many voted for each fruit and write this beside the tally marks. Explain that you have now made a table. Ask questions from the table that involve adding amounts and finding differences and using the vocabulary of more/less popular.

Paired work: Distribute copies of photocopiable page 'Tables' from the CD-ROM. Explain the task: to find out if Martyn's thinking that the most popular vegetable in the class is potatoes is correct. The children add vegetable names to the vegetable column. They ask the class to choose the vegetable they like the best and complete the table.

Progress check: As the children are working on their activity visit pairs and ask questions such as:

• *How are you making your tally? When else might we use a tally?*
• *What are you going to do when you have finished making your tally?*

Review

Take feedback from the activity. Invite pairs to share what they did and what they found out. *Was Martyn correct?* If not which is the favourite vegetable in the class? Which is the least popular? Recap the ways they showed data during the lesson: lists and tables. Discuss when we use lists and tables in real life, such as shopping lists.

Curriculum objectives
● To interpret and construct tally charts and simple tables.
● To ask and answer simple questions by counting the number of object in each category and sorting the categories by quantity.

Success criteria
● I can make lists.
● I can turn the information from a list into a table.

You will need
General resources
'Ways to organise data'
Equipment
Large pieces of sugar paper

Differentiation
Check that the less confident learners have the opportunity to take part in the activity.

Lesson 2 — Oral and mental starter 22

Main teaching activities

Whole-class work: Recap the meaning of data handling as discussed in lesson I and also the vocabulary. Give out copies of photocopiable page 'Ways to organise data' from the CD-ROM to pairs of children. For each sheet ask: *How is the information being shown? What can you tell me from this list/table? What is the most/least common? How many people/children were asked/involved?* Ask as many children as possible to tell you something from the information shown. It might be very simple such as, 'The longest word is...' or more complex, such as 'Six more...had...than...'.

Group work: Remind the children of the activity they did in lesson I and tell them that, today, they will be doing something similar but making up their own topic to investigate. They need to make a list, take a tally and then sort their results into a table. Give each group a large piece of paper on which to work. You could discuss and write up possible topics to help them, such as favourite foods, books, sports or use the children's names or birthdays as in 'Ways to organise data'.

Progress check: Spend a few minutes with each group to make sure they understand their task.

Review
Ask each group to share their work and explain how they decided on their topic and criteria. Ask the class questions to check that they are able to extract information from tables. Ask: *Is this a good way to present information? Why?*

Curriculum objectives
● To interpret and construct simple pictograms.
● To ask and answer simple questions by counting the number of objects in each category and sorting the categories by quantity.

Success criteria
● I can make a pictogram.
● I can tell you information from a pictogram.

You will need
Photocopiable sheets
'Pictograms'
Equipment
Individual whiteboards

Differentiation
Less confident learners
Children work with a higher attaining child for support.
More confident learners
Ask children to do a survey of the class to find out their favourite hobbies. They create a pictogram to show the results.

Lesson 3 — Oral and mental starter 26

Main teaching activities

Whole-class work: The focus of this lesson is pictograms. Ask: *What can you tell me about pictograms? Talk to your partner.* Agree that there are ways of showing information using pictures. Ask the children to give you the names of some sports they like to take part in. Write these on the board. Ask them to vote for their favourite one. Make a tally and together find the totals of the tallies. Ask: *How can we show this information in a pictogram?* Listen to any suggestions. Show them how to construct one for the sports information. One symbol should represent one child.

Ask questions from the pictogram that involve extracting information and finding totals and differences. Repeat this for favourite animals. When you have collected the data, ask the children to sketch their own pictogram on their whiteboard. When they have finished invite children to share their pictograms with the rest of the class.

Paired work: Distribute photocopiable page 'Pictograms'. The children's task is to create a pictogram to show the given information.

Progress check: Spend a few minutes with pairs of children as they create their pictogram and ask such questions as:
● *What is a pictogram?*
● *What do the symbols represent? Can you explain this in a different way?*

Review
Take feedback from the activity. Invite children to share their pictograms and give two or three pieces of information from them that involve finding totals and differences, for example three more people prefer football than reading. Discuss why this is a useful way to show information. Ask: *How is a pictogram the same as a table? How is it different?*

Curriculum objectives
● To interpret and construct simple pictograms, tally charts, block diagrams and simple tables.
● To ask and answer simple questions by counting the number of objects in each category and sorting the categories by quantity.
● To ask and answer questions about totalling and compare categorical data.

Success criteria
● I can order the week days.
● I can find information from a block graph.

You will need
Photocopiable sheets
'Sports block graph'; 'Popular sports'

Differentiation
Let the children work together in mixed-ability groups.

Curriculum objectives
● To interpret and construct block diagrams.
● To ask and answer simple questions by counting the number of objects in each category and sorting the categories by quantity.

Success criteria
● I can find out information from a block graph.

You will need
Photocopiable sheets
'Block graphs'
Equipment
Interlocking cubes: white, pink, yellow, brown; individual whiteboards

Differentiation
Less confident learners
Give children a frame for making their block graph.
More confident learners
Ask the children to carry out a survey of favourite drinks in the class and display the information as a block graph.

Lesson 4 — Oral and mental starter 27

Main teaching activities

Whole-class work: Recap the ways of collecting and presenting data so far from this week. Ensure you include tallies, lists, tables and pictograms. Give pairs of children a copy of photocopiable page 'Sports block graph' from the CD-ROM and ask them to describe what they see. Discuss how it is similar to a pictogram and how it is different. It might be helpful for the children to look at the pictogram they made in lesson 3 in order to compare. Focus on the block graph and ask them to tell you as much information as they can from it. Ask the children who may not find this easy first, so that they can contribute before the most obvious facts have been said. Discuss why this is a useful way of telling people about favourite sports. Elicit that it is clear, simple and easy to interpret.

Paired work: Give mixed-ability groups of up to four children photocopiable page 'Sports block graph' and each child photocopiable page 'Popular sports' from the CD-ROM to complete.

Progress check: As they work through the activity ask questions such as: *What is a block graph? How is it the same as a pictogram? How is it different?*

Review

Invite a group to ask the questions that they made up. Ask the other children to answer them, and to describe in detail how they worked them out. Say: *Tell your partner about the ways of showing information that you have learned this week.* Assess whether they have a good understanding of each one.

Lesson 5 — Oral and mental starter 27

Main teaching activities

Whole-class work: Tell the children that they will be displaying information on block graphs. Remind them that these are similar to pictograms but displayed in a column instead of symbols. Set this problem: *Sally sells ice cream and wants to put in an order for her supplies. She usually sells strawberry, vanilla, chocolate and banana flavours. This year she only wants to sell three flavours and doesn't know which to pick. How can you help her?*

Agree that Sally needs to know which three flavours are the most popular. Suggest that she uses what the class thinks. Give the children a pile of cubes (white, brown, pink and yellow). They decide which their favourite flavour is and take the appropriate cube to a central place to be counted. Discuss how the information could be displayed. Children draw a block graph on their whiteboards. For example:

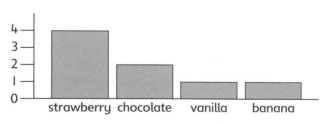

Stress the importance of labels and a title.

Independent work: Give the children photocopiable page 'Block graphs' from the CD-ROM to complete.

Progress check: During the activity ask individuals to explain how they are making their block graphs. Check that everyone is doing this in the correct way. Ask: *What will your block graph look like? What must you remember to put on it?*

Review

Invite some children to share the block graphs they made. The class asks questions about them and the children show answers. The class decides if the answers are correct. Recap the different ways of displaying information: lists, tables, pictograms and block graphs. Assess their confidence in each of these.

■**SCHOLASTIC**

Curriculum objectives
● To recall and use multiplication and division facts for the 2, 5 and 10 multiplication tables.

You will need
1. Check
Oral and mental starters

25 Times tables facts

19 Odd and even numbers

2. Assess
'0–100 number cards'

3. Further practice
Oral and mental starters

16 Counting

24 The equals sign

8 Doubling and halving

15 Multiples

Photocopiable sheets
'Multiplication and division facts'

Multiplication and division

Most children should be able to count on in steps of two, five and ten and use their fingers to link to multiplication and division facts.

Some children will not have made such progress and will require practice. Give them strips with the steps on and gradually cover over the steps as the children begin to remember them.

1. Check

25 Times tables facts

19 Odd and even numbers

Encourage the children to recall the answers by keeping the pace sharp. Observe which children are confident and which need further practice.

Probing questions: *What is 2 × 6? How can you check? Can you give me three odd numbers? How do you know they are odd?* Repeat this for other multiplication facts in the two-, five- and ten-times tables. Encourage the children to use division facts to check their multiplications.

2. Assess

Write 2 on the board. Ask the children to pick a card from a set of 1–9 number cards. They multiply it by 2 and write down the answer. They then pick another card and do the same thing. Repeat this over a minute to see how many numbers the children can multiply by 2. Then do the same for the five-times and ten-times tables. Record the outcomes.

3. Further practice

Photocopiable page 87 'Multiplication and division facts' provides practice in recalling multiplication facts and corresponding divisions. Encourage the children to use their fingers, for example: 2 × 6, count in twos to the sixth finger, answer is 12, 15 ÷ 5, count in fives to 15, third finger is up so 3 is the answer.

Curriculum objectives
● To calculate mathematical statements for multiplication and division.

You will need
1. Check
Oral and mental starters

25 Times tables facts

11 Counting in twos, fives and tens

2. Assess
'0–100 number cards'

3. Further practice
Oral and mental starters

8 Doubling and halving

15 Multiples

Photocopiable sheets
'Multiplying'

Multiplying and dividing

Most children should be able to multiply and divide using repeated addition and subtraction along a number line.

Some children will not have made such progress. Provide concrete apparatus for them to group together when multiplying and dividing.

1. Check

25 Times tables facts

11 Counting in twos, fives and tens

As you do the check-up, ask the children to draw number lines to show repeated addition and subtraction for the times tables facts. Ask: *I have six toy cars, my friend has five times as many. How many does my friend have? How did you work that out? How can you check that you are right? Sam had 12 sweets, he put them in groups of two. How many groups did he have? How do you know?*

2. Assess

Using two sets of 1–9 number cards, ask the children to pick two cards. When they have they multiply them together by repeated addition on a number line. Observe how they do this. Ask them to check their answers using repeated subtraction. Record the outcomes.

3. Further practice

Expect most children to be able to answer the questions on photocopiable page 88 'Multiplying' using repeated addition along a number line and to check using repeated subtraction. Some children may need to use counters or cubes.

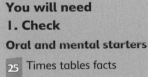

Curriculum objectives
● To recognise, find, name and write fractions ⅓, ¼, ⅔ and ¾.

You will need
1. Check
Oral and mental starter
26 Finding fractions

2. Assess
Counters

3. Further practice
Oral and mental starter
15 Multiples
Photocopiable sheets
'Halves and quarters'
General resources
Interactive activity 'Fractions'

Fractions

Most children should know that half is something that is shared into two equal groups and a quarter is shared equally into four.

Some children will not have made such progress and will require concrete apparatus to physically share them into two and then four piles.

1. Check

26 Finding fractions

Using the oral mental starter to check which children can write halves and quarters of different amounts. Provide counters for children if necessary. Ask: *What is half of 20? How can you check that you are right? What is one quarter of 20? How did you work that out? Is there another way?*

2. Assess

Give the children a pile of counters. Ask them to count out 24. Then ask them to find half. Observe them as they do this. How do they share the counters, individually or in groups? Are they confident that they know how to find half? Repeat this for finding a quarter. *Can you tell me what three quarters of 24 is?* Repeat for other numbers. Record the outcomes.

3. Further practice

Photocopiable page 89 'Halves and quarters' is designed as an activity to practise halving and quartering numbers. Give the children counters to use. Encourage any that don't use counters to draw pictures on the sheet so that you have a record of their thinking.

Curriculum objectives
● To tell and write the time to five minutes, including quarter past/to the hour and draw the hands on a clock face to show these times.

You will need
1. Check
Oral and mental starter
27 Telling the time

2. Assess
Clocks

3. Further practice
Oral and mental starter
11 Counting in twos, fives and tens
Photocopiable sheets
'Telling the time (1)'

Time

Most children should be able to tell o'clock and half past times successfully, some will be able to also tell quarter past and quarter to times.

Some children will not have made such progress and will need to focus on o'clock times.

1. Check

27 Telling the time

Give the children clocks and call out times, for example o'clock and half past times, then quarter past and quarter to. Watch out for children who struggle. Look for opportunities to work on these times during different times of the day. Ask: *What does the short hand on a clock show? What about the long hand? Can you show me half past three?*

2. Assess

Give each child a clock. Ask them to show you 3 o'clock, then one hour earlier. Repeat this for other times asking for different numbers of hours earlier or later. Make up some time stories. Record the outcomes.

3. Further practice

Focus on counting in fives. Give the children a clock each and ask them to count round it in minutes positioning the minute hand on the correct hour number. Photocopiable page 'Telling the time (1)' from the CD-ROM gives the opportunity for children to show you how well they can tell o'clock, half past, quarter to and quarter past times.

Oral and mental starters

Multiplication and division

15 Multiples

Swing the pendulum from side to side. As you do, ask the children to count in multiples of two from 2 to 24 and then back again. Give the children two minutes to write down as many multiples of two as they can. Encourage them to think of those other than the ones they have just counted in. They could extend the count in their heads from 24, double (14 doubled is 28, 20 doubled is 40) or by multiplying by 10 ($8 \times 10 = 80$). Repeat this for multiples of five and ten.

25 Times tables facts

Write 2 on the board. Say that you will call out numbers up to and including ten. When you do the children multiply the number you call out by two and write the answer on their whiteboards. Occasionally ask them to write appropriate multiplication sentences, such as $2 \times 5 = 10$. Repeat for multiplication facts for 5 and 10.

Number and place value

16 Counting

Show the children the counting stick. *One end is 0, the other is 20. What steps will we count in to get from 0 to 20?* Together, count forwards and backwards in twos. Point to different divisions. *What number would go here?* Repeat for the step sizes of five and ten.

17 Counting in tens again

Each child needs a 'Hundred square'. Ask them to put their finger on 13 on their 100 squares. *What is 10 more than 13? How do you know? Which number stays the same? Which number is different?* Ask the children to count on in tens to 93 and back again. Repeat for other teens numbers.

18 Number pairs

Swing the pendulum from side to side. You call out a number from zero to ten as it swings one way. The children call out the number that goes with it to make ten as it swings the other way. Repeat this for other numbers up to ten, for example six - you say four, they say two.

Extension
When the children are ready, practise number pairs for all numbers to 20.

19 Odd and even numbers

Ask the children to stand up. Call out some single and two-digit numbers. If the number is even they clap. If it is odd they jump once. Move onto more complex numbers as this can be fun, such as 1 456 231. Remind them they simply need to consider the ones number.

Addition and subtraction

20 Adding 11

Give each child a 'Hundred square'. They place their finger on 4. Ask them to add 10 and then 1. *Where are you? What have you added onto four?* Agree that as 10 and 1 is 11, they have added on 11. Ask them to add on another 10 and 1 to the 15. Do this several times and then ask them to add 11 to different numbers. Can they use the strategy you have just practised? Repeat this for taking away 11: take away 10 and, because this is one too few, take away another 1 to adjust.

21 Adding nine

Ask the children to place their finger on 7 on a 100 square and then add 10 and take away 1. *Where are you? What have you added onto 7?* Agree that as 10 take away 1 is 9, they have added on 9. Ask them to add on another 10 and take away 1 to the 16. Do this several times and then ask them to add 9 to different numbers. Can they use the strategy you have just practised? Repeat for subtracting 9: take away 10 and, because that is one too many, add 1 to adjust.

22 Adding and subtracting

Ask the children to write down the number eight on their whiteboards. Call out instructions. The children do what you say and write down the new number, for example take away three, add ten, double. After a few instructions ask them to show you the number they now have. Repeat with different starting numbers.

23 Bridging ten

Write this on the board: 6 + 8. Ask the children to tell you how they could add these two numbers. Take feedback and say that you want them to focus on the strategy of bridging ten, 6 + 4 + 4 = 10 + 4 = 14. Repeat with a few examples and then ask questions for the children to answer on their whiteboards. Ensure you include adding two single digits (7 + 8), a two-digit number and a single digit (28 + 5) and two teens numbers (17 + 15).

24 The equals sign

Write = on the board. *Remember what goes on one side must be equal to what is on the other.* Write 8 =. *What could go on the other side so that it is equal to eight?* Discuss the options for example 8, 1 + 7, 9 − 1, 4 + 2 + 2. Repeat with different single and two-digit numbers.

Extension

Write number sentences like this: 7 + 5 = ? − ? The children write down different numbers for the question marks that will make the sentence correct, such as 13 − 1, 20 − 8, 5 + 5 + 2, 2 × 6.

Fractions

26 Finding fractions

Recap that finding half is the same as sharing between two. Call out some even numbers to 20 for the children to halve. They write their answers on their whiteboards. Recap that finding a quarter is the same as sharing between four. Quarters can also be found by halving and halving again. Call out some multiples of four (8, 16, 24). The children find a quarter by halving and halving again and write their answers on their whiteboards and show you.

Measurement

27 Telling the time

Give each child a clock face. Call out times for them to find. These should be a mixture of o'clock, quarter past, half past and quarter to times. As soon as they find each one, they check with their neighbour and then show you their clock. Ask some problems, such as *I left home at 9 o'clock. It took me an hour to get to my friend's house. What time did I get there?*

SCHOLASTIC

Multiplication and division facts

- Answer these multiplication and division facts.
- Use your fingers to help you. For example, 4 × 2.

1. 2 × 6 =

2. 5 × 6 =

3. 2 × 8 =

4. 3 × 8 =

5. 15 ÷ 5 =

6. 24 ÷ 2 =

7. 10 ÷ 5 =

8. 10 ÷ 2 =

9. 10 × 10 =

10. 3 × 10 =

11. 10 × 6 =

12. 12 ÷ 4 =

13. 20 ÷ 10 =

14. 2 × 9 =

Write down your two-times table.

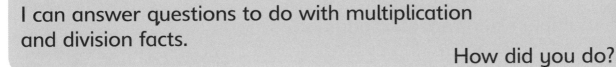

I can answer questions to do with multiplication and division facts.

How did you do?

Multiplying

- Multiply these numbers using repeated addition along the number lines.
- Check using repeated subtraction.

Here is an example:

$5 \times 4 = 20$

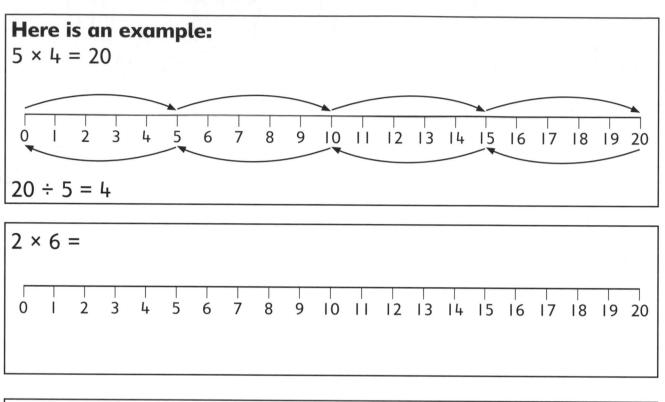

$20 \div 5 = 4$

$2 \times 6 =$

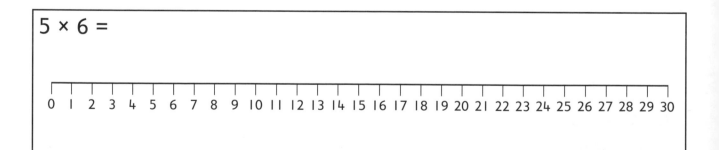

$2 \times 9 =$

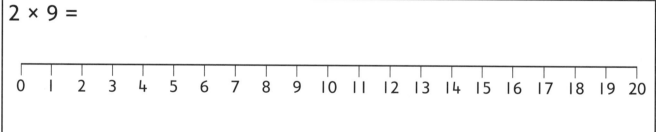

$5 \times 6 =$

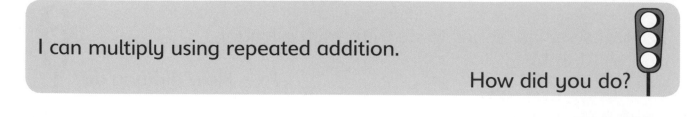

I can multiply using repeated addition.

How did you do?

Name: _____   Date: _____

Halves and quarters

- Find the fractions of these numbers.
- Draw pictures to show your thinking.

Here is an example:

$\frac{1}{2}$ of 12 = 6

● ● ● ●
● ● ● ●
● ● ● ●

Now it's your turn!

1. $\frac{1}{2}$ of 8

2. $\frac{1}{4}$ of 12

3. $\frac{1}{4}$ of 24

4. $\frac{1}{4}$ of 20

5. $\frac{1}{2}$ of 14

6. $\frac{1}{2}$ of 18

7. $\frac{1}{4}$ of 32

8. $\frac{1}{2}$ of 24

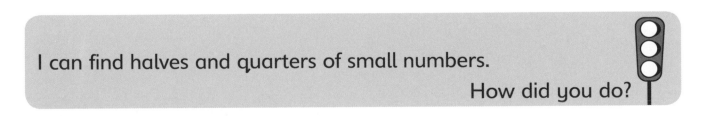

I can find halves and quarters of small numbers.

How did you do?

Number and place value: estimating, counting and comparing

Expected prior learning

Children should be able to:

- count forwards or backwards in steps of two, five and ten
- partition two-digit numbers into tens and ones
- read and write numbers from 1 to 50 in digits and 30 in words
- begin to partition numbers to 100 in different ways.

Topic	Curriculum objectives	Expected outcomes
Number and place value	**Lesson 1**	
	To identify, represent and estimate numbers using different representations, including the number line. To compare and order numbers from 0 up to 100; use <, > and = signs.	Position numbers on a number line. Compare numbers using < and >. Write numbers to 100 in figures. Identify numbers to 100 in words.
	Lesson 2	
	To count in tens from any number, forward or backward. To identify, represent and estimate numbers using different representations, including the number line.	Count forwards and backwards in tens from any number.
	Lesson 3	
	To count in steps of 2, 3, and 5 from 0, and in tens from any number, forward and backward.	Count in steps of two, three, four, five and ten from zero. Position two-digit numbers on number lines.
	Lesson 4	
	To recognise the place value of each digit in a two-digit number (tens, ones). To read and write numbers to at least 100 in numerals and words.	Partition numbers in different ways. Read and write numbers to 100 in numerals. Read and write numbers to 50 in words.
	Lesson 5	
	To use place value and number facts to solve problems.	Use counting to solve simple oral problems.

Preparation

Lesson 1: copy and laminate the number words for use during the week

Lesson 2: photocopy three 'Diamond number line' onto A3 paper

Lesson 4: copy, laminate and cut sets of tens and ones 'Arrow cards' for each child

Lesson 5: prepare some additional simple problems to ask the class

You will need

Photocopiable sheets

'Counting problems'; 'Partitioning (1)'; 'Diamond number line'

General resources

'Number words'; '0–100 number cards'; 'Number lines 0–30 and 0–100'; 'Arrow cards'; interactive activity 'The name game'

Equipment

Individual whiteboards; interlocking cubes; pendulum; counters; 1p coins

Further practice

Interactive activity 'The name game' offers further practice of reading and writing two-digit numbers.

Oral and mental starters for week 1

See bank of starters on page 126. Oral and mental starters are also on the CD-ROM.

28 Counting on a 100 square

29 Counting in steps of two, five and ten

30 Counting in odd and even numbers

Overview of progression

During this week the children will focus on reading and writing numbers in words and figures and describing simple number sequences. They will also reinforce, rehearse and consolidate ordering, comparing and rounding two-digit numbers. They will continue to partition two-digit numbers in different ways. It is a good idea to do this regularly as it really helps the children to get a feel for number.

Watch out for

Some children may have difficulty counting in steps of two, five and/ or ten. Give them written prompts such as cards with sequences counting in steps of two from 0 to 20 and the same for fives and tens. Over time put a sticker over one or two numbers beginning with, for example, 0 then 2.

Creative context

Take the children on a number walk around the school. How many different numbers can they see? They could record these with pictures to show where they found the different numbers and compare them using the symbols < and >.

Vocabulary

continue, count in fives, count in tens, count in twos, **multiple of**, nearest ten, one-digit number, **partitioning,** place, **place value**, predict, represents, sequence, round, stands for, 'teens' number, tens digit, two-digit number

Curriculum objectives
- To identify, represent and estimate numbers using different representations, including the number line.
- To compare and order numbers from 0 up to 100; use <, > and = signs.

Success criteria
- I can write numbers on a number line.
- I can compare numbers using < and >.

You will need

General resources
'0–100 number cards'; 'Number words'

Equipment
Individual whiteboards

Differentiation

Less confident learners
Give the children the two numbers that they need to place at either end of their number line.

More confident learners
After doing the activity, children order their cards from lowest to highest. They draw a number line and position these onto it. When they have done this they make up < and > number sentences.

Lesson 1   Oral and mental starter 28

Main teaching activities

Whole-class work: Explain that this lesson is about writing, ordering and comparing numbers. Each child will need a set of digit cards. Give the children instructions, such as: *Put 7 on the table in front of you. Make it read 74. What did you do? Partition it in different ways and write these ways on your whiteboards.* (70 + 4, 60 + 14, 50 + 24, 40 + 34, 30 + 44, 20 + 54, 10 + 64) *Swap the digits around. What number do you have now? Is that bigger or smaller than 74? Now add a card to make 147. What did you do? How much bigger is 147 than 47? Make the highest three-digit number that you can using the cards. How did you do that? Why? Make it 5 more...100 less...10 more...*This is a very good method for helping children reinforce and rehearse place value and number manipulation. Most children can do this fairly easily after some practice. If any have difficulty, help them or allow them to work with a 'buddy'. Repeat the activity with children writing the numbers on their whiteboards.

Hold up two number cards: *Which number is higher?... lower? How do you know?* Draw a number line on the board and write these numbers at either end. Invite children to suggest numbers that come between the two and to place them on the line. Show the children photocopiable page 'Number words' from the CD-ROM and ask them to find the correct words for some of these numbers. Repeat this several times.

Paired work: Ask the children to work in pairs. Give them about ten number cards. Their task is to pick two, draw a number line and position them at either end. They then write two numbers that come between them on their line. They repeat this for other pairs of numbers.

Progress check: Invite pairs to show the class what they have been doing. They could demonstrate their number lines on the board.
- *Where would you put this number on your number line?*
- *What number could go towards the end of your line? Can you explain why?*

Review

Take feedback about the activity. Invite pairs to show their start and end numbers. The rest of the class suggest numbers that could be placed between them and tell the pair where to write them. Ask the class to match the numbers on the number line to the words on photocopiable page 'Number words'. Write some two-digit numbers on the board. The children write number sentences for them, for example you write 36, they write 30 + 6 = 36. Draw a number line on the board and invite children to plot the numbers on the number line.

Curriculum objectives

● To count in tens from any number, forward or backward.
● To identify, represent and estimate numbers using different representations, including the number line.

Success criteria

● I can count on and back in ones and tens.
● I can place numbers on a number line.

You will need

Photocopiable sheets

'Diamond number line'

General resources

'0–100 number cards'

Differentiation

Less confident learners

Give pairs a starting number below 20 and a pile of digit cards with ten extra one and two digit cards.

More confident learners

Ask pairs to write their starting number in the middle diamond on the line so that they need to count forwards and backwards.

Lesson 2   Oral and mental starter 28

Main teaching activities

Whole-class work: Explain that today, the children will be learning about number sequences that go up or down in ones or tens. Pick a card from a pile of two-digit number cards and ask the children to start counting forwards and then backwards in ones. Repeat counting in tens. Do this for other numbers.

Invite a child to pick a card and write the number on the board. Ask the children to discuss with a partner what they think the next eight numbers will be on either side counting on and back in ones. Ask the children what they notice. Elicit the fact that the ones number is one more each time. Invite some children to write these numbers on the board. Repeat for counting in tens: what do the children notice? (The ones number remains the same.)

Paired work: Ask the children to play a number line game in pairs. Use an A3 copy of photocopiable page 'Diamond number line' from the CD-ROM to explain the game. For example: *I've picked 2 and 4, so I'm going to make 24 and write it in the first diamond. If my partner picks 8 and 2, what two numbers can they make? Can one of them be written in a diamond?* Ask a child to write 28 in the correct place. *If 7 and 5 are picked now, what numbers can we make? Will either of them fit on the line? No, so it's the other player's turn. What about 2 and 5? 25 can be added to the line.* Children must start with a number below 90.

Progress check: Ask pairs to show their diamond number line and to explain how they have filled them so far. Ask the rest of the class to check that they are doing this correctly.

Review

Play the game again as a class, using another A3 copy of 'Diamond number line' but counting in tens. Pick single-digit number cards to make a two-digit number and write it in the middle diamond. Invite the children to pick a single-digit to replace the tens number each time, to make a new number. Ask the class to tell you what the numbers are and invite individuals to write them in the correct places. Each time, ask the children what has happened to the tens and then the ones numbers. Reiterate the fact that the ones number stays the same; only the tens number changes.

Curriculum objectives
● To count in steps of 2, 3 and 5 from 0, and in tens from any number, forward and backward.

Success criteria
● I can count in steps of two, three, four, five, ten from zero.
● I can position two-digit numbers on number lines.

You will need

General resources
'Number lines 0–20, 0–30 and 0–100'

Equipment
Interlocking cubes

Differentiation

Less confident learners
Provide children with a 0–20 number line.

More confident learners
Provide children with a 20–50 number line.

Lesson 3 — Oral and mental starter 30

Main teaching activities

Whole-class work: Explain that this lesson is about counting in steps. Draw a numbered number line from 0–30 on the board. Circle the zero and ask: *If we count in threes from zero, what is the first number we come to?* Draw a loop from zero to three. Continue to 30, each time drawing a loop from one multiple of three to the next. At 30, go back in jumps of three. Help the children to make the inverse connection by drawing inversion loop diagrams.

Ask questions such as: *How many jumps from zero to six? If I make three jumps from zero, will I land on an odd or an even number?* Repeat, starting at different numbers. Focus on odd and even numbers. Ask: *What are they? What numbers do they end with?* Repeat for counting in steps of two and five.

Paired work: Hand out photocopiable sheet 'Number lines 0–30' from the CD-ROM. Ask the children to count in steps of 3, circling the even multiples they land on and putting a cross through the odd ones. Then repeat, counting in multiples of 4, then 5.

Progress check: Ask: *If I count on 4 from 12, where will I land? What can you tell me about the numbers that you have circled?*

Review

Invite pairs to draw one of their number lines on the board and demonstrate what they did. Ask the children to look for patterns. Look for awareness that when we count in fours, the numbers are always even (if the starting number is even); but when we count in fives the ones digit alternates between two digits, one odd and one even.

Curriculum objectives
● To recognise the place value of each digit in a two-digit number (tens, ones).

Success criteria
● I can partition numbers in different ways.

You will need

Photocopiable sheets
'Partitioning (1)'

General resources
'Arrow cards'; interactive activity 'The name game'

Equipment
Individual whiteboards

Differentiation

Less confident learners
Adapt photocopiable page 'Partitioning (1)' so that the children partition numbers to 50.

More confident learners
Children partition the numbers in as many different ways as they can.

Lesson 4 — Oral and mental starter 29

Main teaching activities

Whole-class work: Give each child a set of 'Arrow cards'. Ask them to make 38. *Show me the tens card. How many are there?* (3) *What is the actual number?* (30) *How many ones?* (8). They write the number sentence to show this: 30 + 8 = 38. Ask: *How else can we partition this number? Show me on your whiteboards.* (20 + 18 = 38, 10 + 28 = 38) Repeat for other two-digit numbers. The children make 45. Ask them to show you ten more than 45. They exchange 40 for 50. Next ask them to show you three more. They exchange the 5 for 8. Repeat, each time they show you their new number and talk about the other ways that they can partition it.

With a partner, the children take it in turns to make numbers using the arrow cards. They write number sentences for the numbers and then order the numbers from smallest to largest. Take feedback and write some of the numbers on the board for the class to order from smallest to largest.

Independent work: Distribute photocopiable page 'Partitioning (1)' from the CD-ROM and demonstrate what the children need to do.

Progress check: Invite volunteers to demonstrate partitioning. Ask:
● *How can we partition 39? Is there another way? Can you explain why?*
● *What does the 4 in 45 represent? Can you explain why?*

Review

Take feedback about the activity. Invite children to explain how they partitioned numbers. Discuss other ways to partition. Ask the children to say some three-digit numbers. Invite them to demonstrate how these would be partitioned. Interactive activity 'The name game' on the CD-ROM, can be used for further practice of recognising the place value of two-digit numbers.

Curriculum objectives
● To use place value and number facts to solve problems.

Success criteria
● I can solve word problems by counting.

You will need
Photocopiable sheets
'Counting problems'
General resources
'Number lines 0–20 and 0–30'
Equipment
Pendulum; 1p coins; counters

Differentiation
Less confident learners
Give children numbered number lines to help them during the activity.

More confident learners
Adapt photocopiable page 'Counting problems' so that children count in steps of four.

Lesson 5   Oral and mental starter 29

Main teaching activities

Whole-class work: Recap some of the counting that children rehearsed during the week: counting in ones, twos, threes, fives and tens. Rehearse these using the pendulum. Swing it from side to side and count in steps of a particular size as it swings. Practise all steps. Say: *Freddie counted out five sweets, he then counted another five and another. He carried on doing this until he had 45 sweets. How many lots of five did he count?* Ask the children to talk to a partner about this. Take feedback and then together count in fives to 45. Agree that he counted nine lots of fives. Link this to repeated addition and multiplication by writing 5 + 5 + 5 + 5 + 5 + 5 + 5 + 5 + 5 = 45 and 5 × 9 = 45 on the board. Repeat with similar problems that involve counting in steps of two, three and ten.

Say: *Chelsea had some pennies. She grouped them in piles of ten. She had seven piles. How much money did she have altogether?* Give the children piles of 1p coins or counters to do this practically. Agree that she has 70p altogether. Again, link to repeated addition and multiplication as above. Repeat with similar problems that involve counting in steps of two, three and five.

Independent work: Distribute photocopiable page 'Counting problems' from the CD-ROM. Explain that the children need to solve the problems using counting in steps and then write the process they went through as a repeated addition and multiplication sentence. Once they have completed the activity sheet, ask them to make up some of their own problems for questions to ask the class in the review.

Progress check: Invite volunteers to explain how they answered the first question and to write the repeated addition and multiplication number sentences on the board. Recap counting in steps of two, three, five and ten.

● *If I counted in steps of two to 16, how many steps will I have counted?*
● *If I counted in steps of three to 21, how many steps will I have counted?*

Review

Take feedback about the activity, asking the children to share their results. Invite children to share one of their word problems for others to solve. Set some problems such as: *I had six groups of three marbles. How many marbles did I have? I counted in steps of a number. I stopped counting when I got to 20. In steps of what number did I count? Are there any other possibilities?* Finish the lesson by asking the children a few more problems as in the main activity. Ensure you include problems for the more confident children, for example, *Cheryl had seven piles of four sweets. How many sweets did she have? How did you work that out? Is there another way?*

Addition and subtraction: recall and mental calculation strategies

Expected prior learning

Children should be able to:

- find totals by counting on along a number line
- find differences by counting on
- use the inverse operation to check additions and subtractions.

Topic	Curriculum objectives	Expected outcomes
Addition and subtraction	**Lesson 1**	
	To add and subtract using concrete objects, pictorial representations, and mentally, including: a two-digit number and ones; adding three one-digit numbers.	Add and subtract using number pairs to 10 and 20.
	To recall and use addition and subtraction facts to 20 fluently, and derive and use related facts up to 100.	Use concrete and pictorial representations and number facts to add and subtract.
		Check answers using the inverse operation.
	Lesson 2	
	To add and subtract using concrete objects, pictorial representations, and mentally, including: a two-digit number and ones; adding three one-digit numbers.	Solve simple one-step addition and subtraction problems within the context of money.
	To recognise and use the inverse relationship between addition and subtraction and use this to check calculations and missing number problems.	Use bridging ten.
		Check answers using the inverse operation.
	Lesson 3	
	To show that addition of two numbers can be done in any order (commutative) and subtraction of one number from another cannot.	Solve simple one-step addition and subtraction problems within the context of number and money.
	To recall and use addition and subtraction facts to 20 fluently, and derive and use related facts up to 100.	Know number pairs to 10 and 20 and use these to find totals to 100.
		Show that addition can be done in any order but subtraction cannot.
	Lesson 4	
	To add and subtract using concrete objects, pictorial representations, and mentally, including: a two-digit number and ones; two two-digit numbers.	Solve simple one-step addition and subtraction problems within the context of number.
		Add and subtract by adding/subtracting 9 and 11 by adding/subtracting 10 and adjusting to add and subtract.
	Lesson 5	
	To solve problems with addition and subtraction: using concrete objects and pictorial representations, including those involving numbers, quantities and measures; applying their increasing knowledge of mental and written methods.	Use mental calculation to solve simple addition and subtraction problems within the context of money.

Preparation

Lesson 1: prepare addition and subtraction vocabulary cards using the words in the vocabulary section; enlarge 'Grid for ten' to A3 and laminate for use in the lesson and during oral mental starters; copy, cut out and laminate enough copies of 'Grid for ten' for pairs of children

You will need

Photocopiable sheets

'Adding and subtracting'; 'Measures and money problems'

General resources

'Grid for ten'; '0–100 number cards'; 'Hundred squares'; interactive activity 'Addition and subtraction facts'

Equipment

Individual whiteboards; counting apparatus

Further practice

Photocopiable sheets

'Shopping cards': Children choose three toys and add the amounts using one of the strategies covered during this week. Interactive activity 'Addition and subtraction facts' offers practice of number facts to 20.

Oral and mental starters for week 2

See bank of starters on pages 45, 86 and 126. Oral and mental starters are also on the CD-ROM.

30 Counting in odd and even numbers

7 Number pairs to ten

32 What makes ten?

24 The equals sign

Overview of progression

During this week children will develop their mental calculation strategies for addition and subtraction. These strategies will include using number facts, adding/subtracting 9 and 11 by adding/subtracting 10 and adjusting, bridging ten and partitioning. They will be encouraged to use concrete apparatus, 100 squares and number lines. They will check answers using the inverse operation and begin to understand that addition is commutative and subtraction is not. Throughout they will be solving simple problems within the context of number, money and time.

Watch out for

Some children may still be uncertain about place value. Work with them for some of the time and demonstrate with grouping concrete apparatus in tens and ones and linking to arrow cards to help deepen their understanding.

Creative context

Encourage the children to make up problems involving addition and subtraction using familiar scenarios.

Vocabulary

add, addition, altogether, **bridging ten**, difference, inverse operation, make, more, plus, subtract, sum, take away, **tens boundary**, total

Curriculum objectives

● To add and subtract using concrete objects, pictorial representations, and mentally, including: a two-digit number and ones; adding three one-digit numbers.
● To recall and use addition and subtraction facts to 20 fluently, and derives and use related facts up to 100.

Success criteria

● I can solve addition and subtraction problems by finding number pairs to ten.
● I can tell you pairs of numbers that total ten.

You will need

General resources

'Grid for ten'; interactive activity 'Addition and subtraction facts'

Equipment

Individual whiteboards; interlocking cubes

Differentiation

Less confident learners

Children focus on numbers that make ten.

More confident learners

Encourage children to use an extra set of 'Grid for ten' and make pairs of numbers to 30.

Lesson 1

Oral and mental starter 30

Main teaching activities

Whole-class work: Tell the class that they are going to practise some mental addition and subtraction strategies and learn some new ones. Revise the vocabulary for addition and subtraction, holding up the word cards you have prepared as the children suggest them and attach them to the board. *I have 12 red beads and 8 blue ones. How many beads do I have altogether? Talk to your partner about how you could answer this.* Take feedback and agree that they could count on from the largest number. They could also use their number pairs to ten and add two and eight, then add this to the other ten. Demonstrate this using cubes. Say that they are going to practise this strategy. Show the children photocopiable page 'Grid for ten' from the CD-ROM and look at the grid with ten circles. Ask: *How many more will I need to add to this to make ten? Write what you think on your whiteboards.* Agree nothing. Next show the card with nine circles. Agree that they need to add one. Repeat for all the cards in order and then jumble them up and do it again. Now put two cards together, for example those showing ten and nine and ask them to write down what is needed to make 20.

Write some single-digits on the board such as 2, 7 and 8. Invite a child to circle the two numbers that total ten. Together add this to the seven. Repeat for other sets of single-digit numbers. Each time, ask a volunteer to demonstrate using cubes. Ask: *George bought a DVD for £16 and a CD for £8. How much did he spend? Talk to your partner about how you could use number pairs to ten to find the total.* Write £16 + £4 on the board. Agree that they could add £6 and £4 to make £10 and then add this to the other £10 to total £20. Then they add the £4 left from the £8 to make a total of £24. Repeat for other similar problems.

Paired work: Give pairs of children two copies of 'Grid for ten'. They pick pairs of cards that make 10 and then 20 and make up problems to go with them.

Progress check: Invite a pair to show two of their cards that total ten and to share their problem for the class to solve.

Review

Write on the board: 16 + 9 + 4. Ask: *How can we use the strategy we have practised today to solve this?* Aim towards adding the 6 and the 4 to make 10, which with the other 10 makes 20, then adding the 9. Write a few more such examples on the board for the children to answer.

At the end of the lesson, check children's current understanding of number facts to 20 using the interactive activity 'Addition and subtraction facts' on the CD-ROM.

Curriculum objectives

● To add and subtract using concrete objects, pictorial representations, and mentally, including: a two-digit number and ones; adding three one-digit numbers.
● To recognise and use the inverse relationship between addition and subtraction and use this to check calculations and missing number.

Success criteria

● I can solve addition and subtraction problems by bridging ten.
● I can check answers using the inverse operation.

You will need

General resources
'0–100 number cards'

Differentiation

Less confident learners
Children work with numbers to 20.

More confident learners
Children work with numbers beyond 50.

Lesson 2   Oral and mental starter 7

Main teaching activities

Whole-class work: Set this problem: *Marcus had £27, his aunt gave him £6 more. How much does Marcus have now?* Take feedback and agree that they could count on £6 from £27. Agree that they could also partition £6 into £3 and £3, add one £3 to £27 to make £30 and then add the other making a total of £33. Ask: *How can we check that we are correct?* For example, take £6 from the answer to get back to £27 by taking away £3 and then another £3. Demonstrate on a number line. Explain that this strategy is called bridging ten. Repeat for similar problems.

Say: *Suzie had £24, she spent £7 on a toy. How much did she have left?* Agree that they could partition £7 into £4 and £3 and take away £4 then £3. Demonstrate on a number line. Check by adding £3 and then £4 to the £17 to give £24. Repeat with similar money problems.

Independent work: Give each child some number cards to 50 with ones numbers of 6 and above and digit cards 5, 6, 7, 8 and 9. They pick one of each card and add using the bridging ten strategy. For each, they check and make up a money related problem.

Progress check: Invite children to share how they added their numbers and checked their answers. Check that everyone is using the required strategy.

Review

Invite children to share the problems they made up and ask the class to answer them. As they answer, ask children to demonstrate on a number line.

Curriculum objectives

● To show that addition can be done in any order and subtraction cannot.
● To recall and use addition and subtraction facts to 20 fluently, and derive and use related facts up to 100.

Success criteria

● I can use number pairs to 10 and 20 to add multiples of 10.
● I can show that addition can be done in any order but subtraction cannot.

You will need

Equipment
Individual whiteboards

Differentiation

Less confident learners
Give children a 'Hundred square' for support. Ensure they focus on the tens column.

More confident learners
Children work with multiples of 10 to 200.

Lesson 3   Oral and mental starter 7

Main teaching activities

Whole-class work: Write 6 + 4 = 10 on the board. Ask the children to write down as many other facts from this as they can on their whiteboards, such as. 4 + 6 = 10, 10 − 4 = 6, 10 − 6 = 4, 40 + 60 = 100, 60 + 40 = 100, 100 − 60 = 40, 100 − 40 = 60. Ask: *Is 10 = 4 + 6 another example?* Agree that it is. Revisit the meaning of the = symbol (whatever is on one side of it must equal what is on the other). Ask: *Is 6 − 10 = 4 another example?* Agree that it is not. Revisit the fact that it doesn't matter which way round you add numbers the answer will be the same but it does matter with subtraction because the answer will be different. Repeat with other examples. Ask: *Katy had a 50p and a 20p coin in her pocket. How much does she have in total?* Agree that if 5 and 2 equals 7, then 50p and 20p will equal 70p. Ask similar problems and move onto numbers such as 35 + 14, 56 − 24.

Independent work: Ask the children to write down the tens numbers from 10 to 100. They pick pairs of these numbers to add together and then make up a problem to go with their calculation.

Progress check: Ask volunteers to demonstrate some of their calculations to the class describing how they worked out the answers.

● *How can we check that the answer is correct?*

Review

Take feedback from the activity. Invite children to share their problems for the class to answer. Ask the children to assess their confidence in using this strategy.

Curriculum objectives

- To add and subtract using concrete objects, pictorial representations, and mentally, including: a two-digit number and ones; two two-digit numbers.

Success criteria

- I can add by adding a multiple of 10 and adjusting.
- I can subtract by taking away a multiple of 10 and adjusting.

You will need

Photocopiable sheets
'Adding and subtracting'

General resources
'Hundred square'

Differentiation

Less confident learners

Adapt photocopiable page 'Adding and subtracting' so that the children add and subtract 9 to and from numbers up to 20. If necessary give them a 'Hundred square' to help.

More confident learners

Adapt photocopiable page 'Adding and subtracting' so that the children add and subtract higher numbers.

Lesson 4   Oral and mental starter 32

Main teaching activities

Whole-class work: Say: *Devon had a collection of 23 shells. Ava gave her another 9. How many does she have now? How would you work this out? Talk to your partner.* Agree that the children need to add 9 to 23. *How can you do this?* Take feedback of all their ideas. Consider these two strategies: count on 9 in ones, partition 9 into 7 and 2, add 7 to make the next 10 and then 2. Next focus on adding 10 and taking away 1: 23 + 10 − 1. Discuss which is the most efficient of the three strategies. Suggest that counting in ones is not the most efficient method and that they should try to use the other two strategies for numbers like these. Make up similar problems to Devon's. Include adding numbers such as 19, 29 and ask the children to use this strategy to find the totals. Say: *If Devon had 23 shells and gave 9 away, how would we use this strategy to find out how many she had left?* Agree that they should take away 10 and because they have taken away one too many they need to add 1 (23 − 10 + 1).

Discuss what the children could do if they had to add 11 (add 10 and then another 1) and take away 11 (take away 10 and then another 1). Ask some problems so they can practise.

Ask the children to work with a partner and make up a problem to share with the class.

Paired work: Distribute photocopiable page 'Adding and subtracting' from the CD-ROM and demonstrate what the children need to do: pick a number from the left side of the page (26, 38, 43) and one from the right (9, 11, 19). The children need to add them together using the strategy focused on during the lesson. They then subtract in the same way.

Progress check: Check to make sure everyone has understood what to do by asking two or three children to give examples. Ask questions such as:

- *What is 34 + 19? Can you explain your strategy?*
- *What is 45 − 11? How did you work that out?*

Review

Take feedback from the activity. Invite children to share the numbers they chose and to describe the strategies they used to find their answer. Invite the class to make up problems to go with the children's calculations.

Curriculum objectives

● To solve problems with addition: using concrete objects and pictorial representations, including those involving numbers, quantities and measures: applying their increasing knowledge of mental and written methods.

Success criteria

● I can solve word problems using mental calculations.
● I can check my answers using a different strategy.

You will need

Photocopiable sheets

'Measures and money problems'

Equipment

Individual whiteboards

Differentiation

Less confident learners

Adapt photocopiable page 'Measures and money problems' so children work with simpler quantities. Work with children, taking them through the problems step-by-step, giving guidance and discussing strategies.

More confident learners

Adapt photocopiable page 'Measures and money problems' so children work with more complex problems.

Lesson 5
Oral and mental starter 24

Main teaching activities

Whole-class work: Explain that this lesson is about solving problems. The children will be thinking about how to solve problems and the best strategies to use. Discuss the strategies that they have been thinking about this week: number pairs, using known number pairs, bridging ten and adding multiples of ten and adjusting. Write some calculations on the board to practise these, such as 28 + 12, 80 − 30, 36 + 7, 34 − 9. The children answer on their whiteboards and show you. Ask: *Suzie cut a piece of string into three lengths. They measure 9cm, 15cm and 16cm. What was the total length of the string?* Discuss the steps involved in solving the problem. Agree they need to look for the relevant information, decide what they need to do with it, do the calculation, make sure the answer seems sensible and check. For Suzie's problem, agree that they need to add 9cm, 15cm and 16cm. Discuss ways to do this. Establish that they could add 9cm to 15cm by adding 10 and taking away 1 to give 24cm. They could then add 6 to make 30cm and then add the other 10 to give 40cm. Discuss how they could check. Agree that they could add in a different order or take away two numbers from 40cm to see if they get the third one. Repeat for other problems.

Paired/Independent work: Ask the children to work with a partner or individually on photocopiable page 'Measures and money problems' from the CD-ROM, finding the best strategy to solve each one. Model an example from the sheet.

Progress check: Ask different children these questions:

● *Which is the best strategy to use to solve this?*
● *How could you check? Is there another way?*

Review

Invite some children to explain how they solved their problems. Question them carefully about the steps they used and why they chose particular strategies. Ask how they could check their answers. Encourage them to think about using the inverse operation. Demonstrate this using arrow diagrams.

Addition and subtraction: using partitioning and counting on strategies

Expected prior learning

Children should be able to:

● add and subtract using mental calculation strategies
● use the inverse operation to check additions and subtractions.

Topic	Curriculum objectives	Expected outcomes
Addition and subtraction	**Lesson 1**	
	To add and subtract using concrete objects, pictorial representations, and mentally, including: two two-digit numbers.	Add and subtract using partitioning and sequencing.
	Lesson 2	
	To add and subtract using concrete objects, pictorial representations, and mentally, including: two two-digit numbers.	Add and subtract using partitioning and sequencing.
	Lesson 3	
	To add and subtract using concrete objects, pictorial representations, and mentally, including: a two-digit number and ones. To recognise and use the inverse relationship between addition and subtraction and use this to check calculations and solve missing number problems. To show that addition of two numbers can be done in any order (commutative) and subtraction of one number from another cannot.	Add and subtract using counting on. Use concrete and pictorial representations and number lines to add and subtract. Check answers using the inverse operation. Know that addition can be done in any order, subtraction cannot.
	Lesson 4	
	To add and subtract using concrete objects, pictorial representations, and mentally, including: two two-digit numbers. To recognise and use the inverse relationship between addition and subtraction and use this to check calculations and solve missing number problems.	Add and subtract using counting on. Use concrete and pictorial representations and number lines to add and subtract. Check answers using the inverse operation. Complete missing number sentences.
	Lesson 5	
	To solve problems with addition and subtraction: ● using concrete objects and pictorial representations, including those involving numbers, quantities and measures ● applying their increasing knowledge of mental and written methods.	Use partitioning and counting on to solve simple addition and subtraction problems within the context of money.

■SCHOLASTIC

Preparation

Lesson 2: prepare sets of eight cards that are about 4cm by 5cm in size for the activity

You will need

Photocopiable sheets
'Partitioning and sequencing'; 'What am I?'
General resources
'0–100 number cards'
Equipment
Individual whiteboards; price labels

Further practice

Photocopiable sheets
'Ivor Dog's dog and puppy food'

Oral and mental starters for week 3

See bank of starters on pages 44, 126 and 127. Oral and mental starters are also on the CD-ROM.

3 Partitioning

31 Number pairs to 20

32 What makes ten?

33 Ordering numbers

34 Bridging ten again

Overview of progression

During this week children will continue to develop their understanding of addition and subtraction. They will be rehearsing strategies that include partitioning and counting on. They will be encouraged to use concrete apparatus and number lines as appropriate. They will check answers using the inverse operation. Throughout they will be solving simple problems within the context of number, money and time. Lesson 5 gives opportunity for children to use and apply their facts and skills to solve multiplication problems.

Watch out for

Some children may still find it difficult to visualise a two-digit number when it has been partitioned. Let these children work with arrow cards. When they gain confidence ask them to think what each number will be and write the number sentence first. They use the cards to check.

Creative context

Set up a class shop. Encourage the children to price items in the shop and make up shopping problems for each other involving addition and subtraction of prices.

Vocabulary

add, addition, altogether, **bridging ten**, difference, **inverse operation,** make, more, partitioning, plus, subtract, sum, take away, **tens boundary**, total

Curriculum objectives
● To add and subtract using concrete objects, pictorial representations, and mentally, including: two two-digit numbers.

Success criteria
● I can add and subtract by partitioning numbers.
● I can check an answer by using a different strategy.

You will need
Photocopiable sheets
'Partitioning and sequencing'
General resources
'0–100 number cards'
Equipment
Individual whiteboards

Differentiation
Less confident learners
Adapt photocopiable page 'Partitioning and sequencing' so that the children add single-digit numbers.
More confident learners
Encourage children to think of a third strategy to add their numbers.

Lesson 1   Oral and mental starter 31

Main teaching activities

Whole-class work: *Emily saw 46 girls at the start of the tennis match. Just as it started another 32 girls arrived. How many were at the match altogether?* Ask the children to work with a partner and discuss strategies for finding the total. Invite them to demonstrate any methods that they might have. Celebrate those that give the correct answer. Focus on partitioning. Demonstrate this strategy: $46 + 32 = 40 + 30 + 6 + 2 = 70 + 8 = 78$. *How can we check to see if we are correct?* Listen to the children's suggestions and tell them that you are going to show them how they could add in a different way to check. Demonstrate this (sequencing): $46 + 30 = 76. 76 + 2 = 78$.

Give the children two two-digit numbers (10–50) to add and check in the ways described above on their whiteboards.

Set similar problems to Emily's. Include those with numbers where the ones total is more than ten. Ask: *If 25 girls leave the tennis match early, how many will be left? Talk to your partner about what you need to do to find the answer.* Discuss how to answer the question by partitioning. Partition 78, take 20 from 70 and 5 from 8 and recombine. Next demonstrate checking by sequencing: $78 - 20 - 5$. Practise this for other examples which can be answered without exchanging any tens, for example $56 - 34$, $89 - 43$.

Independent work: Give the children two-digit number cards (10–50) and photocopiable page 'Partitioning and sequencing' from the CD-ROM. Explain that they need to pick two two-digit number cards and add them using one of the strategies above and check using sequencing.

Progress check: Invite several children to demonstrate their methods for partitioning and sequencing. Ask the rest of the class to check that they are using these strategies. Ask:
- *How would you add 65 and 23 by partitioning?*
- *What about sequencing?*

Review
Take feedback from the activity. Invite the children to share their methods for the numbers they picked, demonstrating on the board. Ask the class to make up some problems for these. Ask: *How are partitioning and sequencing the same? How are they different?* Ask the children which strategy they prefer and why.

Curriculum objectives
● To add and subtract using concrete objects, pictorial representations, and mentally, including: two two-digit numbers.

Success criteria
● I can add and subtract using partitioning.
● I can add and subtract using sequencing.

You will need
Equipment
Individual whiteboards; price labels

Differentiation
Organise the children to work in mixed attainment groups. Encourage the more confident learners to support the less confident. However, ensure they do not dominate the group.

Lesson 2   Oral and mental starter 3

Main teaching activities

Whole-class work: Set this problem: *Peter's mum spent £37 on school uniform. Dan's mum spent £48. How much did the mums spend all together? Talk to your partner about how you would find the answer?* Take feedback and agree that they need to add the amounts of money. Recap the strategies used in lesson 1. Ask the children to add the amounts using partitioning on their whiteboards: £37 + £48 = £30 + £40 + £7 + £8 = £70 + £15 = £85. Next they add the same amount using sequencing: £37 + £40 + £8 = £85. Ask: *How much more did Dan's mum spend?* Ask the children to find out using partitioning: £40 − £30 = £10, £8 − £7 = £1, recombine to give £11 and sequencing: £48 − £30 − £7 = £11. Repeat with similar money problems. Ensure that none involve exchanging in the subtractions at this stage.

Group work: Working in mixed attainment groups of four, the children collect eight items from around the classroom. They decide how much each will cost between 20p and 90p. They write price labels on the cards. They then take it in turns to work out the totals and differences between pairs of items using the strategies discussed in the lesson.

Progress check: Move around the groups checking that they understand what to do. Ask questions such as: *How are you going to add those amounts together? Is there another strategy that you can use?*

Review
Invite groups to show the items they chose and the prices they gave them. Ask children from the rest of the class to pick pairs of items and demonstrate how they would find the total price and the difference.

Curriculum objectives
● To add and subtract using objects, pictorial representations.
● To recognise and use the inverse relationship between addition and subtraction and use this to check calculations.
● To show that addition can be done in any order and subtraction cannot.

Success criteria
● I can add and subtract by counting on.
● I can check a calculation by doing the opposite operation.

You will need
General resources
'0–100 number cards'

Differentiation
Less confident learners
Children work with numbers to 20. Provide counting apparatus if necessary.
More confident learners
Children add single digits to numbers up to 50.

Lesson 3   Oral and mental starter 32

Main teaching activities

Whole-class work: Say: *Tammy has 15 dolls. Charlie has 9. How many do they have altogether? Talk to your partner about the strategies you could use to find the answer.* Take feedback. Expect the children to be able to tell you that they could add by bridging ten (partitioning 9 into 5 and 4, add 5 to 15 to make 20 then add the other 4). They could also add 10 and take away 1. Invite volunteers to demonstrate each using a number line, plotting 15 and counting on 9. Discuss whether it would work if they placed 9 on the number line and then added 15. Agree they can because it doesn't matter which way an addition is carried out, the answer will be the same. Demonstrate on the number line. Discuss checking answers using the inverse operation.

Independent work: Give each child a set of number cards 1–30. They pick pairs of a single-digit and a two-digit number and work out the totals and differences drawing their own number lines.

Progress check: Check to make sure everyone has understood what to do by asking two or three children to give examples.

Review
Take feedback about the activity. Invite children to share the numbers they chose and to demonstrate how they found the totals and differences using their number lines.

Invite the class to make up problems to go with the children's calculations.

Curriculum objectives

● To add and subtract using concrete objects, pictorial representations, and mentally, including: a two-digit number and ones; two two-digit numbers.
● To recognise and use the inverse relationship between addition and subtraction and use this to check calculations and solve missing number problems.

Success criteria

● I can add by counting on along a number line.
● I can find differences by counting on.

You will need

General resources

'0–100 number cards'

Equipment

Individual whiteboards

Differentiation

Less confident learners

Give children a selection of number cards 10–20. Provide numbered number lines for them to use.

More confident learners

Give children a selection of number cards 50–70.

Main teaching activities

Whole-class work: Say: *Shannon has a collection of 47 stamps. Sam has 38. How many do they have altogether? Talk to you partner about the strategies you could use to find the answer.* Take feedback. Expect the children to be able to tell you that they could add by partitioning and also sequencing. Invite volunteers to demonstrate. *How could we use a number line to add these numbers?* Agree they could draw a number line from 0 to 100, plot 47 and then make a jump of 30 to 77 and then 3 and 5 to give 85. Demonstrate this. *What other strategies have we used to do this?* Agree sequencing and bridging ten. Help the children see the links between these. Discuss checking answers using the inverse operation.

Ask: *How can we use a number line to find out how many more stamps Shannon has than Sam?* Agree that they could count on from the smallest number. Demonstrate by first drawing rectangles to represent the whole amounts. Next plot the numbers on a number line from zero. Cross out the part from 0 to 38 to show these numbers have been taken away and count up from 38 to 40 then 47.

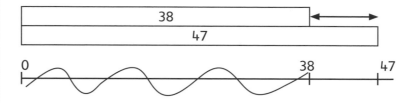

Repeat for other examples. Again, check using the inverse operation.

Independent work: Give each child a set of number cards 20–50. They pick pairs and work out the totals and differences drawing their own number lines.

Progress check: Ask volunteers to demonstrate some of their addition and subtraction calculations. Check that everyone is using a number line.

● *How can we check that the answer is correct?*

Review

Take feedback. Invite children to share how they found their totals and differences. Ask them to work with a partner to make up a problem for one of the pairs of numbers. They share their problems with the class.

Curriculum objectives
● To solve simple problems with addition: using concrete objects and pictorial representations, including those involving numbers, quantities and measures; applying their increasing knowledge of mental and written methods.

Success criteria
● I can solve word problems using a number line.
● I can check my answers using the opposite operation.

You will need
Photocopiable sheets
'What am I?'
Equipment
Individual whiteboards

Differentiation
Less confident learners
Adapt photocopiable page 'What am I?' so children only work with numbers to 20. Provide counters if necessary.

More confident learners
Adapt photocopiable page 'What am I?' so children work with numbers to 100.

Lesson 5   Oral and mental starter 34

Main teaching activities

Whole-class work: Explain: *Today we are going to use the strategies we have been learning to help us solve missing number problems.* Discuss the strategies that have been looked at this week: partitioning, sequencing, counting on along the number line to add and find the difference. Write some calculations on the board to practise these, for example $38 + 25$, $45 - 32$, $56 + 12$, $34 - 29$. Recap the fact that they can use subtraction to check addition and addition to check subtraction. Ask them to check the answers to the practice calculations. Recap that it doesn't matter which way round you add numbers, the answer will be the same but it does matter which way round you subtract because the two answers will be different. Demonstrate with the practice questions.

Write on the board: $32 + \square = 40$. Ask: *Which of the strategies will help us here?* Agree that a number line would work and demonstrate counting on from 32 to 40 on the line. Repeat for similar problems.

Write on the board: $\square + 32 = 54$ and ask the children to discuss how they would find the missing number. Take feedback, celebrating any that work. Remind them that they could use the opposite operation. They could find the missing number by taking the known number from the answer. They could do this on a number line or by partitioning or sequencing. Repeat for similar problems. Move onto subtraction: $20 - \square = 13$. Discuss how a number line can help. Go over a few more examples.

Independent work: The children practise the strategy using photocopiable page 'What am I?' from the CD-ROM. It asks them to find missing numbers and explain how they find them. The activity concentrates on addition. You may wish to add a few subtractions.

Progress check: Ask children:
● *Which is the best strategy to use to solve this?*
● *How could you check that you are correct?*

Review
Go through examples of each level of the activity inviting children to share their thinking. Ask questions such as: *Is there another way you could have done this? Is your method the same as your neighbour's?*

Multiplication and division: grouping, sharing and times tables facts

Expected prior learning

Children should be able to:

- answer multiplication calculations using repeated addition
- answer division calculations using repeated subtraction
- describe arrays.

Topic	Curriculum objectives	Expected outcomes
Multiplication and division	**Lesson 1**	
	To calculate mathematical statements for multiplication and division within the multiplication tables and write them using the multiplication (×), division (÷) and equals (=) signs. To recall and use multiplication and division facts for the 2, 5 and 10 multiplication tables, including recognising odd and even numbers.	Multiply using repeated addition. Understand the link between repeated addition and arrays.
	Lesson 2	
	To calculate mathematical statements for multiplication and division within the multiplication tables and write them using the multiplication (×), division (÷) and equals (=) signs.	Understand the links between repeated subtraction and grouping. Use times tables facts to answer division calculations.
	Lesson 3	
	To calculate mathematical statements for multiplication and division within the multiplication tables and write them using the multiplication (×), division (÷) and equals (=) signs. To show that multiplication of two numbers can be done in any order (commutative) and division of one number by another cannot.	Understand the link between repeated subtraction, grouping and arrays. Use tables facts to solve multiplication and division.
	Lesson 4	
	To calculate mathematical statements for multiplication and division within the multiplication tables and write them using the multiplication (×), division (÷) and equals (=) signs.	Understand division as grouping. Check answers by multiplying.
	Lesson 5	
	To solve problems involving multiplication and division, using materials, arrays, repeated addition, mental methods and multiplication and division facts, including problems in contexts.	Use multiplication and division to solve simple problems.

Preparation

Lesson 1: photocopy, cut and laminate the cards from photocopiable pages 'Multiplication and division vocabulary'

Further practice: Prepare sets of 'Multiplication facts for 2-, 5- and 10-times tables' cards, one per group

You will need

Photocopiable sheets

'Array for maths! (2)'; 'Group that!'; 'Grouping (1)'; 'Home we go!'; 'Party problems example'; 'Party problems'

General resources

'0–100 number cards'; 'Multiplication and division vocabulary'; 'Multiplication facts for 2-, 5- and 10-times tables'

Equipment

Individual whiteboards; interlocking cubes; counters

Further practice

Give groups of children a set of 'Multiplication facts for 2-, 5- and 10-times tables' cards face down. Each child picks a card in turn, and keeps it if they know the answer. The winner is the player with the most cards at the end.

Oral and mental starters for week 4

See bank of starters on pages 85, 126 and127. Oral and mental starters are also on the CD-ROM.

 Times tables facts

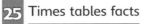 Multiples

29 Counting in steps of two, five and ten

35 Two-times, five-times and ten-times tables

Overview of progression

During this week children will consolidate and extend their knowledge of multiplication and division. They will continue to develop the idea that multiplication is repeated addition and division is repeated subtraction using practical apparatus, arrays and number lines. They will check answers by using the inverse operation and learn that multiplication is commutative. They will begin to extend repeated subtraction into grouping. They will rehearse and develop the mental calculation strategies of doubling and halving and recalling multiplication table facts. They will use the strategies considered during the week to solve simple problems in familiar contexts.

Watch out for

Some children may have difficulty recalling times tables facts. Encourage them to count on in multiples using their fingers.

Creative context

You could ask the children to make up a musical rap to help them recall times tables facts.

Vocabulary

array, column, divide, divided by, equal groups, grouping, groups of, lots of, multiply, **multiple of,** multiplied by, repeated addition, repeated subtraction, row, times

Curriculum objectives
● To recall and use multiplication and division facts for the 2, 5 and 10 multiplication tables, including recognising odd and even numbers.
● To calculate mathematical statements for multiplication and division within the multiplication tables and write them using the multiplication (×), division (÷) and equals (=) signs.

Success criteria
● I can multiply using repeated addition.
● I can make arrays and describe them.

You will need
Photocopiable sheets
'Array for maths! (2)'
General resources
'Multiplication and division vocabulary'

Differentiation
Less confident learners
Adapt photocopiable page 'Array for maths! (2)' so children work with lower numbers. If possible, ask a teaching assistant to work with these children. Let them make the arrays with counters before drawing them.

More confident learners
Adapt photocopiable page 'Array for maths! (2)' so that children find three different arrays for 24.

Lesson 1
Oral and mental starter 29

Main teaching activities

Whole-class work: Revise the meaning of *multiply* and *divide* and ask for the related vocabulary that the children can remember. If they say any of those on the vocabulary cards prepared from photocopiable page 'Multiplication and division vocabulary' stick these on the board. Discuss any words that have not been mentioned. Sort the words into two groups: multiplication and division. *Could any of these be in both groups?* Agree *groups of* and *lots of* could refer to both. Say: *Today we will focus on the words repeated addition, repeated subtraction, arrays and groups.* Ask the children to discuss with a partner what each of these words is about. Take feedback and invite volunteers to demonstrate using practical equipment or with drawings on the board.

Write the number 6 on the board. Ask the children to make an array using counters and then to draw an array of six dots on their whiteboards. After they have done this, draw one on the board. There are several possibilities so celebrate any that are correct. Ensure you draw one that has two rows of three dots. Draw loops around the columns for groups of two dots and ask the class how this can be recorded as a number sentence: 2 + 2 + 2 = 6 which is two three times or 2 × 3. Link this to the two-times table by counting two, four, six on fingers. Ask whether there is another way of 'reading' the array. This time loop the two rows: 3 + 3 = 6 and 3 × 2. Link this to the three-times table by counting three, six on fingers. Repeat for two arrays for ten (5 × 2 and 2 × 5). Ask the children to draw arrays of eight on their whiteboards and write the number sentences. Ask those that do this quickly to try 12. Can they find more than two arrays?

Paired work: Distribute photocopiable page 'Array for maths! (2)' on the CD-ROM and model an example to show the children what to do.

Progress check: Check that the children are doing what is expected by inviting pairs to share some of the arrays they have made. The class then work out, for each, the different number sentences that can be made.

Paired work: Give pairs who have finished 'Array for maths! (2)' a container of counters. Ask them to make arrays and derive two number sentences from each.

Review

Invite one pair to draw and explain one of their arrays. Use their work to introduce division in terms of repeated subtraction. Explain that because division is the opposite of multiplication and multiplication is repeated addition, division must be repeated subtraction.

Curriculum objectives
● To calculate mathematical statements for multiplication and division.
Success criteria
● I can divide by grouping.
● I can check my answer using my times tables.

You will need
Photocopiable sheets
'Group that!'
Equipment
Interlocking cubes or counters; individual whiteboards

Differentiation
Less confident learners
Adapt photocopiable page so children work with numbers to 12.
More confident learners
Adapt photocopiable page so children draw arrays.

Lesson 2   Oral and mental starter 35

Main teaching activities

Whole-class work: Recap on arrays and the link to division as in the review from lesson 1. Use interlocking cubes or similar objects to demonstrate 12 in an array of three rows of four. Ask the children to tell you the two possible repeated subtraction number sentences for division and to write what they say on the board ($12 - 4 - 4 - 4 = 0$, $12 - 3 - 3 - 3 - 3 = 0$). Demonstrate on a number line.

Next, focus on grouping, demonstrating with cubes. Say: *I have 12 cubes and I am going to divide them into groups of four.* Take away groups of four. Agree three. Write the number sentence $12 \div 4 = 3$. Show this on a number line and agree this is the same as repeated subtraction. Repeat with similar calculations. Use the children to demonstrate. For each show what you have done on a number line and write the appropriate division number sentence.

Independent work: Distribute photocopiable page 'Group that!' from the CD-ROM and demonstrate what the children need to do.

Progress check: To check their understanding, ask the children:
● *What are you doing?*
● *What number sentence can you write to show what you have done?*

Review

Ask one child from each level to show the class an example of their work. Explain that for a division, e.g. $12 \div 2$ we can say 'How many twos make 12?' and that our times tables knowledge can help us. Work through a few examples, such as $15 \div 5$, $18 \div 3$.

Curriculum objectives
● To calculate mathematical statements for multiplication and division.
Success criteria
● I can solve a division using arrays

You will need
Photocopiable sheets
'Home we go!'; 'Home we go! gameboard'
General resources
'0–100 number cards'
Equipment
Individual whiteboards; counters

Differentiation
Less confident learners
Children make even numbers to 20.
More confident learners
Children find and draw other arrays for the numbers of counters they pick.

Lesson 3   Oral and mental starter 25

Main teaching activities

Whole-class work: Write $18 \div 2$ on the board and ask: *How can we answer this? Let's work out $18 \div 2$ by counting in twos together, using our fingers: 2, 4, 6… 18. How many twos is that?* (9) *Try $15 \div 3$. What should we count in this time?* (threes) Ask similar questions for the children to answer on their whiteboards. Make the divisors the numbers they have counted in steps of: 2, 3, 5 and 10. Make the link that division and multiplication are opposite operations and one can be used to answer the other or as a check. Demonstrate with $15 \div 3 = 5$, $3 \times 5 = 15$.

Group work: Children practise division by playing the game 'Home we go!' in groups of three or four.

Progress check: Visit each group to ensure that they are playing the game correctly.

Review

Play 'Home we go!' in two class teams. Make sure everyone counts. Use this as an opportunity to bring in remainders very briefly. For example, with $11 \div 3$, count in threes: 3, 6, 9, 12. 11 is higher than 9 but lower than 12. Draw 11 dots on the board and say: *We can get three groups of three from 11, but then we have two left over. So we can say $11 \div 3$ is 3 remainder 2.* Repeat these with a few similar examples.

Curriculum objectives
● To calculate mathematical statements for multiplication and division within the multiplication tables and write them using the multiplication (×), division (÷) and equals (=) signs.

Success criteria
● I can divide by grouping.
● I can group using arrays.

You will need
Photocopiable sheets
'Grouping (1)'
Equipment
Counters; individual whiteboards; cubes

Differentiation
Less confident learners
Provide the children with counters so that they can physically make the arrays.

More confident learners
Once the children have finished the activity, ask them to make up some more calculations and problems.

Lesson 4   Oral and mental starter 15

Main teaching activities

Whole-class work: Explain that this lesson is about solving problems using grouping. Ask the children to tell you what is meant by grouping: taking groups of the same number away from an amount. Set this problem: *Yukesh had 12 cookies. If he wanted to put two on each plate how many plates would he need?* Give the children a few minutes to think about this. Take feedback. Show 12 cubes and say these represent cookies. Give two of them to a child who comes to the front of the class. Repeat this until there are no more cubes. Agree that Yukesh needs six plates. Show this on a number line and as a number sentence: 12 ÷ 2 = 6. Next ask the children how they could check that they are correct: 6 × 2. Show this as an array and make the links between division and multiplication.

Repeat for this problem: *Olivia had 20 dolls, she put them in groups of five. How many groups did she have?* Give the children 20 counters. Ask them to group them in groups of five to form an array. How many groups do they have? How can they check? Ask them to write this as a number sentence and to make up a story to go with their sentence. Repeat for other numbers of counters.

Independent work: Distribute copies of photocopiable page 'Grouping (1)' from the CD-ROM and demonstrate what the children need to do using the example.

Progress check: Invite individuals to demonstrate one of the questions. Ask:
- *How can we check they are correct?*
- *What does grouping mean? Can you explain in a different way?*
- *If I had 14 pencils and put them into groups of two, how many groups would I have? How do you know?*
- *Can you make up a story for 15 ÷ 3? Can you make up another?*

Review

Ask: *What did you notice during your activity?* Aim towards the fact that they can answer division questions by working with arrays. Ask them which method for division they prefer: grouping, arrays or repeated addition. Point out that they are basically the same but the visual representation is different. Remind them that multiplication and division are inverse or opposite operations.

Curriculum objectives

● To solve problems involving multiplication and division, using materials, arrays, repeated addition, mental methods and multiplication and division facts, including problems in contexts.

Success criteria

● I can solve simple problems involving multiplication and division.

You will need

Photocopiable sheets

'Party problems example'; 'Party problems'

Differentiation

Less confident learners

Adapt photocopiable page 'Party problems' so children work with smaller numbers. Make counting apparatus available if needed.

More confident learners

Adapt photocopiable page 'Party problems' so children work with larger numbers.

Lesson 5   Oral and mental starter 35

Main teaching activities

Whole-class work: Explain that this lesson is about solving problems using multiplication and division. Display photocopiable page 'Party problems example' from the CD-ROM. Read through it with the children. Discuss what the children need to do to solve the problem: look for the important information; decide what to do with the numbers; answer the problem; decide if the answer makes sense and check. Together work through the problem, asking: *What is the question? What do we need to know to find the answer? How many packets of biscuits can you see? How many biscuits are in each one? What are four lots of ten? What else do we need to find out? How many biscuits are there altogether? How did you work out the last part?*

Paired work: Distribute photocopiable page 'Party problems' from the CD-ROM. Explain what the children need to do. Tell them that they can jot down their workings on the back of the sheet.

Progress check: Visit each pair to check that they understand what to do and are working correctly.

Review

Invite a few children, particularly any you want to assess, to explain how they solved one of their problems. Discuss and compare methods. Ask questions such as: *How did you know what was being asked? Explain how you worked out your answer. How did you know if you were right? What did you do if there were some things left over?*

If time is available, give children, in groups, a set of 'Multiplication facts' cards to further practice the 2, 5 and 10 times tables.

Geometry: properties of 3D and 2D shapes

Expected prior learning

Children should be able to:

● identify and describe the properties of 3D shapes including edges, vertices and faces
● identify 2D shapes on the surface of 3D shapes.

Topic	Curriculum objectives	Expected outcomes
Geometry: properties of shapes	**Lesson 1**	
	To identify and describe the properties of 3D shapes including the number of edges, vertices and faces.	Identify and describe the properties of spheres, cones, cylinders, cubes, cuboids, square-based pyramids.
	Lesson 2	
	To identify and describe the properties of 3D shapes including the number of edges, vertices and faces. To identify 2D shapes on the surface of 3D shapes [for example, a circle on a cylinder and a triangle on a pyramid].	Make 3D shapes. Identify and name the 2D shapes on the surface of 3D shapes.
	Lesson 3	
	To identify 2D shapes on the surface of 3D shapes, for example circle on a cylinder and a triangle on a pyramid. To identify and describe the properties of 2D shapes, including the number of sides and line symmetry in a vertical line.	Identify the 2D shapes of the faces of 3D shapes. Use 2D shapes to make symmetrical patterns.
	Lesson 4	
	To identify and describe the properties of 2D shapes, including the number of sides and line symmetry in a vertical line.	Sort 2D shapes according to the property of symmetry.
	Lesson 5	
	To identify and describe the properties of 2D shapes, including the number of sides and line symmetry in a vertical line.	Use shapes to solve different types of problems that involve reasoning.

Preparation

Lesson 1: prepare sets of 3D shapes enough for groups of four: sphere, cone, cylinder, cube, cuboid and square-based pyramid; copy, cut out and laminate the shape names from '3D shape vocabulary' enough for groups of four

Lesson 2: prepare a small amount of Plasticine® for each child to use

Lesson 3: fold in half or draw a line down the middle of A3 paper for pairs of children

Lesson 4: copy 'Templates for irregular shapes', and 'Templates for regular shapes' for use by pairs of children; draw two-column tables on A3 paper for those that need them; fold some shapes ready for the review part of the lesson

Lesson 5: fold or draw a line down the middle of A3 paper for pairs of children

You will need

Photocopiable sheets
'Shapes'; '3D shapes'

General resources
'3D shape vocabulary'; 'Templates for regular shapes'; 'Templates for irregular shapes'

Equipment
Individual whiteboards; 3D shapes: spheres, cones, cylinders, cubes, cuboids, square-based pyramids, triangular prism; Plasticine®; feely bag; A3 paper; scissors; glue

Further practice

Photocopiable sheets
'Creating patterns'

Oral and mental starters for week 5

See bank of starters on pages 126 to 127. Oral and mental starters are also on the CD-ROM.

29 Counting in steps of two, five and ten

30 Counting in odd and even numbers

34 Bridging ten again

35 Two-times, five-times and ten-times tables

36 Arrays

Overview of progression

During this week children will extend their knowledge of 3D and 2D shape. They will begin by identifying familiar 3D shapes. They will describe their properties in terms of faces, edges and vertices. They will identify the properties of the 2D shapes that make up the faces of 3D shapes. They will explore symmetry. From their explorations of 3D and their 2D faces, they will begin to visualise how these can be made. They will also sort 3D and 2D shapes including those that they can see in the environment.

> ### Watch out for
> Some children may find it difficult to visualise shapes. Provide these children with real shapes for the activities that they carry out and interlocking shapes so that they can explore how 3D shapes are made.

Creative context

Encourage the children to use their knowledge of shape in art and topic work, for example in designing patterns and model making.

Vocabulary

apex, circle, cone, corner, cube, cuboid, curve, cylinder, edge, face, hexagon, octagon, pentagon, pyramid, rectangle, side, sphere, square, symmetry, triangle, **triangular prism**, **vertex,** vertices

Curriculum objectives
● To identify and describe the properties of 3D shapes including the number of edges, vertices and faces.

Success criteria
● I can name 3D shapes.
● I can describe 3D shapes.

You will need
General resource
'3D shape vocabulary'
Equipment
Sphere; cone; cylinder; cube; cuboid; square-based pyramid; triangular prism

Differentiation
The children work in mixed-ability groups. Check that the less confident learners are taking an active part in the discussions and make sure the more confident learners do not dominate the proceedings.

Lesson I
Oral and mental starter 29

Main teaching activities

Whole-class work: Ask the children to think about all they can remember to do with shape. First they share their thoughts with a partner and then with the rest of the class. Bring out these points, showing/drawing/discussing examples as you do: 3D, 2D, regular, irregular, all the shape names they should know (see vocabulary list), the different properties of face, corner, edge, side and symmetry. Remind them of the work they covered in Autumn term I and say that today they are going to rehearse and reinforce 3D shape. Describe the properties of each of the shapes on photocopiable page '3D shape vocabulary' and ask the children to identify the shape you are describing. Show each 3D shape as it is identified and place the label beside it. Pick up each shape in turn and ask the children to describe its properties in terms of edges, vertices and curved surfaces or flat faces. Inform the children that a face is flat, so the faces on a sphere, cone and cylinder are not faces but curved surfaces. A vertex is made when edges meet so a cone does not have a vertex because there are no edges meeting. The name of the cone's point is an apex. It is important that the children hear the correct terminology, even if they don't remember it at first.

Group work: The children should work in mixed-ability groups of about four. They need at least one of each shape on the table in front of them plus a set of shape name labels made from photocopiable page '3D shape vocabulary' from the CD-ROM. As a group, they match each shape with its name label. They then take it in turns to describe all the shapes one at a time, using the properties discussed in the main part of the lesson but not their names. The others guess what shape they are describing. They should find that the third and fourth children will describe more quickly because they have listened to the descriptions of the other two. Once they have all had a go, they should come up with a good, written description for all the shapes.

Progress check: Visit each group in turn to make sure everyone is taking part. Ask questions such as:

- *What are the properties of a cube?*
- *How is a cube the same as a cuboid? How is it different?*
- *What are the properties of a cone?*

Review

Take feedback from the activity by listening to the groups' descriptions of the shapes. Pick one description for each from different groups and repeat the group activity with the class. Describe and expect the children to tell you quickly which shape you are describing.

Curriculum objectives
● To identify and describe the properties of 3D shapes.
● To identify 2D shapes on the surface of 3D shapes.

Success criteria
● I can describe 3D shapes.
● I can name the faces on a 3D shape.

You will need

Photocopiable sheets
'3D shapes'

Equipment
Sphere; cone; cylinder; cube; cuboid; square-based pyramid; triangular prism; Plasticine®; feely bag

Differentiation
Place less confident learners with more confident learners so that they have someone to support them if necessary. Encourage all the children to take an active part in examining the 3D shapes during the review.

Lesson 2 — Oral and mental starter 30

Main teaching activities

Whole-class work: This is a whole-class lesson. Recap what the class did in the previous lesson. In turn, show the sphere, cone, cylinder, cube, cuboid, square-based pyramid and triangular prism. Discuss the properties of each (edges, vertices, faces, curved surfaces and apex) as well as the names of their 2D faces. Recap on the terms as they occur. For each, ask where they might see these shapes in real life and also anything that they can do, for example, can they roll, stack?

Remind the children of the work they did in the Autumn term with Plasticine® and say that they are going to do this again but making other shapes. Quickly follow the instruction and discussion prompts on photocopiable page '3D shapes' from the CD-ROM and demonstrate as you go along, guiding the children through the instructions. It is important for continuity to follow the instructions in order. The discussion of each 3D shape and the 2D shapes of its faces should follow on naturally from the previous one.

Progress check: Ask questions such as:
● *How do you know this is a cube?*
● *Where might you see a cube in real life?*

Review

Put a 3D shape in a feely bag. Invite a child to feel the shape and describe it. Encourage the child to use the properties that were discussed in the lesson, including the shapes of the faces. The class has to work out what the shape is.

Curriculum objectives
● To identify 2D shapes on the surface of 3D shapes.
● To identify and describe the properties of 2D shapes.

Success criteria
● I can name 2D shapes.
● I can use 2D shapes to make symmetrical patterns.

You will need

Photocopiable sheets
'Shapes'

General resources
'Templates for irregular shapes'; 'Templates for regular shapes'

Equipment
Sphere; cone; cylinder; cube; cuboid; square-based pyramid; triangular prism; A3 paper; scissors; glue; individual whiteboards

Differentiation
Let the children work together in mixed ability pairs. Ask more confident learners to help their partners with cutting out and labelling 2D shapes.

Lesson 3 — Oral and mental starter 36

Main teaching activities

Whole-class work: Recap the work done in the previous lesson. Show the different faces and/or curved surfaces of each 3D shape, ask the children to look at each carefully and draw what they see on their whiteboards. They should see a 2D shape. Use this as a lead into a discussion of 2D shapes and their properties. Show the shapes from photocopiable pages 'Templates for irregular shapes' and 'Templates for regular shapes', one type at a time. For each, discuss their properties including regularity and symmetry.

Paired work: Give mixed-ability pairs a copy of photocopiable page 'Shapes' from the CD-ROM each and one piece of A3 paper folded or with a line drawn down the middle. Demonstrate their task which is to label each shape, then cut it out and together make a symmetrical pattern as follows: one child should put a shape on one side of the fold/line, the other takes their matching shape and puts in the same position on the other side of the fold/line. They stick these down and then continue with another shape until all the shapes are stuck down.

Progress check: Visit each pair in turn and ask questions such as:
● *What shape is this one?*
● *How are you going to place this shape so it is symmetrical to the one on the other side?*

Review

Look at each pair's pattern and as a class assess their accuracy. Ask the class to think of an accurate definition of symmetry.

Curriculum objectives
● To identify and describe the properties of 2D shapes.
Success criteria
● I can recognise line symmetry in 2D shapes.

You will need
General resources
'Templates for irregular shapes'; 'Templates for regular shapes'
Equipment
Individual whiteboards; scissors; glue; A3 paper

Differentiation
Less confident learners
Give children a ready-made table with headings.
More confident learners
Children make a table with six columns, (with headings from 'no lines' to 'more than four lines'). They place at least two shapes in each column.

Lesson 4
Oral and mental starter 34

Main teaching activities

Whole-class work: Discuss what the children did in lesson 3 recapping their work on symmetry. Hold up regular and irregular shapes made from photocopiable pages. Ask the children to name them and describe their properties in terms of regularity, sides and corners. Ensure that at least one of the shapes you hold up has no lines of symmetry. Ask the children to draw a shape on their whiteboards that has one line of symmetry, then two and ask them to identify the name of their shape. Next ask them to draw a shape that has no lines of symmetry and justify this to a partner.

Paired work: Give each pair a copy of photocopiable pages 'Templates for regular shapes' and 'Templates for irregular shapes' from the CD-ROM. They cut the shapes out and label them. They draw a two-column table on A3 paper, with the columns headed 'symmetry' and 'no symmetry' and stick all their shapes in the appropriate section.

Progress check: Visit the pairs of children you might wish to assess. Ask questions such as:

- *What is meant by the word symmetry?*
- *Is this shape symmetrical? How do you know?*

Review

Take feedback from the activity, inviting pairs to share where they placed the shapes on their table and explain why they did this. Finish by showing the children a shape that you have folded. Ask them to imagine opening it up and then to draw the shape they think will be made. Repeat this a few times.

Curriculum objectives
● To identify and describe the properties of 2D shapes.
Success criteria
● I can solve simple problems involving symmetry.

You will need
General resources
'Templates for irregular shapes'; 'Templates for regular shapes'
Equipment
A3 paper; scissors; glue

Differentiation
Organise the children in mixed-ability pairs. More confident learners can assist any that may have difficulty recognising how to make their pattern symmetrical.

Lesson 5
Oral and mental starter 35

Main teaching activities

Whole-class work: Recap the work that the children have covered over the previous four lessons by holding up different 3D and 2D shapes and asking the children to name them and describe their properties and identify whether they have symmetry or not. Say: *Samir wants to make a symmetrical design for the cover of his book. Can you give him some ideas?* Put a regular card shape from the photocopiable sheet on the board and draw round it. Demonstrate how you can flip if over so that one of its sides is still joined to the original shape to make a new shape that is symmetrical: the two halves are the same. Highlight the middle line and explain that is called the line of symmetry because it shows where the two halves are. Repeat this a few times with other regular and irregular shapes.

Paired work: Say: *You are going to make some designs for Samir.* Give pairs of children sets of shape templates from the photocopiable sheets. They make two copies of five shapes. They stick one on one side of an A3 folded piece of paper. They flip the other shapes across the fold. When they have made a symmetrical pattern they stick it in place and colour the shapes so they are symmetrical too.

Progress check: Visit the pairs you wish to assess as they work to watch what they are doing. Ask questions such as:

- *How do you know your pattern will be symmetrical?*

Review

Take feedback from the activity by asking pairs of children to show their results. They explain what they did and point out the line of symmetry.

■SCHOLASTIC

Measures and money

Expected prior learning

Children should be able to:

- estimate, measure and compare lengths, masses (weights) and capacities
- recognise that a thermometer measures temperature.

Topic	Curriculum objectives	Expected outcomes
Measurement	**Lesson 1**	
	To choose and use appropriate standard units to estimate and measure length/height in any direction (m/cm); mass (kg/g); temperature (°C); capacity (litres/ml) to the nearest appropriate unit using rulers, scales, thermometers and measuring vessels. To compare and order lengths, mass, volume/capacity and record the results using >, < and =.	Use standard units of measurement. Use the appropriate language and abbreviations. Compare using >, <, = and order lengths. Read scales to the nearest sensible division.
	Lesson 2	
	To choose and use appropriate standard units to estimate and measure length/height in any direction (m/cm); mass (kg/g); temperature (°C); capacity (litres/ml) to the nearest appropriate unit using rulers, scales, thermometers and measuring vessels. To compare and order lengths, mass, volume/capacity and record the results using >, < and =.	Use standard units of measurement. Use the appropriate language and abbreviations. Compare using >, <, = and order masses. Read scales to the nearest sensible division.
	Lesson 3	
	To choose and use appropriate standard units to estimate and measure length/height in any direction (m/cm); mass (kg/g); temperature (°C); capacity (litres/ml) to the nearest appropriate unit using rulers, scales, thermometers and measuring vessels.	Use standard units of measurement. Use the appropriate language and abbreviations. Read scales to the nearest sensible division.
	Lesson 4	
	To choose and use appropriate standard units to estimate and measure length/height in any direction (m/cm); mass (kg/g); temperature (°C); capacity (litres/ml) to the nearest appropriate unit using rulers, scales, thermometers and measuring vessels.	Understand that temperature measures how hot or cold something is. Use thermometers to read temperatures.
	Lesson 5	
	To choose and use appropriate standard units to estimate and measure length/height in any direction (m/cm); mass (kg/g); temperature (°C); capacity (litres/ml) to the nearest appropriate unit, using rulers, scales, thermometers and measuring vessels.	Solve problems involving measures.

Preparation

Lesson 1: enlarge the cards from photocopiable page 'Measures vocabulary' to A3; prepare strips of paper that are longer than 1m but shorter than 2m

Lesson 2: ensure that the vocabulary words from lesson 1 are available for the children to see; prepare mixed colours of Plasticine® for the fruit weighing in total about 1kg

Lesson 3: ensure that the vocabulary words from lesson 1 are available for the children to see; make a collection of different-sized bottles and containers for the activity

Lesson 5: prepare problems similar to those suggested to ask during the activity

You will need

Photocopiable sheets

'Measures activities'; 'Thermometer'

General resources

'Lengths'; 'Measures vocabulary'; interactive teaching resource 'Measuring jug'; interactive teaching resource 'Thermometer'; '0–100 number cards'

Equipment

Strips of paper; scissors; sticky tape; rulers; metre sticks; modelling material in red, green, orange and yellow; weighing scales; individual whiteboards; litre bottles; drinks containers; containers; measuring jugs; water

Further practice

Give children further practice of measuring using rulers, metre sticks, measuring jugs and weighing scales. The interactive teaching resources can also be used for this purpose.

Oral and mental starters for week 6

See bank of starters on page 127. Oral and mental starters are also on the CD-ROM.

35 Two-times, five-times and ten-times tables

36 Arrays

37 Changing numbers

Overview of progression

During this week children will extend their knowledge of measures. They will estimate, measure and compare lengths, masses, capacities and volumes and look at the units used to describe them and their equivalences and abbreviations. They will also explore temperature. They will solve word problems involving length, mass, capacity and temperature.

> ### Watch out for
>
> Some children may find it difficult to read scales. Provide them with rulers and pictures of measuring jugs and weighing scales and use these as number lines. Ask the children to put their fingers on certain numbers and count on and back different amounts.

Creative context

Encourage the children to use their knowledge of measures in DT activities, especially when making things and cooking.

Vocabulary

capacity, Celsius, Centigrade, centimetre, degrees, empty, full, gram, heavy, kilogram, length, light, litre, mass, measure, measuring jug, metre, millilitre, short, **temperature, thermometer,** volume, weigh

Curriculum objectives
● To choose and use appropriate standard units to estimate and measure length/height in any direction (m/cm) to the nearest appropriate unit using rulers.
● To compare and order lengths and record the results using >, < and =.

Success criteria
● I can measure in centimetres and metres.
● I can compare and order lengths.

You will need
General resources
'Measures vocabulary'; 'Lengths'
Equipment
Strips of paper; scissors; sticky tape; rulers; metre sticks; individual whiteboards

Differentiation
Some children may benefit from measuring multiples of 10cm only, others might be able to measure to the nearest centimetre.

Lesson 1   Oral and mental starter 37

Main teaching activities

Whole-class work: Say: *Over the next few days you will be solving problems that involve length, weight (mass), capacity, volume and temperature.* Ask the children to tell you what each of these is a measure of, for example how long, high, wide something is, how heavy something is, how much a container can hold, how much liquid is in a container, how hot or cold something is. Ask them to tell you any words that they can remember to do with these measures and list them on the board under appropriate headings.

Say: *My friend Miss Singh is a teacher and she would like your help in preparing some classroom resources. Her class is going to be working on length and she would like you to make strips of paper of different lengths for her class to compare.*

Discuss the vocabulary for length, writing down the words the children tell you. Display all the words from photocopiable page 'Measures vocabulary' from the CD-ROM and ask the children to tell you which are to do with length. Then match them to the list on the board. Ask them to identify any that they didn't think of. Sort them into descriptive words (for example, long), units of measure (for example, metres) and measuring equipment (for example, ruler), discussing the meaning of each with examples as appropriate. Recap how many centimetres there are in a metre and ask questions relating to this, for example, how many centimetres in 2m/½m/1 ½m. Discuss the abbreviations used for metres and centimetres.

Remind the children that they need to make strips of paper to compare and ask how they might do this. Aim towards measuring different lengths using a ruler. Demonstrate how this is done with particular emphasis on starting at zero.

Paired work: The children work in mixed-ability pairs. Give each pair a selection of cards from photocopiable page 'Lengths' from the CD-ROM strips of paper, scissors, sticky tape, ruler and metre stick. Their task is to cut strips to the lengths on their cards as accurately as possible. If they have lengths longer than the strips, they need to stick some together. Encourage them to estimate how long each strip will be before they actually measure.

Progress check: Visit pairs of children as they work to check that they are using their rulers correctly. Ask questions such as:
- *How long is that strip?*
- *Can you show me how you measured this strip?*
- *Which part of your ruler did you start measuring from?*

Review

Take feedback from the activity. Compare different pair's strips and ask: *Which of these is the longest/shortest? How long do you think this is?* Ask the children to write < and > number sentences for these strips on their whiteboards. Show a strip that is 20cm in length and say: *This strip is 20cm long. How could you use it to find a book that is about 40cm tall? How could you use it to find a book that is about 10cm wide? Show me how you would use it to check that this book is about 23cm tall.*

Curriculum objectives
● To estimate and measure mass (kg/g) to the most appropriate unit using scales.
● To compare and order mass and record the results using >, < and =.

Success criteria
● I can estimate and measure in kilograms and grams.

You will need
General resources
'Measures vocabulary'
Equipment
Modelling material; weighing scales; strips of paper from the previous lesson

Differentiation
Children work in mixed-ability groups. Ensure everyone takes part and that more confident learners do not dominate.

Lesson 2
Oral and mental starter 37

Main teaching activities

Whole-class work: Recap the length work the children did in lesson 1. Include the vocabulary, the equivalent units and abbreviations. Show some of the strips they cut and ask them to estimate their length. Invite volunteers to measure them and together compare their estimates with the actual. Say: *My friend Miss Singh wants your help again! Her children are thinking about how heavy things are. So, this time she would like you to make some fruit so the children can order them from lightest to heaviest.*

Show the cards from photocopiable page 'Measures vocabulary' from the CD-ROM and ask the children to identify those to do with weight (mass). Discuss how many grams there are in different numbers of kilograms and the abbreviations used for each measure.

Group work: The children work in mixed-ability groups of four. Give each group 1kg of modelling material to make an apple, a banana, an orange and a melon. The apple must be the lightest and the melon the heaviest. They estimate the weights of the fruit then check using a set of scales. They write the weight of each fruit on paper and place the appropriate fruit onto it.

Progress check: Visit the groups to make sure they understand what to do and that everyone is taking part.

Review

Compare fruits from two groups. Ask: *Which of these do you think is the heaviest/lightest? Why?* Put each fruit on the scales to find out. Together make up some < and > number sentences. *How many of these fruits do you think will weigh a kilogram?* Use the scales to find out how close the children's estimates were.

Curriculum objectives
● To estimate and measure volume and capacity (litres/ml) to the nearest appropriate unit using measuring vessels.

Success criteria
● I can estimate and measure in litres and millilitres.

You will need
General resources
'Measures vocabulary'; 'Capacities'; interactive teaching resource 'Measuring jug'
Equipment
Litre bottles; drinks cartons; containers; measuring jugs; water; individual whiteboards

Differentiation
Differentiate by selecting which capacity cards children are given. Some are specific amounts while others are not.

Lesson 3
Oral and mental starter 36

Main teaching activities

Whole-class work: Show the cards from photocopiable page 'Measures vocabulary' from the CD-ROM and ask the children to identify those that refer to capacity and volume. Sort these into descriptive words, units and measuring equipment. Discuss the abbreviations for litres and millilitres and their equivalent units. Remind the children that capacity is the amount of liquid a container will hold and volume is the amount of liquid in a container.

Show the interactive teaching resource 'Measuring jug' on the CD-ROM and set the scale up to 1000, explaining that this is 1 litre and the smaller marks are ml. Set the subdivisions to 2. Count in hundreds to 1000 and discuss halfway marks. Show litre bottles, drinks cartons for ml measures and fill a measuring jug to these amounts, asking the children to write down the measurements on their whiteboards.

Paired work: Give each pair a selection of cards from photocopiable page 'Capacities' from the CD-ROM, some containers, measuring jugs and access to water. Their task is to estimate and then measure the volumes on the cards.

Progress check: Visit each pair to ensure they understand the task. Ask: *How far will you fill this bottle for that amount? How can you check your estimate?*

Review

Take feedback about the practical activity, comparing containers: *Which of these has the most/least water in it? Which containers do you think will hold about one litre?*

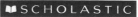

Curriculum objectives
● To estimate and measure temperature (°C) to the nearest appropriate unit using thermometers.
Success criteria
● I can describe temperature.
● I can read a thermometer.

You will need
General resources
'Thermometer'; '0–100 number cards'; interactive teaching resource 'Thermometer'
Equipment
Individual whiteboards

Differentiation
Less confident learners
Give children a vertical numbered line to use alongside the thermometers.
More confident learners
Ask children to find the differences in the temperatures for all the different pairs of places on the photocopiable sheets.

Lesson 4
Oral and mental starter 35

Main teaching activities

Whole-class work: Ask: *What can you tell me about temperature?* Children discuss with a partner. Take feedback. Find out if they know what temperature is measured in. Establish that it is a unit called degrees and that these are commonly measured in Celsius or Centigrade. Ask the children to tell you the seasons of the year. *In which season do we usually have the coldest weather? In which season do we have the hottest?*

Show the interactive teaching resource 'Thermometer' on the CD-ROM and tell the children that it is like a number line. Click at different points on it and ask the children to write down the temperature on their whiteboard. Use the arrow to see if they are correct. Increase and decrease temperatures, asking them to tell you the temperature is each time. Invite children to tell you by how many degrees the temperature has risen or dropped.

Paired work: Distribute photocopiable page 'Thermometer' from the CD-ROM. In pairs, the children make up temperatures for the imaginary places, using number cards 1–9. They pick two – for example 2 and 7 – and make a temperature: 27°C. They plot it on the first thermometer and label it. They repeat for all four thermometers and then compare.

Progress check: Invite pairs to share the temperatures they made. Ask questions such as:
- *If I pick 1 and 9, what temperature could I make that will fit on the thermometer?*
- *Which is the hottest/coldest temperature you have made?*

Review

Take feedback from the children's activity, positioning some of their temperatures on the interactive teaching resource 'Thermometer' on the CD-ROM. Compare these using the symbols < and >. Identify odd and even numbers and partition some of the two-digit numbers.

Curriculum objectives
● To choose and use appropriate standard units to estimate and measure length/height in any direction; mass; temperature; capacity to the nearest appropriate unit.
Success criteria
● I can solve simple problems involving measures.

You will need
Equipment
Individual whiteboards

Differentiation
Less confident learners
Work with the children discussing each problem and how it can be solved.
More confident learners
Provide more complex problems for the children to solve.

Lesson 5
Oral and mental starter 35

Main teaching activities

Whole-class work: Say: *There are 3kg of apples in a box. How many kilograms are there in two boxes?* Invite responses and ask: *How did you work that out?* Write the number sentence $3 \times 2 = 6$ on the board. Now say: *A bag of sugar weighs 2kg. How many bags will I need to buy so that I have 10kg?* Again, ask for responses and how the children worked out the answer. Write the number sentences to show the possible methods: $2 \times 5 = 10$ and $10 \div 2 = 5$. Discuss how the children can use mental calculation strategies to solve problems involving measures.

Independent work: Write some word problems on the board for the children to solve, such as:
- There are two parcels to be delivered which weigh 22kg and 15kg. How much do the parcels weigh altogether?
- Sally had 30cm of string. She cut it into three equal lengths. How long was each length?

Progress check: Ask questions such as: *How would you find the difference in the two weights? How would you find the total? What is meant by twice as far?*

Review

Invite children to explain how they worked out their answers and which mental strategies they used. Invite others to write the appropriate number sentence on the board. Ask: *How did you work this out? Who chose a different way? Which way do you think is the best? Why do you think that?*

Curriculum objectives
• To count in tens from any number, forward or backward.
• To compare and order numbers from 0 up to 100; use <, > and = signs.

You will need
1. Check

Oral and mental starter

29 Counting in steps of two, five and ten

2. Assess
'Hundred square'

3. Further practice

Oral and mental starters

2 Counting in tens

6 Counting in tens and ones

Photocopiable sheets
'Counting in tens'

Place value

These activities assess the children's understanding of what happens when ten is added to or taken from a two-digit number. Most children should be able to understand that the value of tens increases or decreases and the value of the ones number remains the same.

Some children require additional practice at counting backwards and forwards in tens from zero first and then gradually progress to counting from one, then two.

1. Check

29 Counting in steps of two, five and ten

Encourage the children to count forwards and backwards in tens keeping the pace sharp. Observe which children are confident and which need further practice. *What is 10 more than 63? How do you know? What is 10 less than 29? How do you know?*

2. Assess

Give each child a 'Hundred square'. Ask them to place their finger on the number 3. Give instructions for them to follow that involve counting forwards and backwards in ones and tens, for example, add 10, take away 1, add two lots of 10, add 4, take away 10. Record the outcomes.

3. Further practice

Photocopiable page 'Counting in tens' from the CD-ROM provides practice in counting forwards and backwards in tens. This will help reinforce the skills needed for children who are having difficulty in this area. They should work on this independently.

Curriculum objectives
• To add and subtract using pictorial representations and mentally, including: a two-digit number and ones.

You will need
1. Check

Oral and mental starter

32 What makes ten?

2. Assess
'0–100 number cards';
'Number line 0–100'

3. Further practice

Oral and mental starters

31 Number pairs to 20

34 Bridging ten again

7 Number pairs to ten

Photocopiable sheets
'Adding problems (1)'

Addition facts to 10

Most children should be able to partition a single number in order to add one part to make a multiple of ten and then the second part to find totals of two-digit and single-digit numbers by bridging ten.

Some children will not have made such progress and will require concrete apparatus or number lines to assist them.

1. Check

32 What makes ten?

Use the oral and mental starter to check which children can confidently show you the number pairs that make 10 and then 20. Provide further opportunities to practise this through a matching activity. Ask:

- *What goes with 4 to make 10? How do you know? What goes with 12 to make 20? How do you know? How does knowing your number pairs to ten help?*

2. Assess

Ask the children to pick a two-digit card and a single-digit card (use numbers with ones digits 5 and higher). They add the single-digit number to the two-digit number. Ask them to partition the single-digit number so that they can make the next multiple of ten. Observe how confident children are. Give the less confident a numbered number line to count along. Record the outcomes.

3. Further practice

Photocopiable page 128 'Adding problems (1)' is designed to practise addition using the bridging ten strategy. Expect most children to be able to do this with the aid of a number line. Some children will need concrete apparatus in the form of counters or small cubes.

Curriculum objectives
- To add and subtract using concrete objects, pictorial representations, and mentally, including: two two-digit numbers.

You will need
1. Check

Oral and mental starters

3 Partitioning

9 Inversion loops

2. Assess
'0–100 number cards'; 'Arrow cards'

3. Further practice
Photocopiable sheets
'Partitioning (2)'

Addition by partitioning

Most children should be able to add two two-digit numbers by partitioning.

Some children will not have made such progress and will require number lines or concrete apparatus to assist them.

1. Check

3 Partitioning

9 Inversion loops

Use photocopiable page 129 'Partitioning (2)' to check which children can now partition two-digit numbers in different ways. Provide further opportunities to practise this using number lines. Adapt photocopiable page 'Inversions' to use two-digit numbers and ask the children to explain how they can check their answer to an addition by subtracting. Ask: *How can you add 36 and 24? Is there another way? How can you check that you are right?*

2. Assess

Give each child two number cards. Ask them to add the numbers together and write a number sentence to show how they could do this using partitioning. Repeat this several times. Watch out for children who are not confident and provide them with arrow cards so that they can 'see' what their numbers are when they are partitioned. Record the outcomes.

3. Further practice

Use photocopiable page 129 'Partitioning (2)' to assess how successful the children are at adding two two-digit numbers by partitioning within a word problem context.

Curriculum objectives
- To calculate mathematical statements for multiplication and division within the multiplication tables and write them using the multiplication (×), division (÷) and equals (=) signs.

You will need
1. Check

Oral and mental starter

36 Arrays

2. Assess
Counters

3. Further practice
Oral and mental starters

25 Times tables facts

15 Multiples

35 Two-times, five-times and ten-times tables

Photocopiable sheets
'Arrays'

Multiplication and division

Most children should be able to successfully make arrays and write number sentences with numbers to 50.

Some children will not have made such progress and will require smaller arrays to describe.

1. Check

36 Arrays

Use the oral and mental starter to assess children's confidence in making and interpreting arrays. Ask: *What multiplication can you make from an array that has six rows of three counters? Is there another? What division can you make from this array? Is there another?*

2. Assess

Give each child 15 counters. Ask them to make an array of their choice. Ask them to explain the two multiplication number sentences that they can make, for example 3 × 5 = 15, 5 × 3 = 15, 1 × 15 = 15, 15 × 1 = 15. Next ask them to show you the two ways in which the array can be grouped and explain the two division number sentences that they can make, such as. 15 ÷ 3 = 5, 15 ÷ 3 = 5. Give more confident leaners more counters (say, 36) and fewer counters (say, 10) to less confident learners. Record the outcomes.

3. Further practice

Photocopiable page 130 'Arrays' asks the children to explore the different arrays that they can make with 24 counters and to interpret these as multiplication and division number sentences. Encourage them to explain how they arrive at their solutions.

Oral and mental starters

Number and place value

28 Counting on a 100 square

Tell the children that they will practise counting in ones and tens. Give each child a 'Hundred square'. They place their finger on four. Call out instructions for them to follow, such as count on ten, back one, forward two tens, forward one, back ten. Once you have given five or six instructions, ask the children to tell you what number they are on.

Repeat several times. Then extend to include counting on 9 and 11.

29 Counting in steps of two, five and ten

Tell the children that they will rehearse counting in steps of two, five and ten.

Call out ten numbers which the children write down, for example 12, 5, 24, 30, and so on. They circle the numbers that they would say if counting, from zero, in steps of two, tick the multiples of five and cross out the multiples of ten. Take feedback finding out how they knew which numbers to circle, tick and cross out. Link to multiples: steps of two will be even, five will end with 5 and 0, ten will end with 0. *Which numbers were circled, ticked and crossed?* Count together from zero in these steps to check they are correct. Next count on in multiples of two, five and ten from other starting numbers which are multiples of these numbers, e.g. 6, 25, 40. Repeat with other numbers. Extend to counting in steps of three.

30 Counting in odd and even numbers

Give single digit starting numbers and ask the children to count from them in odd and even numbers. For example, give a starting number of 6, ask the children to count in even numbers to 50. These could be in steps of two, four or ten. Ask them what they notice about the ones number (it is always even). Repeat, but ask them to count in an odd number, for example, one, three or five. Ask them what they notice this time (ones number alternates between even and odd).

31 Number pairs to 20

Swing the pendulum from side to side. As it swings one way, call out a number to ten. As it swings the other way the children call out the number that goes with it to make ten, for example, you say 6 and the children say 4. Repeat for numbers to 20 and then other numbers up to 20, for example, 5 (4 and 1, 3 and 2 and so on), 11, 15.

32 What makes ten?

Show the 'Grid for ten' cards one at a time. As you do, the children write down the number that goes with it to make ten on their whiteboards. Give a set of these cards to some of the children. This time, as you show a card, the child with the one that goes with it to make ten holds it up. Repeat this with other children.

Extension
Repeat for pairs of numbers that make 20.

33 Ordering numbers

Give each child a number card at random from 0–99. Ask five children to come to the front and stand with their numbers held up, ordered from lowest to highest. Invite other children to stand in the place appropriate to their number. Ask the class to check that they are standing in the right places and explain why. When the line is ten children long, ask the original five to sit down and another five to go to the places appropriate to their numbers. Repeat until everyone has had a go. Ask questions such as: *Who is holding the number closest to 34? Who is holding an odd number between 20 and 30?*

37 Changing numbers

Ask the children to follow your instructions, writing and changing the two- and three-digit numbers on their whiteboards. They should record all of the numbers. For example: *Write ten. Double it.* (20) *Add five.* (25) *Add nine.* (34) *Add 100.* (134) *Swap the three and the one. What is your number?* (314) Repeat with different starting numbers and instructions. Try to include mental calculation strategies that the children need to practise, for example, adding 9 or 11 by adding a multiple of ten and adjusting, bridging ten, doubling.

Addition and subtraction

34 Bridging ten again

Write this calculation on the board: $24 + 7$. Ask the children to tell you how they could add this. Aim towards bridging ten by partitioning 7 into 6 and 1. Write similar calculations on the board. Repeat this for subtraction, for example $35 - 8$ ($35 - 5 - 3$).

Multiplication and division

35 Two-times, five-times and ten-times tables

Count in twos from zero to 12 and back. Ask the children to close their eyes as they count and imagine jumping up and down a number line. Show them the spider chart for multiplying by two from 'Spider charts for multiplying' from the CD-ROM. Point randomly around the outside of the chart. The children call out the answer when the number is multiplied. Now show the spider chart for dividing by two: *What would you multiply two by to get the numbers around the outside? If I point to 18 what would you call out? That's right, nine.* Draw their attention to the fact that finding out what you would multiply two by to get 18 is one way of working out $18 \div 2$. Repeat for facts for the five-times and ten-times tables.

36 Arrays

Ask the children to draw a dot array on their whiteboards to show three rows of four. Ask them to work out how many dots there are altogether and to write down the two multiplication sentences which show this ($3 \times 4 = 12$, $4 \times 3 = 12$). Next ask them to draw loops to show how they can group the 12 into threes. They draw a second array and show how they can group the dots into fours. For each they write the division number sentence ($12 \div 3 = 4$, $12 \div 4 = 3$). Repeat for other numbers.

Adding problems (1)

■ Find the answers to the following problems using the bridging ten strategy.

> **Here is an example:**
> Sunshine had 17 sweets. Her friend gave her another 8. How many does she have now?
> Partition 8 into 3 and 5. Add 3 to 17 to make 20 then add 5.
> 17 + 3 + 5 = 25

1. Jenni baked 26 cakes. Hope baked 7. How many did they bake altogether?

2. Tim had 27 toy cars. His friend gave him another 6. How many does he have now?

3. Faith saw 14 swans in the lake. Hope saw 9. How many did they see altogether?

4. Bobby stuck 48 stamps on one page of his scrapbook. He stuck another 5 on the next page. How many stamps did he stick in his scrapbook?

I can add pairs of two-digit numbers.

How did you do?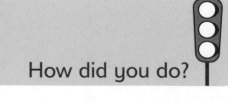

Partitioning (2)

■ Solve the following problems using partitioning.

> **Here is an example:**
> Sophie's mum spent £25 on some clothes for her. She spent £36 on clothes for her sister. How much did Sophie's mum spend altogether?
> £25 + £36 = £20 + £30 + £5 + £6 = £50 + £11 = £61
> Sophie's mum spent £61.

1. Harry had 23 tadpoles in his fish tank. Ben had 48. How many tadpoles did they have altogether?

They had _____ tadpoles altogether.

2. Henri took 45 seconds to count to 50. Samir took 38 seconds. How many seconds did they take altogether?

They took _____ seconds altogether.

3. Casey had 24 counters. Her friend had 47. How many counters did they have altogether?

They had _____ counters.

4. Billy had 36 toy cars. Ben had 26. How many toy cars did they have altogether?

They had _____ toy cars.

I can add by partitioning.

How did you do?

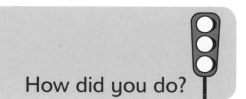

Name: _____   Date: _____

Arrays

- You will need 24 counters.
- Your task is to make as many different arrays as you can.
- You need to make them with your counters and then draw them on this sheet.
- For each one write the multiplication and division number sentence.

Here is an example:

●●●●●●●●●●●●
●●●●●●●●●●●●

Number sentences: $12 \times 2 = 24$, $2 \times 12 = 24$, $24 \div 2 = 12$, $24 \div 12 = 2$

First array

Number sentences:

Second array

Number sentences:

- Turn over the sheet and make up some more on the back.

I can make arrays.

How did you do?

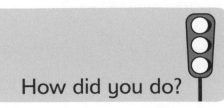

PHOTOCOPIABLE

SCHOLASTIC
www.scholastic.co.uk

Number and place value: counting, comparing and ordering

Expected prior learning

Children should be able to:

- count forwards or backwards in steps of two, five and ten
- partition two-digit numbers into tens and ones
- read and write numbers from 1 to 50 in digits and 30 in words
- begin to partition numbers to 100 in different ways.

Topic	Curriculum objectives	Expected outcomes
Number and place value	**Lesson 1**	
	To count in steps of 2, 3, and 5 from 0, and in tens from any number, forward and backward.	Count in steps of 2, 5 and 10 from 0 and forwards and backwards in 10s from any number.
		Begin to count in 3s from 0.
	Lesson 2	
	To identify, represent and estimate numbers using different representations, including the number line.	Estimate, count efficiently and compare amounts. Position numbers on a number line.
	To compare and order numbers from 0 up to 100; use <, > and = signs.	Compare numbers using < and >.
		Understand the purpose of =.
	Lesson 3	
	To recognise the place value of each digit in a two-digit number (tens, ones).	Continue to partition numbers in different ways and use this to find totals of pairs of numbers.
	To read and write numbers to at least 100 in numerals and in words.	
	To compare and order numbers from 0 up to 100; use <, > and = signs.	
	Lesson 4	
	To recognise the place value of each digit in a two-digit number (tens, ones).	Partition numbers in different ways.
	To read and write numbers to at least 100 in numerals and in words.	Read and write numbers to 100 in numerals. Read and write numbers to 50 in words.
	To compare and order numbers from 0 up to 100; use <, > and = signs.	Compare numbers using < and >.
	Lesson 5	
	To use counting to solve problems.	Use counting to solve simple oral problems.

Preparation

Lesson 2: prepare vocabulary cards for estimating; copy the photocopiable sheets 'Dots (1)', 'Dots (2)' and 'Dots (3)' onto A2 paper; fill string bags, or similar with cubes, three bags per group

Lesson 3: copy photocopiable page 'Number words' onto A3 paper and provide a set of cards for pairs of children; copy photocopiable sheet '0–100 number lines' for most of the class

Lesson 4: if you haven't already, copy, cut out and laminate photocopiable page 'Arrow cards' for each child

Lesson 5: copy and cut into strips photocopiable page 'Money problem cards', at least one strip per group

You will need

Photocopiable sheets
'Missing number sentences'; 'Missing number sentences recording sheet'; 'Money problem cards'; 'Greater or less?'

General resources
'Number lines 0–100'; '0–100 number cards'; 'Number words'; 'Arrow cards'; interactive activity 'Fill your ladder'

Equipment
Blu-Tack®; counting stick; individual whiteboards; A2 paper; small string bags or similar; interlocking cubes; £1, 50p, 20p, 10p, 5p, 2p and 1p coins

Further practice

'Greater or less?' can be used at other times to practice comparing and ordering numbers to 100. Children also need a set of 0–99 number cards for this activity. The interactive activity 'Fill your ladder' can also be used for this purpose.

Oral and mental starters for week 1

See bank of starters on pages 126 and 167. Oral and mental starters are also on the CD-ROM.

38 More doubling and halving

39 Counting in steps

33 Ordering numbers

40 Taking away

Overview of progression

During this week the children will extend their counting skills by counting in steps of two, three, five and ten from and to zero. They will practise and extend reading and writing numbers in words and figures. They will reinforce and continue to consolidate partitioning numbers in different ways, estimating, counting, comparing and ordering numbers both practically and on a number line. They will finish the week by using and applying some of these skills as they visualise, draw and act out problems.

> ### Watch out for
> Some children may have difficulty counting in steps of different sizes. Give them written prompts such as number cards with sequences counting in steps of, for example, two from 0 to 20. Ask them to practise using the cards and then only refer to them when they get stuck.

Creative context

Give the children food packages, for example cereal boxes. Ask them to write down all the numbers they can find and then compare them using the symbols < and >.

Vocabulary

count in twos , count in fives, count in tens, continue, **multiple of**, nearest ten, one-digit number, place, **place value**, predict, represents, round, sequence, stands for, tens digit, two-digit number, 'teens' number

Curriculum objectives
● To count in steps of 2, 3, and 5 from 0, and in tens from any number, forward and backward.

Success criteria
● I can count in steps of two and five from zero.
● I can count in steps of ten forwards and backwards from any number.
● I am beginning to count in steps of three from zero.

You will need
Photocopiable sheets
'Missing number sentences'; 'Missing number sentences recording sheet'
General resources
'0–100 number cards'
Equipment
Counting stick; individual whiteboards

Differentiation
Less confident learners
Give the children 0–20 number cards.
More confident learners
Give the children a range of number cards up to 100.

Lesson 1

Oral and mental starter 38

Main teaching activities

Whole-class work: Tell the children that this lesson will focus on counting in steps of two, three, five and ten from zero and back again and also steps of ten forwards and backwards from any number. Using a counting stick, move your finger up and down, asking the children to count in jumps of two, then five and then three. Make jumps along the stick, asking the children to predict what number you are pointing to and to say how they know. Expect answers such as: *That is 35 because it is 7 jumps of 5.* Encourage them to write the appropriate number sentence on their whiteboards: $5 \times 7 = 35$.

Write some missing number sentences on the board, for example, $2 \times ? = 16$. Ask the children how they can work out the missing number: counting in steps of two, in this example, to 16 or counting back in twos from 20. Bring in the inverse operation: $16 \div 2 = 8$. Repeat for counting in steps of two, five, ten and then three.

Move on to counting in tens from any number. Begin with 23. Can the children get to 103 and back? Ask them what they notice about the digits. Bring out the fact that the ones remain the same and the tens go up and down in one ten each time. For 103, make the link that this is ten tens which is 100. Challenge the children by writing up missing number sentences where they have to work out how many tens are needed to complete the sentence, for example: $46 + ? = 76$.

Group work: The children work in ability groups of three or four for this game and use the cards from photocopiable page 'Missing number sentences' from the CD-ROM. They spread the cards face down on the table and pick two. They then try to make a missing number sentence using both numbers. Their number sentence must relate to the activities they practised during the lesson. If they can, they score two points. Model the activity first. For example, *If you pick ten and five, the number sentence could be $10 \div ? = 5$ to score two points.* The children should use photocopiable page 'Missing number sentences recording sheet' to write their sentences and scores.

Progress check: Visit each group in turn to make sure they understand what to do. You may need to support the less confident learners. Ask:
● *What number sentence can you make with seven and five? Is there another?*

Review

Take feedback about the game, asking volunteers to show some of their missing number sentences. Challenge the children by asking: *How would you work out the missing number in this number sentence: $24 \div ? = 4$?* Agree that they could count in fours to 24.

Curriculum objectives

● To identify, represent and estimate numbers using different representations, including the number line.
● To compare and order numbers from 0 up to 100; use <, > and = signs.

Success criteria

● I can make a sensible estimate.
● I can compare numbers using <, > and =.

You will need

General resources

'Dots (1)'; 'Dots (2)'; 'Dots (3)'

Equipment

A2 paper; small string bags; interlocking cubes; individual whiteboards

Differentiation

The children work in mixed-ability groups. Check to make sure the less confident learners take an active part and that the more confident don't dominate the group discussions.

Lesson 2

Main teaching activities

Whole-class work: This lesson is about estimating and approximating amounts up to 50. Ask: *What do we mean by estimating? Can anyone tell me any estimating words?* Display the prepared vocabulary cards relating to estimating and discuss any words the children leave out. Show photocopiable page 'Dots (1)' from the CD-ROM, on the interactive whiteboard or enlarged on a piece of A2 paper. Discuss using fingers to help make a sensible estimate. Ask: *Are there more dots than you have fingers? Yes, so there are more than ten. Put your hands next to a friend's. Are there more dots or fingers now?* Build up groups of ten fingers until the number is close: *Do you think we have exactly the same amount, just over or just under?* Finally count, drawing loops around groups of ten. Repeat using 'Dots (2)' and 'Dots (3)'.

Write the three numbers of dots on the board and ask the children to order them from smallest to greatest. Use this as an opportunity to make number sentences to practise using the symbols < and >. You could include the = symbol. Write two of the numbers, one on each side, and ask the children what to do to make a correct number sentence (take a number from the highest, add a number to the smallest).

Group work: The children work in mixed-ability groups of four. Give each group three string bags with different numbers of cubes in them. For each bag, they take it in turns to feel the cubes and estimate how many there are in the bag, recording their estimates on a sheet of paper. Set a short time limit so that they can't count the cubes. Once everyone has made a guess, they count the cubes to find out who was closest.

Progress check: Ask groups to share how they are making their estimates. Are they using the first number of cubes to inform their estimate for the others? If not, suggest they do this.

Review

Discuss whether the children found it easy or hard to make sensible estimates. Did it help them to use their first amount to estimate the others? Ask each group to give you one of the totals that they had. Write these on the board. Ask the children to order these numbers on their whiteboards. They then write some < and > number sentences. You could also ask them to make up some = sentences as described in the lesson.

Curriculum objectives

- To recognise the place value of each digit in a two-digit number (tens, ones).
- To compare and order numbers from 0 up to 100.

Success criteria

- I can partition numbers.
- I can compare and order numbers from 0 up to 100.

You will need

General resources

'0–100 number cards'; 'Number lines 0–100'; 'Number words'; interactive activity 'Fill your ladder'

Equipment

Individual whiteboards

Differentiation

Less confident learners

Ask children to order sets of numbers to 50.

More confident learners

Ask children to draw and complete blank number lines.

Lesson 3 — Oral and mental starter 33

Main teaching activities

Whole-class work: Hold up two two-digit number cards. Write these at either end of a number line without divisions. Hold up some cards from photocopiable page 'Number words' from the CD-ROM and ask volunteers to write the number in the correct position on the line. For each, ask the children to partition them on their whiteboards in as many ways as they can.

Paired work: The children work in similar ability pairs. Each pair has a pile of number cards face down on the table in front of them. They pick five cards and order them from smallest to largest on the 0–100 number line.

Progress check: Visit pairs to check that the children are following your instructions correctly. Spend time with those you wish to assess. Ask:

- *How do you know that number goes there?*
- *How could you partition that number? Is there another way?*

Review

Invite some pairs to explain how they positioned their numbers on their lines. Ask others to place numbers picked from a pile of number cards as accurately as they can on a line you have drawn on the board. Invite the rest of the class to comment on their accuracy. If time, go through the interactive activity 'Fill your ladder' on the CD-ROM, to further practice ordering numbers to 100.

Curriculum objectives

- To recognise the place value of each digit in a two-digit number (tens, ones).
- To compare and order numbers from 0 up to 100; use <, > and = signs.

Success criteria

- I can partition numbers in different ways.
- I can order numbers.

You will need

Photocopiable sheets

'Greater or less?'

General resources

'Arrow cards'; '0–100 number cards'

Equipment

Individual whiteboards; Blu-Tack®

Differentiation

Less confident learners

Adapt the photocopiable sheet so that children work with cards to 20.

More confident learners

Ask the children to think of three-digit numbers that can be placed on either side of the > and < symbols.

Lesson 4 — Oral and mental starter 40

Main teaching activities

Whole-class work: Give each child a set of arrow cards. Ask them to make two-digit numbers, such as 78. Discuss each digit's place value (7: 7 tens or 70, 8: 8 ones). They write number sentences to show how they can be partitioned, for example 70 + 8, 60 + 18. Hand out to each child a number card from photocopiable page '0-100 number cards'. The children make their number using arrow cards explaining the place value of its digits to a partner. Invite ten children to order themselves from smallest to largest number. Invite others to place themselves between those that have been ordered. Repeat so that you involve everyone. Write > (greater than) on the board. Invite two children to stick their numbers on either side of the symbol using Blu-Tack®. Repeat a few times and then do the same for < (less than).

Independent work: Distribute photocopiable page 'Greater or less?' from the CD-ROM and five number cards from '0–100 number cards'. Demonstrate using the instructions on the sheet.

Progress check: Invite volunteers to show one of their number sentences and to explain how they knew where each number went. Ask questions such as:

- *What can you tell me about the 4 in 47? What else?*
- *Which is the greater number, 36 or 63? How do you know?*
- *Can you give me an odd number that is greater than 23? ...an even number? Are there any others?*

Review

Take feedback from the photocopiable activity by inviting children to demonstrate what they did and write their number sentences on the board. Ask them which numbers they looked at to determine which was the greatest. Expect them to tell you that they looked at the tens number.

Curriculum objectives
• To use counting to solve problems.

Success criteria
• I can solve word problems by counting in steps of different sizes.
• I can visualise a problem.

You will need
Photocopiable sheets
'Money problem cards'
Equipment
£1.50p, 20p, 10p, 5p, 2p, 1p coins

Differentiation
The children work together in mixed-ability groups. Ensure that everyone takes an active part.

Lesson 5

Main teaching activities

Whole-class work: Tell the children that they will spend this lesson visualising problems in their heads, drawing them and acting them out. Ask them to close their eyes and visualise what you say. *You are sitting in your bedroom with a money box. It is shaped like a pig. It is blue and has a yellow flower on it. You take out the stopper from underneath its tummy and tip the money onto your bed. You pick up a 10p coin, another 10p coin and another and another. How many 10p coins are you holding? How much is that altogether?* Discuss how they could work this out: count in tens four times, use multiplication facts, for example 10 × 4 or 4 × 10. Act this out, asking the children to collect the correct coins. Next ask them to draw a simple picture of the problem. Give them a few minutes to do this. Repeat in the same way with different scenarios that all involve counting in steps of two, three, five and ten.

Group work: The children work in mixed-ability groups to act out some mathematical problems so that the rest of the class can identify each problem and work out the answer. They will need a selection of coins. After discussing each problem, they draw a picture to describe it and make up a short play (without any written or spoken words). Use a problem from photocopiable page 'Money problem cards' from the CD-ROM to demonstrate, then give each group a strip from that sheet. Allow time for groups to plan their scenario.

Progress check: Visit groups to make sure they are all on task and everyone is taking an active part. Discuss any drawings they might have done and how these might have helped them solve their problem.

Review

Ask groups of children to act out their 'plays' and invite the class to try to interpret them, saying what they think the problem is and then they solve it. Ask whether the activities of drawing and acting out have helped them to problem solve and in what way. Ask: *What do you need to be able to do to solve a problem?* Expect answers such as: find out what the problem is about and what they need to do to solve it; look for the important information; plan how to solve it; check any answers they get.

Addition and subtraction: using mental calculation strategies

Expected prior learning

Children should be able to:

- add and subtract using mental calculation strategies
- use the inverse operation to check additions and subtractions.

Topic	Curriculum objectives	Expected outcomes
Addition and subtraction	**Lesson 1**	
	To add and subtract numbers using concrete objects, pictorial representations, and mentally, including: two two-digit numbers.	Add and subtract using partitioning and sequencing.
	Lesson 2	
	To add and subtract numbers using concrete objects, pictorial representations, and mentally, including: two two-digit numbers.	Add and subtract using partitioning and sequencing.
	Lesson 3	
	To add and subtract numbers using concrete objects, pictorial representations, and mentally, including: two two-digit numbers.	Add and subtract using counting on.
	To recognise and use the inverse relationship between addition and subtraction and use this to check calculations and solve missing number problems.	Use concrete and pictorial representations and number lines to add and subtract.
		Check answers using the inverse operation.
	To show that addition of two numbers can be done in any order (commutative) and subtraction of one number from another cannot.	Know that addition can be done in any order, subtraction cannot.
	Lesson 4	
	To add and subtract numbers using concrete objects, pictorial representations, and mentally, including: two two-digit numbers.	Add and subtract using counting on.
	To recognise and use the inverse relationship between addition and subtraction and use this to check calculations and solve missing number problems.	Use concrete and pictorial representations and number lines to add and subtract.
		Check answers using the inverse operation.
		Complete missing number sentences.
	Lesson 5	
	To solve problems with addition and subtraction:	Use partitioning and counting on to solve simple addition and subtraction problems within the context of money.
	• using concrete objects and pictorial representations, including those involving numbers, quantities and measures	
	• applying their increasing knowledge of mental and written methods.	

Preparation

Lesson 2: copy photocopiable page 'Make your own' for pairs of children

Lesson 4: copy photocopiable page 'Finding the difference' for pairs of children.

You will need

Photocopiable sheets
'Make your own'; 'Finding the difference'

General resources
'0–100 number cards'

Equipment
Individual whiteboards; A2 paper; interlocking cubes; counters

Further practice

Photocopiable sheets
'Problems at the zoo'

Oral and mental starters for week 2

See bank of starters on pages 85, 167 to 168. Oral and mental starters are also on the CD-ROM.

40 Taking away

41 Spider charts

15 Multiples

38 More doubling and halving

34 Bridging ten again

Overview of progression

During this week children will continue to develop their understanding of addition and subtraction. They will be rehearsing strategies that include partitioning, sequencing and counting on and back. They will be encouraged to use number lines as appropriate. They will check answers using the inverse operation and reinforce their understanding that addition can be done in any order but subtraction cannot. Throughout they will be solving simple problems within the context of number and measures.

Watch out for

Some children may find it difficult to draw their own number lines in order to count on and back. Give these children numbered number lines to use: the important thing is to enable them to access the problem-solving elements of each lesson.

Creative context

Set up a post office selling stamps of different prices and single items such as envelopes. Encourage the children to use the items to make up problems to give each other involving addition and subtraction.

Vocabulary

add, addition, altogether, **bridging ten**, counting on, difference, **inverse operation**, make, more, **partitioning**, plus, subtract , sum, take away, **tens boundary**, total

Curriculum objectives

● To add and subtract using concrete objects, pictorial representations, and mentally, including: two two-digit numbers.

Success criteria

● I can add and subtract using mental calculation strategies.

You will need

Equipment

Individual whiteboards; A2 paper

Differentiation

Less confident learners

Children focus on making up one-step problems with numbers up to 50.

More confident learners

Children focus on making up two-step problems.

Lesson 1 — Oral and mental starter 40

Main teaching activities

Whole-class work: Explain that in this lesson the children will be using mental calculation strategies to solve addition and subtraction problems. Say: *Georgie drew a line 24cm long. Tia continued that line for another 36cm. How long was the line now?* Display the 'How to solve a problem' poster. Use the poster to talk through the steps needed to solve the problem. When you reach step 4, ask the children to think of a strategy to work out the answer. Agree that they could partition and use number pairs to ten (20 + 30 + 10 = 60) or use sequencing (36 + 20 + 4 = 60). Invite two children to demonstrate a strategy each.

Say: *Elvis had a length of string 80cm long, he cut off 65cm. How much was left?* Again, talk through the solving steps. At step 4 invite learners to share their ideas for finding out the answer. Agree that they could count on from 65 to 80 using their ability to count in steps of five and ten (65 + 5 + 10, 5 + 10 = 15) or sequence (80 − 60 − 5 = 15). Invite the children to do this on their whiteboards.

Say: *Greta saved £9, she was given another £25 for her birthday. How much does she have now?* Repeat the procedure above. Agree that they could add £10 and take away £1 or partition £9 into £5 and £4. Repeat with other problems that involve adding and subtracting using the calculation strategies that the children have previously learned about.

Write basic facts on the board, for example, '50p', 'potatoes', 'how much?' Ask the children to talk to a partner and make up a problem involving this information. Use this example: *I bought 3kg of potatoes. Each kilogram cost 50p. How much did I spend?* Discuss how knowledge of tables or counting on in fives can help: 5p × 3 = 15p, so, 50p × 3 = 150p or £1.50. Next demonstrate checking by sequencing: 78 − 20 − 5. Practise this for other examples which can be answered without exchanging any tens, such as 56 − 34, 89 − 43.

Paired work: Explain that the children need to work with a similar-ability partner to make up and answer problems. List some basic information on the board that involves one or two steps. Encourage them to make jottings or draw their problems so that they don't waste time writing too many words. For example: *14 monkeys and 28 bananas. What might your problem be? You have five ice cream cones, 50p and £5. What might your problem be?*

Progress check: Visit pairs of children to make sure they understand what to do. Ask questions such as:

● *What problem could you make up with these numbers?*
● *What strategy could you use to find out the answer to your problem?*

Review

Invite pairs to share their problems for the class to solve. Each time ask: *How did you solve the problem? How many steps did you need to take?*

Curriculum objectives
● To add and subtract using concrete objects, pictorial representations, and mentally, including: two two-digit numbers.

Success criteria
● I can add using partitioning and number facts that I know.
● I can subtract by finding the difference.

You will need
Photocopiable sheets
'Make your own'
Equipment
Individual whiteboards

Differentiation
Less confident learners
Children work with numbers to 30.
More confident learners
When the children have completed the activity they make up problems to go with their calculations.

Curriculum objectives
● To add and subtract using pictorial representations, and mentally, including: two two-digit numbers.
● To recognise and use the inverse relationship between addition and subtraction.
● To show that addition can be done in any order and subtraction cannot.

Success criteria
● I can add numbers in any order.
● I can check a calculation by doing the opposite operation.

You will need
General resources
'0–100 number cards'
Equipment
Interlocking cubes; counters

Differentiation
Less confident learners
Children work with number cards 10–20.
More confident learners
Children work with two-digit numbers up to 100.

Lesson 2
Oral and mental starter 41

Main teaching activities

Whole-class work: Explain that in this lesson the children will be adding numbers using partitioning and also using facts that they already know and subtracting by counting on. Write the numbers 36 and 54 on the board. Together partition them into 30 + 6 and 50 + 4. Ask them to add the tens using this thinking: *I know that 3 + 5 = 8, so 30 + 50 must be 80.* Then the ones: *I know my number pairs to ten, so 6 + 4 = 10.* Finally recombine 80 and 10 to make 90. Ask: *What is the difference between 36 and 54?* Listen to their responses accepting anything that they say which is correct. Then ask them to focus on the numerical difference and ask how they could find this out by counting on. Invite a volunteer to demonstrate on the board. Repeat for other two-digit numbers. The children use their whiteboards to show their strategies and answers.

Paired work: Distribute photocopiable page 'Make your own' from the CD-ROM and demonstrate what the children need to do. They add two two-digit numbers together and find the numerical difference using one of the methods used in the lesson. They then check their answers using another strategy of their choice, which could include using the inverse operation.

Progress check: Invite some children to share their numbers and their strategies for adding and subtracting. Check that everyone is doing something similar.

Review

Invite pairs of children to share examples of their work, demonstrating on the board and explaining exactly what they did.

Lesson 3
Oral and mental starter 15

Main teaching activities

Whole-class work: Ask: *What can you tell me about addition and subtraction?* Take feedback. Draw out the fact that numbers can be added in any order as the answer will be the same. With subtraction the answers will always be different; addition and subtraction are inverse operations or processes. Write examples of these concepts on the board demonstrating on number lines and with arrow diagrams as appropriate, for example, 23 + 14= 37, 14 + 23 = 37, 23 − 14 = 9, 14 − 23 = −9

Independent work: Give each child a set of number cards 10–50. They pick a pair of numbers and add them together. They then draw an arrow diagram to show how they can subtract them using the inverse operation of subtraction.

Progress check: Check to make sure everyone has understood what to do by asking two or three children to give examples.

Review

Take feedback from the activity. Invite children to share the numbers they chose and to demonstrate how they found the totals and differences using the number lines.

Invite the class to make up problems to go with the children's calculations.

Curriculum objectives

- To add and subtract using concrete objects, pictorial representations, and mentally, including: a two-digit number and ones; two two-digit numbers.
- To recognise and use the inverse relationship between addition and subtraction and use this to check calculations and solve missing number problems.

Success criteria

- I can add by counting on along a number line.
- I can find differences by counting on.

You will need

Photocopiable sheets

'Finding the difference'

General resources

'0–100 number cards'

Equipment

Individual whiteboards

Differentiation

Less confident learners

Children work with numbers 0–30. Provide numbered number lines for them to use if this would be helpful.

More confident learners

Children work with numbers 0–100.

Lesson 4   Oral and mental starter 38

Main teaching activities

Whole-class work: *Sam would like to find out what 37 take away 29 is. Can you tell him how he can do this?* Ask the children to discuss this with a partner. Agree and demonstrate these strategies using a number line:

I draw a number line and plot 37 and 29 onto it. If Sam takes 29 away we can cross out that part of the number line. Sam needs to count on from 29 to 37.

Explain that Sam could also work this out by counting back 29 from 37.

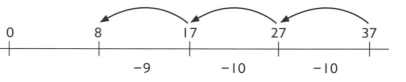

Which method is the best to use? Agree counting on, because the numbers are quite close together.

How can we check that we are correct? Agree: add the smaller number to the answer.

Repeat both strategies for subtracting 45 and 8. Agree that, because the numbers are far apart it is probably more efficient to count back.

Paired work: Distribute photocopiable page 'Finding the difference' from the CD-ROM. The children work with a similar-ability partner. They pick two number cards. One finds the difference between the two numbers using the counting on strategy. The other counts back. They explain what they are doing to each other and decide which method they prefer.

Progress check: Ask pairs to demonstrate some of their subtraction calculations. Check that everyone is counting on and back using a number line.

- *How can we check that the answer is correct?*

Review

Take feedback from the task inviting pairs to share their numbers and methods. Ask them to demonstrate on the board. For each pair of subtractions ask the class to discuss which of the two methods was the most efficient. Finish the lesson by asking:

- *Ali wants to take 4 from 37. Can you explain how he could do this? Is there another way? Which is the best way?*
- *Sasha wants to take 35 from 42. She says that she is going to count on from 35. Is this a good method? Why?*
- *How can we check that the answer to a subtraction is correct?*

Curriculum objectives
● To solve problems with addition: using concrete objects and pictorial representations, including those involving numbers, quantities and measures; applying their increasing knowledge of mental and written methods.

Success criteria
● I can solve word problems using a number line.
● I can check my answers using the opposite operation.

You will need
General resources
'0–100 number cards'
Equipment
Individual whiteboards

Differentiation
Less confident learners
Children make up problems using number cards 0–30.
More confident learners
Children work with number cards 50–100.

Lesson 5   Oral and mental starter 34

Main teaching activities

Whole-class work: Explain: *Today we are going to use the strategies we have been practising to help us solve problems.* Discuss the strategies that the children have been thinking about this week: partitioning, sequencing and counting on and back to subtract. Write some calculations on the board to practise these, for example. 58 + 37, 48 − 29, 35 + 26, 54 − 38. Recap what will help, for example the fact that they can use subtraction to check addition and addition to check subtraction, it doesn't matter which way round you add numbers the answer will be the same but it does matter which way round you subtract because the two answers will usually be different. Ask them to check the answers to the practice calculations.

Ask: *Sanjit and Jono both had collections of stamps. Sanjit had 53 and Jono had 38. How many stamps did they have altogether? How many more stamps did Sanjit have?* Ask the children to discuss how they would find the total and difference with a partner. Then take feedback and invite volunteers to share their strategies for finding the answer.

Paired work: Give the children a set of number cards 10–50 and ask them to pick two at a time. They make up a problem to solve that involves adding and subtracting as in the example in the lesson.

Progress check: Ask different pairs of children who you wish to assess these questions:
● *Which is the best strategy to use to solve this?*
● *How could you check that you are correct?*

Review
Take feedback from the task. Invite pairs to ask their problem and the class to solve it sharing the strategies they used to do this. Ask them to assess their confidence at finding totals and differences using the different strategies involved in this week's series of lessons.

Multiplication and division: grouping and using times tables facts

Expected prior learning

Children should be able to:
- use multiplication facts to help them answer multiplication and division problems
- answer multiplication and division calculations using arrays.

Topic	Curriculum objectives	Expected outcomes
Multiplication and division	**Lesson 1** To calculate mathematical statements for multiplication and division within the multiplication tables and write them using the multiplication (×), division (÷) and equals (=) signs. To recall and use multiplication and division facts for the 2, 5 and 10 multiplication tables, including recognising odd and even numbers.	Use two-, five- and ten-times table facts to solve problems. Use counting to solve problems. Use partitioning to multiply. Use grouping for division.
	Lesson 2 To calculate mathematical statements for multiplication and division within the multiplication tables and write them using the multiplication (×), division (÷) and equals (=) signs. To recall and use multiplication and division facts for the 2, 5 and 10 multiplication tables, including recognising odd and even numbers.	Complete missing number sentences. Understand multiplication and division are inverse operations. Use times tables facts to answer division calculations.
	Lesson 3 To calculate mathematical statements for multiplication and division within the multiplication tables and write them using the multiplication (×), division (÷) and equals (=) signs.	Understand multiplication as repeated addition and division as repeated subtraction. Understand that one can be used to check the other.
	Lesson 4 To calculate mathematical statements for multiplication and division within the multiplication tables and write them using the multiplication (×), division (÷) and equals (=) signs.	Understand division as grouping. Understand that there might be a remainder when dividing.
	Lesson 5 To solve problems involving multiplication and division, using materials, arrays, repeated addition, mental methods, and multiplication and division facts, including problems in contexts.	Use multiplication and division to solve and check simple problems. Make up multiplication problems.

■ SCHOLASTIC

Preparation

Lesson 1: enlarge a copy of the photocopiable sheets 'Spider charts for multiplying' and 'Spider charts for ×5 and ÷5'

You will need

Photocopiable sheets

'Sally's sweet shop'; Opposites'; 'Remainders'; 'Missing number sentences'; 'Missing number sentences recording sheet'

General resources

'Spider charts for ×5 and ÷5'; 'Spider charts for multiplying'; 'Shopping cards'; 'Number lines 0–30'

Equipment

Individual whiteboards; coins counting stick; counters; interlocking cubes

Further practice

Photocopiable sheets

'Party problems'

Oral and mental starters for week 3

See bank of starters on pages 85, 126 and 167. Oral and mental starters are also on the CD-ROM.

29 Counting in steps of two, five and ten

39 Counting in steps

41 Spider charts

15 Multiples

Overview of progression

During this week children will consolidate and extend their knowledge of multiplication and division. They will continue to develop the idea that multiplication is repeated addition and division is repeated subtraction. They will check answers by using the inverse operation. They will begin to extend repeated subtraction into grouping. They will make use of their multiplication table facts to solve problems.

Watch out for

Some children may have difficulty using number lines. Give them laminated numbered number lines to work with so that they can make jumps with the option to rub out if any errors are made.

Creative context

Ask the children to look for arrays inside and outside the classroom and use these to find out how many of a particular thing there are, for example, window panes.

Vocabulary

divide, divided by, equal groups of, grouping, groups of, **inverse operation,** lots of, **multiple of,** multiplied by, multiply, **remainder,** repeated addition, repeated subtraction, times

Curriculum objectives

● To recall and use multiplication and division facts for the 2, 5 and 10 multiplication tables, including recognising odd and even numbers.
● To calculate mathematical statements for multiplication and division within the multiplication tables and write them using the multiplication (×), division (÷) and equals (=) signs.

Success criteria

● I can multiply using partitioning.
● I can use my times tables facts to help me solve problems.

You will need

Photocopiable sheets

'Sally's sweet shop'

General resources

'Spider charts for multiplying'; 'Spider charts for ×5 and ÷5'

Equipment

A selection of coins

Differentiation

Less confident learners

Adapt photocopiable page 'Sally's sweet shop' so that the children are working with amounts per bag of up to 20p.

More confident learners

Adapt photocopiable page 'Sally's sweet shop' so that the children are working with more complex amounts above 50p, for example 69p.

Lesson 1
Oral and mental starter 29

Main teaching activities

Whole-class work: Tell the children that they will be thinking about multiplication and division this week and that today they will be solving problems involving mental calculation strategies. Say: *I bought five gobstoppers at 15p each. I paid the exact amount. Which coins could I have given the shopkeeper?* Discuss what the question is asking and ask the children to talk to a partner about what they think they need to do. Take feedback, then ask for suggestions as to how they might find the answer. Agree that they could use their five-times table facts and partitioning: partition 15p into 10p and 5p, multiply both numbers by five and then add to make 75p. Give pairs of children a collection of coins and ask them to find ways of paying 75p. Ask: *What are the fewest coins that I could have given? If I wanted three gobstoppers, how much would that cost? How do you know? What about ten gobstoppers?* Discuss doubling for buying two gobstoppers. For each ask the children to find that amount using the coins.

Set a problem for division such as: *I bought three chews. They cost me 24p. How much was one chew?* Explore ways to find the solution, for example, grouping in threes, counting on in threes using fingers until reaching 24.

Paired work: The children need to work in similar-ability pairs. Distribute photocopiable page 'Sally's sweet shop' from the CD-ROM and explain that the children need to work out how much was spent. They should do this using the strategies for multiplication discussed during the lesson.

Progress check: Focus on pairs that you wish to assess. Watch how they find the answers. Can they partition and multiply using their tables facts efficiently?

Review

Invite pairs to share how they answered their problems. They should demonstrate on the board. Finish the lesson by rehearsing multiplication tables using large versions of the 'Spider charts for multiplying', and 'Spider charts for ×5 and ÷5' from the CD-ROM.

Curriculum objectives
● To recall and use multiplication and division facts for the 2, 5 and 10 multiplication tables, including recognising odd and even numbers.
● To calculate mathematical statements for multiplication and division within the multiplication tables and write them using the multiplication (×), division (÷) and equals (=) signs.

Success criteria
● I can solve missing number problems.

You will need
Photocopiable sheets
'Missing number sentences'; 'Missing numbers recording sheet'

General resources
'0–100 number cards'

Equipment
Counting stick; individual whiteboards

Differentiation
Less confident learners
Give children numbers 0–20.

More confident learners
Give children a range of number cards up to 100 using '0–100 number cards'.

Lesson 2
Oral and mental starter 39

Main teaching activities
Whole-class work: Explain that this lesson will focus on counting backwards and forwards from zero in steps of two, three, five and ten and linking these to times tables facts. Using a counting stick, move your finger up and down the stick, asking the children to predict what number you are pointing to and say how they know, first telling them what steps you are counting in. Expect answers such as: *That is 35 because it is 7 jumps of 5.* Encourage them to write the appropriate number sentence: 5 × 7 = 35. Repeat a few times counting in different steps.

Write some missing number sentences on the board, for example, 5 × ☐ = 45 and ask the children how they can work this out. Aim towards counting in fives to 45. Bring in the inverse operation: 45 ÷ 5 = 9. Next write ☐ × 6 = 60 and ask them to tell you how they know what is in the box, again bringing in the inverse. Next write ◯ × ☐ = 24 and ask the children to work with a partner to find out what the possible missing numbers might be. Encourage them to write the missing number sentences and their inverses. Repeat with similar examples.

Paired work: The children work in similar-ability pairs for this game and use the cards from photocopiable page 'Missing number sentences' from the CD-ROM. They spread the cards face down on the table and pick two. They then try to make a missing number sentence using one of the cards as the answer. If they can they score two points. If they can't they replace their cards and try again. Encourage them to use both multiplication and division sentences. You may need to model this first. They use photocopiable page 'Missing number sentences recording sheet' to write their sentences and scores.

Progress check: To check their understanding, ask the children:
● *How can you work out the missing number? Is there another way?*
● *How can you use your multiplication tables to help you?*
● *Can you find your answer using the inverse operation?*

Review
Take feedback from the game, asking volunteers to show some of their missing number sentences. Write some missing number sentences on the board for the children to complete. Finish the lesson by recalling tables facts.

Curriculum objectives

● To calculate mathematical statements for multiplication and division within the multiplication tables and write them using the multiplication (×), division (÷) and equals (=) signs.

Success criteria

● I can multiply using repeated addition.
● I can divide using repeated subtraction.
● I can explain that multiplication and division are inverse operations.

You will need

Photocopiable sheets
'Opposites'

Photocopiable sheets
'Number lines 0–30'

Equipment
Individual whiteboards

Differentiation

Less confident learners

Give children photocopiable page 'Number lines 0–30' to count along. You might need to support them when doing the activity.

More confident learners

After the children have completed the photocopiable sheet, they make up stories to go with their calculations.

Lesson 3   Oral and mental starter 15

Main teaching activities

Whole-class work: Recap what the children know about multiplication and division. Agree that multiplication is totalling groups of the same number and division is taking groups of the same number away from a whole amount. Establish that multiplication is repeated addition and division repeated subtraction. These can be shown on number lines and in arrays. Discuss the idea that multiplication and division are opposite or inverse operations. You could say that division is un-doing multiplication.

Demonstrate this on a number line, for example 6 × 5 and 30 ÷ 5. Describe how you are adding six groups of five for multiplication and taking away six groups of five for division.

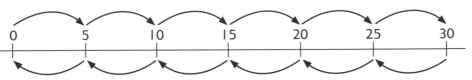

Ask: *What can we use to help us?* Agree that they could count in multiples of five using their fingers to work out both. Together do this. Ask: *What story could we make up for 6 × 5? Talk to your partner.* Invite the children to share their stories, for example: *Sally has six bowls. In each bowl are five sweets. How many sweets does she have?* Repeat for 30 ÷ 5. Repeat for other calculations and ask the children to show these using number lines on their whiteboards.

Independent work: Distribute photocopiable page 'Opposites' from the CD-ROM and explain they need to use the number lines to show that multiplication and division are inverse operations as demonstrated in the lesson.

Progress check: Ask individuals to demonstrate one of their number lines. Ask questions such as:

● *What do we mean by inverse operations? Can you explain in a different way?*
● *How can we count on to work out 15 ÷ 5?*

Review

Invite the children to demonstrate some of the number line work they did in the task.

Ask the children who made up stories to share them with the class. The class then works out which calculation each story goes with.

Curriculum objectives

● To calculate mathematical statements for multiplication and division.

Success criteria

● I can divide by grouping.
● I can tell you if there will be a remainder when I group.

You will need

Photocopiable sheets

'Remainders'

Equipment

Counters; individual whiteboards; interlocking cubes

Differentiation

Less confident learners

Adapt the photocopiable sheet so the children find groups of six instead of eight.

More confident learners

Once the children have finished the activity, ask them to make up some more calculations and problems.

Lesson 4
Oral and mental starter 41

Main teaching activities

Whole-class work: Say: *Kurtis had 20 building blocks. He wanted to put them into equal groups. How many groups could he put them into? Talk to your partner.* Invite the children to share their thinking and to demonstrate using cubes. Agree that he could put them into one group of 20, two groups of ten, four groups of five, five groups of four, ten groups of two and 20 groups of one. *What would happen if he grouped them in threes?* Demonstrate using the cubes. Establish that he would have six groups and two left over. Explain that those left are known as the remainder.

Give pairs of children cubes and ask them to work out how many would be in each group and the remainder if Kurtis made groups of six, seven, eight and nine. Repeat with other examples.

Paired work: Distribute copies of photocopiable page 'Remainders' from the CD-ROM. The children work together to group counters finding how many in each group and how many remaining.

Progress check: Visit pairs that you wish to assess and ask questions such as:

● If I have 20 biscuits how could I group them equally? Is there another way? How many ways are there?
● If I grouped 23 toys into groups of ten, what would the remainder be? How do you know?

Review

Take feedback about the task. Invite pairs of children to share the grouping they did. They could draw counters on the board or use real ones. Say: *Fatima had 12 counters. If she made two groups of five, how many would she have left over?* Invite the children to describe how they would find out. Repeat for similar problems.

Curriculum objectives

● To solve problems involving multiplication and division.

Success criteria

● I can solve problems involving multiplication and division.

You will need

Photocopiable sheets

'Shopping cards'

Differentiation

Less confident learners

Children focus on multiplying and checking by two and ten.

More confident learners

Children make up problems where two different toys are bought and find the total.

Lesson 5
Oral and mental starter 41

Main teaching activities

Whole-class work: Recap the important things to remember about multiplication and division as highlighted in lesson 3. Explain that today the children will make up and solve problems involving multiplying and checking by dividing. Display 'Shopping cards' and say: *Poppy wants to buy three toy kites. How much money will she need?* Ask the children what they need to do to find the answer. Agree multiply 4p by three. Demonstrate repeated addition on a number line. *How can we check?* Agree they can divide by taking groups of 4p away. Again demonstrate this. Repeat for other examples.

Independent work: Distribute photocopiable page 'Shopping cards' from the CD-ROM and explain that they need to make up problems like Poppy's. They pick a toy and decide how many they will buy, choosing from two, three, five or ten. Encourage them to vary these numbers for different problems. They demonstrate how they can find their answer using a number line and then check as in the lesson.

Progress check: Ask the children who you might want to assess to give an example of a problem they made up, how they found the answer and checked they were correct.

Review

Invite a few children to share one of their problems. Invite someone from the class to demonstrate how this could be answered and checked using a number line. Ask the class how else they could have found their answers. Agree counting on in steps using their fingers or using their knowledge of tables facts.

Fractions: finding fractions of quantities, shapes and sets of objects

Expected prior learning

Children should be able to:

- know that fractions are part of a whole
- know that two halves make a whole
- know that four quarters make a whole.

Topic	Curriculum objectives	Expected outcomes
Fractions	**Lesson 1**	
	To recognise, find, name and write fractions ⅓, ¼, ²⁄₄ and ¾ of a length, shape, set of objects or quantity. To write simple fractions, for example ½ of 6 = 3 and recognise the equivalence of ²⁄₄ and ½.	Understand that a fraction is part of a whole. Find halves and quarters. Explain that finding quarters is the same as halving and halving again.
	Lesson 2	
	To recognise, find, name and write fractions ⅓, ¼, ²⁄₄ and ¾ of a length, shape, set of objects or quantity.	Understand that a fraction is part of a whole. Understand that the size of each quarter is the same even if it doesn't look the same.
	Lesson 3	
	To recognise, find, name and write fractions ⅓, ¼, ²⁄₄ and ¾ of a length, shape, set of objects or quantity. To write simple fractions, for example ½ of 6 = 3 and recognise the equivalence of ²⁄₄ and ½.	Understand the equivalence between halves and quarters. Find halves and quarters of amounts.
	Lesson 4	
	To recognise, find, name and write fractions ⅓, ¼, ²⁄₄ and ¾ of a length, shape, set of objects or quantity.	Find fractions of shapes.
	Lesson 5	
	To recognise, find, name and write fractions ⅓, ¼, ²⁄₄ and ¾ of a length, shape, set of objects or quantity. To write simple fractions, for example ½ of 6 = 3 and recognise the equivalence of ²⁄₄ and ½.	Use concrete and pictorial representations to solve simple problems.

Preparation

Lesson 1: prepare three strips of paper for each child; each needs to be approximately 3cm wide and the length of the width of A4

Lesson 2: make towers using interlocking cubes in the following combination of colours: 2 red, 1 yellow, 1 green; 3 red, 2 yellow, 1 green; 4 red, 2 yellow, 2 green 4; 5 red, 2 yellow, 3 green; 6 red, 3 yellow, 3 green

Lesson 4: copy the shapes on photocopiable page 'Shapes to fold' onto A3 paper; if any children need help cutting out their shapes, do it for them before the lesson

You will need

Photocopiable sheets

'Pennies game'; Pennies game recording sheet'; 'My fraction problems'; 'Spin a fraction'; 'Fraction spinner'; 'Shapes to fold'

General resources

'Fraction number line'; 'Fraction cards'; '0–100 number cards'

Equipment

Individual whiteboards; strips of paper; 1p coins; A4 paper; interlocking cubes; Plasticine®; counters

Further practice

Photocopiable sheets

'Clock faces'

Oral and mental starters for week 4

See bank of starters on pages 86, 167 and 168. The oral and mental starters are also on the CD-ROM.

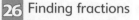

26 Finding fractions

38 More doubling and halving

41 Spider charts

43 Counting in fractions

Overview of progression

During this week children will extend their knowledge of fractions. They will recap the key ideas that they have learned so far. They will begin to link finding fractions to division and use this knowledge to find fractions of shapes and small numbers. They will use their understanding gained during the week to make up and solve simple problems in familiar contexts.

> ### Watch out for
> Some children may still think a quarter is bigger than a half because four is bigger than two. Give them plenty of practice at finding halves and quarters of the same amounts so that they can 'see' that a quarter is a smaller amount because it has been shared into more groups. It is very important that this possible issue is addressed as early as possible.

Creative context

You could explore artists, such as Mondrian and his Komposition painting, and investigate the fractions the children can see in their work.

Vocabulary

equal parts, **equivalent**, four quarters, fraction, one half, one quarter, one whole, part, three quarters, two halves, two quarters

Curriculum objectives

● To recognise, find, name and write fractions ⅓, ¼, ¾ and ¾ of a length, shape, set of objects or quantity.
● To write simple fractions, for example ½ of 6 = 3 and recognise the equivalence of ¾ and ½.

Success criteria

● I can explain that a fraction is part of a whole thing.
● I can find halves and quarters.

You will need

General resources

'0–100 number cards'

Equipment

Three strips of paper per child; 1p coins; counters

Differentiation

Less confident learners

Children use number cards 0–20.

More confident learners

Children could use random, even number cards 0–100. Encourage them to find other fractions.

Lesson 1
Oral and mental starter 41

Main teaching activities

Whole-class work: Say: *Who can tell me something about fractions?* Write down what the children say on the board. Look for (and if necessary prompt) these statements: a fraction is part of a whole; a half is when you divide something into two equal parts; a quarter is when you divide something into four equal parts. Spend some time focusing on the following relationships: two halves and four quarters make a whole; two quarters are the same as a half, therefore one quarter is a half of a half; three quarters is half plus one quarter. Ask the children to make fractions strips to demonstrate this (see autumn 2, week 4, lesson 3).

Focus on fractions of amounts. Give each child 16 1p coins. They take four coins. Tell them that this is the whole amount. They place the four 1p coins on the whole strip. Next ask them to put them in equal amounts onto the half strip. Establish that half of 4p is 2p. Now ask them to place them equally on the quarter strips and agree that a quarter of 4p is 1p. Ask them what three quarters of 4p would be. Agree 3p. Repeat for eight pennies, then 12 and 16. Now try ten pennies. Ask: *What happens? Why?* Agree that ten can be halved but the resulting five cannot be halved again and to make quarters they need to be. Ask the children to tell you other numbers that can only be halved.

Paired work: Give each pair a collection of 1p coins or, if not available, counters and about 15 number cards 0–30. Ask them to select a card, put that number of counters on the whole strip and then work out how many half the number is and then a quarter. Demonstrate this, explaining that they might not always be able to make the fractions as they saw earlier. They should record their findings on a piece of paper as they go along.

Progress check: Check that the children are doing what is expected by inviting individuals to share the numbers they picked and how they found halves and quarters or not if it wasn't possible.

Review

Take feedback from the activity, writing number sentences to show what they say, for example, ½ of 14 = 7. Recap why five pennies cannot be halved and ask the children to give you examples of numbers they picked that couldn't be halved or quartered. Ask: *Can you think of a number that can be divided into quarters but not halves? Can you explain why this is impossible?*

Curriculum objectives
- To recognise, find, name and write fractions.
- To write simple fractions and recognise the equivalence of ¾ and ½.

Success criteria
- I can find halves and quarters of amounts.
- I can record what I have done.

You will need

Photocopiable sheets
'Spin a fraction'; 'Fraction spinner'

Equipment
1p coins; A4 paper; interlocking cubes; counters; individual whiteboards

Differentiation
This is a whole class activity. Less confident learners find halves only if they wish.

Lesson 2
Oral and mental starter 38

Main teaching activities

Whole-class work: Recap all the points from the last lesson with amounts of 1p coins or counters. For example, whole = 24, ½ of 24 = 12, ¼ of 24 = 6, ¾ = ½ = 12, ¾ = ½ + ¼ = 18. This time expect the children to write these number sentences on their whiteboards. Repeat for other numbers that can be halved and quartered.

Group work: Demonstrate the children's task which is to practise finding fractions of numbers by playing the 'Spin a fraction' game. They use the 'Fraction spinner' to generate a fraction. Children record their work.

Progress check: Visit each group to ensure they know what to do. You could ask questions such as:
- *What is half of 18? How do you know?*
- *Can you find a quarter of 18? Why not?*

Review

Take feedback for the task, inviting groups to give examples of the fractions they found. Show some towers made from interlocking cubes. Make statements, asking the children to tell you whether they are true or false. Expect them to explain why. Take a sheet of A4 paper and fold it once but not in half. Say: *I have folded this paper in half. True or false?* Make up other statements for the towers and paper. Here are some examples:
- *I am folding this paper into four equal pieces so I have folded it in half.* (F)
- Make a tower with three yellow cubes, six green cubes, two red cubes, 1 pink cube. Say: *One quarter of this tower is yellow.* (T) *Three quarters are a mix of yellow and green.* (T) *One quarter of this tower is red.* (F)

Curriculum objectives
- To recognise, find, name and write fractions.
- To write simple fractions and recognise the equivalence of ¾ and ½.

Success criteria
- I can work out halves and quarters of amounts.
- I can show that two quarters are the same as a half.

You will need

Photocopiable sheets
'Pennies game'; 'Pennies game recording sheet'; 'Fraction number line'; 'Fraction cards'

Equipment
Individual whiteboards; 1p coins

Differentiation

Less confident learners
Children can play the game using up to 20 1p coins.

More confident learners
Children use up to 80 1p coins.

Lesson 3
Oral and mental starter 26

Main teaching activities

Whole-class work: Recap what the children should know about fractions. Compare this with what they said in lesson1. Are they more confident? Ask them to write ½, ¼ and ¾ on their whiteboards and show you. They then give you information about each one, for example, ½ is a whole amount divided into two equal groups, ¾ is a whole amount divided into four and you need three of the four groups. Explain that they are going to continue to practise working out halves and quarters and looking for patterns, but this time with a game.

Paired work: Model the game 'Pennies game' from the CD-ROM. The children play in similar-ability pairs taking 1p coins from a pile of up to 40. They record their work in fraction number sentences on photocopiable page 'Pennies game recording sheet'.

Progress check: Ask the children to give examples of the fractions that they have found. You could ask questions such as:
- *Which is smaller, a half or a quarter?*
- *Can you tell me any equivalent fractions?*

Review

Discuss the game. Did any children notice which numbers could be divided into halves and quarters? Agree that multiples of four can be. Show the children the photocopiable sheets 'Fraction number line' and 'Fraction cards' and ask them to place some of the fraction cards correctly on the line. Discuss where each card should go and what clues the number line provides.

Curriculum objectives

● To recognise, find, name and write fractions ⅓, ¼, ⅔ and ¾ of a length, shape, set of objects or quantity.

Success criteria

● I can find halves of shapes.
● I can find quarters of shapes.

You will need

Photocopiable sheets

'Shapes to fold'

Equipment

Plasticine®; individual whiteboards; scissors

Differentiation

Less confident learners

Children focus on finding half of the shapes.

More confident learners

Children find as many different ways as possible to find a half and a quarter of the shapes.

Lesson 4   Oral and mental starter 43

Main teaching activities

Whole-class work: Recap on finding fractions of amounts from the previous two lessons. Call out some numbers and ask the children to find a half and a quarter of these, giving a whole number answer. If it is not possible to find either, ask them to explain why, for example, you can only halve an even number, or you can only find a quarter of a multiple of four.

Give each child a piece of Plasticine®. Ask them to roll it into a worm shape and then break it into two halves. Say: *Compare your worm with your neighbour's. Is your half the same as theirs? Does that mean that it isn't a half? Why can all the halves be different sizes?* It's because half sizes are different if the whole lengths are different. Relate this to finding halves of different numbers. Ask the children to take half their Plasticine® and halve it again. Ask: *What fraction do you have now?* Agree a quarter and emphasise that a quarter is a half of a half. Repeat the questioning from above.

Paired work: Model the activity on photocopiable page 'Shapes to fold' from the CD-ROM by cutting out and folding the shapes. Ask: *What shape is this? How many parts will I have if I fold it in half? How many ways can I fold it in half? Can I fold it in half in a different way? Can I fold it into quarters? Why/why not?* Give the sheet of shapes to each pair of children. Ask them to cut out the shapes and fold them in as many ways as they can to make equal halves and then quarters.

Progress check: Invite pairs to demonstrate how they find halves and quarters of the shapes so that the class can check that they are working correctly.

Review

Compare the ways the children found to fold their shapes in half and in quarter. Invite a few children, particularly any whom you wish to assess, to demonstrate their ways.

Curriculum objectives
● To understand that a fraction is part of a whole.
● To find halves and quarters.
● To explain that finding quarters is the same as halving and halving again.

Success criteria
● I can solve simple problems involving fractions.

You will need
Equipment
Individual whiteboard

Differentiation
Less confident learners
Children work with numbers to 20 and find a half.

More confident learners
Children work with higher numbers and find a half, a quarter and three quarters.

Lesson 5   Oral and mental starter 43

Main teaching activities

Whole-class work: Recap on what the children have done during the week. Reinforce that the bottom number of the fraction (denominator) tells them how many to share into, and fractions are equal amounts but do not necessarily look the same. Talk through the equivalences for halves and quarters. Set this problem: *Frankie was offered half of 20 toy cars or three quarters of 12. He collects toy cars and wants the most. Which offer should he choose?* Give the children a few minutes to work out how they could find the answer. Take feedback and establish that they need to find half of 20 is and also three quarters of 12. Agree that half of 20 is 10 and three quarters of 12 is three lots of quarter which is 9. So, Frankie should choose the first offer. Ask similar problems.

Tell the children that they will now use their knowledge of fractions to solve problems. Write on the board:

Pick a number: 24, 16, 30, 20, 36, 12

Pick a fraction: ½ ,¼

Tell them to make up a problem. Then repeat three more times. Ask: *How can we find half? What is an easy way of finding a quarter? What do we know that helps us to find three quarters?*

Paired work: The children's task involves making up problems for another pair to solve using the numbers and fraction above. Model an example and then give the children between 10 and 15 minutes to make up as many as they can. After their time is up, they swap problems with another pair of a similar ability and try to solve them. They could then move on and make their own numbers up.

Progress check: Visit the pairs to find out how they are getting on. Resolve any issues. If there are any common issues, stop the class to address these.

Review
Go through some examples of the children's problems. Ask them to self-assess their confidence in finding halves and then quarters and finally three quarters of amounts.

Geometry and measurement

Expected prior learning

Children should be able to:

- describe position, directions and movements, including clockwise and anticlockwise turns
- tell the time to the quarter hour and draw the hands on a clock face to show these times.

Topic	Curriculum objectives	Expected outcomes
Geometry: position and direction	**Lesson 1**	
	To use mathematical vocabulary to describe position, direction and movement including movement in a straight line and distinguishing between rotation as a turn and in terms of right angles for quarter, half and three-quarter turns (clockwise and anti-clockwise).	Use the appropriate vocabulary to describe the position and movement of shapes. Explore turns of a right angle in clockwise and anticlockwise directions.
	Lesson 2	
	To use mathematical vocabulary to describe position, direction and movement including movement in a straight line and distinguishing between rotation as a turn and in terms of right angles for quarter, half and three-quarter turns (clockwise and anti-clockwise).	Use the appropriate vocabulary to describe the position and movement of shapes. Make mazes and instructions to move around them.
Measurement: Time	**Lesson 3**	
	To tell and write the time to five minutes, including quarter past/to the hour and draw the hands on a clock face to show these times. To know the number of minutes in an hour and the number of hours in a day.	Find o'clock, quarter past, half past and quarter to times on a clock.
	Lesson 4	
	To tell and write the time to five minutes, including quarter past/to the hour and draw the hands on a clock face to show these times. To know the number of minutes in an hour and the number of hours in a day.	Tell and write o'clock, quarter past, half past and quarter to times. Solve problems involving time.
	Lesson 5	
	To tell and write the time to five minutes, including quarter past/to the hour and draw the hands on a clock face to show these times. To know the number of minutes in an hour and the number of hours in a day.	Solve problems involving time.

Preparation

Lesson 1: prepare position vocabulary cards

Lesson 3: enlarge photocopiable page 'Up the mountain gameboard' for whole class use; copy for use by pairs of children; copy and cut up the cards from the photocopiable pages 'Analogue time cards' and 'Time vocabulary'

Lesson 4: enlarge copies of 'Up the mountain gameboard' for pairs of children

You will need

Photocopiable sheets
'Time problems'; 'Up the mountain gameboard'; 'Amazing race'

General resources
Interactive activity 'Right angles'; 'Time vocabulary'; 'Analogue time cards'; interactive activity 'How long does it take?'

Equipment
Floor robot; individual whiteboards; small clocks class clock; toy car; dice; A3 paper

Further practice

Interactive activity 'How long does it take?' offers practice of working out time differences.

Photocopiable sheets
'Time differences'

Oral and mental starters for week 5

See bank of starters on pages 167 to 168. Oral and mental starters are also on the CD-ROM.

40 Taking away

44 Adding

43 Counting in fractions

Overview of progression

During this week children will extend their knowledge of position, direction and motion. They will explore the vocabulary of position and direction through practical activities. They will also extend their knowledge of time. They will find o'clock, quarter to, half past and quarter to times on clocks. They will use their ability to do this to solve problems within the context of time.

> ### Watch out for
> Some children may still not be able to tell o'clock and half past times on a clock. Provide these children with clock faces and ask them to match them with different o'clock and half past times on the class clock during the day and to tell you the times they have made.

Creative context

Position, direction and motion could be included in PE activities. Also, encourage the children to tell the time at different times of the day, e.g. lunch time, home time, time when literacy starts.

Vocabulary

April, analogue clock/watch, **anticlockwise**, August, **clockwise**, day, December, digital clock/watch, February, fortnight, half turn, hands, hour, January, July, June, left, March, May, minute, month, November, o'clock, October, quarter past, quarter to, quarter turn, right, second, September, straight line, today, tomorrow, week, weekend, whole turn, year, yesterday

Curriculum objectives

● To use mathematical vocabulary to describe position, direction and movement including movement in a straight line and distinguishing between rotation as a turn and in terms of right angles for quarter, half and three-quarter turns (clockwise and anti-clockwise).

Success criteria

● I can use appropriate vocabulary to describe direction and movement.

You will need

General resources

Interactive activity 'Right angles'

Equipment

Floor robot; individual whiteboards

Differentiation

Less confident learners

Encourage peer buddying for any child who is having difficulty.

More confident learners

Ask the children for more complicated programming.

Lesson 1
Oral and mental starter 43

Main teaching activities

Whole-class work: Explain that today, the children will revise their knowledge of positions of objects and then think about moving and turning them. Ask them to give you some position vocabulary. As they do hold up the appropriate card and explore the meaning of each word. Ask the children to use their whiteboards and to draw following your instructions: *Draw a circle under a line and draw a square above the circle. Draw a pentagon beside a triangle and another triangle below the pentagon.*

Write these words on the board: clockwise, anticlockwise, whole turn, half turn, quarter turn, right angle, straight line. Point to the words and say: *Who can tell me what a turn is? Can you show me? What is a quarter turn? What type of angle does it make? Which direction is clockwise? What about anticlockwise?* Ask everyone to stand up. *Turn clockwise for a quarter of a turn. Turn anticlockwise to make a right angle turn, turn anticlockwise to make a turn the size of a straight line. Where are you facing?* Repeat with similar instructions. Link quarter and half turns to the fractions work they covered in Week 4.

Paired work: Demonstrate the interactive activity 'Right angles' on the CD-ROM. Let pairs of children complete this activity. If a floor robot is available demonstrate how it works, then ask each pair to take it in turns to be a 'robot' and ask each partner to orally 'program' them with instructions to move around the classroom/hall.

Progress check: Check that the children are giving the correct instructions to the robot. Assess progress with the interactive activity.

Review

Check responses to the interactive activity. Invite some children to 'program' a human robot (an adult or child) to get around the classroom by moving and turning using the vocabulary covered in the main part of the lesson. Assess whether they know the necessary vocabulary and use it correctly.

Curriculum objectives
- To use mathematical vocabulary to describe direction and movement.

Success criteria
- I can use words to describe different positions.

You will need
Photocopiable sheets
'Amazing race'

Equipment
Small clocks; A3 paper; toy car

Differentiation
The children will be working in mixed-attainment pairs. Check that the less confident learners are taking an active part in designing a maze and that more confident learners are not dominating the activity.

Lesson 2 — Oral and mental starter 43

Main teaching activities

Whole-class work: Revisit the vocabulary of direction and movement from the previous lesson. Ask: *Who can show me what a half turn is? What about a quarter turn? What angle does a quarter turn make? Which direction is clockwise?... anticlockwise?* Give the children clocks. Ask: *Show me 12 o'clock. Move the minute hand a quarter turn clockwise. How many minutes past 12 o'clock is that? Now move it half a turn clockwise. How many minutes past 12 o'clock is that? Put the hands back to show 12 o'clock. Move the minute hand a whole turn clockwise. What time will you have made?* Repeat with the children moving: *Everyone stand up. Turn clockwise for a quarter turn, now anticlockwise for half a turn...and so on.*

Show the photocopiable page 'Amazing race' and ask the children to tell you how to move a counter through the maze.

Paired work: The children work in pairs to design a maze on A3 paper with right-angled turns (clockwise and anticlockwise) and straight line moves, then give each other instructions to steer a toy car through the maze. Demonstrate this by drawing an example of a maze on the board.

Progress check: Spend a few minutes with pairs of children to make sure they understand what to do.

Review

Take feedback from the children's task by asking them to give directions through each of the mazes created. Ask the children to make a right angle with their hands. Ask them to look around the room and point to any right angles they can see. Ask: *What shapes have right angles?* Discuss right angles in real life: in objects, shapes and turns.

Curriculum objectives
- To tell and write the time to five minutes.
- To know the number of minutes in an hour.

Success criteria
- I can show o'clock half past, quarter past and quarter to times on a clock.

You will need
Photocopiable sheets
'Up the mountain gameboard'

General resources
'Analogue time cards'; 'Time vocabulary'

Equipment
Small clocks; dice

Differentiation
Less confident learners
Children work with o'clock and half past times.

More confident learners
Children make up cards to use that include times to five minutes.

Lesson 3 — Oral and mental starter 40

Main teaching activities

Whole-class work: Give each child a clock. Ask them to give you some facts about it, for example *The little marks in between the hours number show minutes; there are five minutes from one hour number to the next; for quarter to the minutes hand will be on the 9.*

Ask the children to put a finger on the 12 and then move it to the 1. *How many minutes is that?* Carry on so that the children are counting in fives. Count round in fives again; when you reach 3, ask them how many minutes past the o'clock that is. Write on the board 15 minutes past 12. Ask them how else we can say that, reminding them that the minute hand has gone a quarter of the way round (quarter past 12).

Call out analogue times from the photocopiable sheet for the children to show on their clocks. Divide the class into two teams to play 'Up the mountain'. Call out a time, wait until everyone has shown it on their clocks (the children can help each other) and then throw a dice. If an even number is thrown, the first team moves up the mountain, if an odd number is thrown the second team moves.

Paired work: The children work in similar-ability pairs and play a game using photocopiable page 'Up the mountain gameboard' as in the lesson.

Progress check: Spend a few minutes with pairs of children to make sure they can find the times they need to make.

Review

Ask the children to show you how confident they are with times by showing a thumbs up, down or level sign. Recap the vocabulary of time.

Curriculum objectives
- To tell and write the time to five minutes.
- To know the number of minutes in an hour and the number of hours in a day.

Success criteria
- I can show o'clock and half past times on a clock.
- I can show quarter past and quarter to times on a clock.

You will need
Photocopiable sheets

'Up the mountain gameboard'

Equipment

Small clocks

Differentiation
The children work in mixed-ability groups.

Curriculum objectives
- To tell and write the time to five minutes.
- To know the number of minutes in an hour and the number of hours in a day.

Success criteria
- I can read and draw o'clock and half past times.
- I can read and draw quarter past and quarter to times.

You will need
Photocopiable sheets

'Time problems'

General resources

Interactive activity 'How long does it take?'

Equipment

Class clock; small clocks; individual whiteboards

Differentiation
Less confident learners

Adapt the photocopiable sheet so that the children are working with whole hours and o'clock times.

More confident learners

Adapt the photocopiable sheet so that the children are working with o'clock, half past and quarter to and past times.

Lesson 4 — Oral and mental starter 44

Main teaching activities

Whole-class work: Give each child a clock. Call out different times to the quarter of an hour and ask them to show you them on their clocks. Discuss the units of time and their equivalences: 60 seconds in a minute, 60 minutes in an hour, etc. Focus on days of the week and months of the year. Give seven children one of the days of the week cards. Ask them to order themselves. The class checks to see if they agree. Repeat this for the months of the year.

Tell the children that they will be practising finding different times on a clock like they did yesterday by playing the 'Up the mountain' game again.

Paired work: The children work in mixed-ability groups to play the game 'Up the mountain' as they did in lesson 3.

Progress check: Visit groups to make sure that they are on task.

Review

Ask the children to give a thumbs up sign if they think they can find times more quickly than they could before. Make a note of any who cannot, so that you can target them specifically during oral and mental starter activities related to time. Set the children some problems that they can answer using their clocks.

Lesson 5 — Oral and mental starter 43

Main teaching activities

Whole-class work: Ask: *What do we use to tell the time?* Agree clocks. *Where in real life can we see clocks?* Discuss the difference between analogue and digital clocks. Give each child a small clock. They find different o'clock, quarter past, half past and quarter to times. For each time write the digital equivalent on the board.

Ask: *Yukesh played with his friends from 6 o'clock until half past 7. How long did he play?* Discuss how they could work this out. Draw a number line on the board using digital and analogue times.

Agree that he played for an hour and a half. *Does this sound right? How could we check?* Agree that they could count back 1½ hours from 7:30 or use a clock. Ask them to check using their clocks. Repeat with similar problems.

Independent work: Distribute photocopiable page 'Time problems' from the CD-ROM and explain the task. Demonstrate finding the difference between two times using a number line and a clock.

Progress check: During the activity ask: *How are digital clocks different from the ones with hands? How are they the same? If it is now 10 o'clock, what time will it be in an hour and a half? How did you work that out?*

Review

Work through the problems from the children's task. Invite them to help you find the answers on time number lines and clocks. Finish the lesson by asking the children to self-assess how confident they are at solving problems involving time. If time is available, go through the interactive activity 'How long does it take?' on the CD-ROM and ask the children to write the time differences in this activity on their whiteboards. Say: *Show me* to establish who is confident with time differences and who needs more support.

Statistics: collecting and representing data

Expected prior learning

Children should be able to:

- answer a question by collecting and recording information in a pictogram
- present outcomes using pictograms
- use diagrams to sort objects into groups according to given criteria.

Topic	Curriculum objectives	Expected outcomes
Statistics	**Lesson 1**	
	To interpret and construct simple pictograms, tally charts, block diagrams and simple tables.	Gather information using a tally.
	To ask and answer simple questions by counting the number of objects in each category and sorting the categories by quantity.	Make and interpreting lists and tables.
	To ask and answer questions about totalling and comparing categorical data.	
	Lesson 2	
	To interpret and construct simple pictograms, tally charts, block diagrams and simple tables.	Make and interpreting pictograms.
	To ask and answer simple questions by counting the number of objects in each category and sorting the categories by quantity.	
	To ask and answer questions about totalling and comparing categorical data.	
	Lesson 3	
	To interpret and construct simple pictograms, tally charts, block diagrams and simple tables.	Make and interpreting pictograms.
	To ask and answer simple questions by counting the number of objects in each category and sorting the categories by quantity.	
	To ask and answer questions about totalling and comparing categorical data.	
	Lesson 4	
	To interpret and construct simple pictograms, tally charts, block diagrams and simple tables.	Make and interpreting block graphs.
	To ask and answer simple questions by counting the number of objects in each category and sorting the categories by quantity.	
	To ask and answer questions about totalling and comparing categorical data.	
	Lesson 5	
	To interpret and construct simple pictograms, tally charts, block diagrams and simple tables.	Make and interpreting block graphs.
	To ask and answer simple questions by counting the number of objects in each category and sorting the categories by quantity.	
	To ask and answer questions about totalling and comparing categorical data.	

Preparation

Lesson 1: enlarge and photocopy 'Organising data vocabulary cards' onto card and cut out

Lesson 2: on A1 paper draw a vertical and a horizontal axis, label them 'Number of children' and 'Colour of paint' respectively

Lesson 4: on A1 paper draw a vertical and a horizontal axis, label them 'Number of children' and 'Favourite sport' respectively. Mark the numbers 1–20 on the vertical axis

You will need

Photocopiable sheets

'Lists and tables'; 'Which colour?'; 'Sports block graph'; 'Pictograms'; 'Our sports graph'

General resources

'Organising data vocabulary cards'; 'Ways to organise data'; '0–100 number cards'; interactive activity 'Sorting it out'

Equipment

Individual whiteboards; sticky notes; large squared paper; A1 paper

Further practice

Interactive activity 'Sorting it out' offers practice of representing data in a block graph.

Photocopiable sheets

'Popular sports'

Oral and mental starters for week 6

See bank of starters on pages 167 to 168. Oral and mental starters are on the CD-ROM.

38 More doubling and halving

40 Taking away

43 Counting in fractions

45 Days of the week, months of the year

46 Time differences

Overview of progression

During this week children will extend their understanding of handling data. The children will do this by being given problems to solve. They will be encouraged to evaluate the different methods of presenting information with regard to their suitability in each case. They will explore and make lists, tables, pictograms and block charts.

Watch out for

Some children may not be able to collect, record and interpret information in lists and simple tables. Making and interpreting lists and tables are the early stages in data handling so it is important that the children are able to do this. Provide opportunities to practise in other area of mathematics.

Creative context

Ask children to make lists during the day and then make a representation of their choice, for example, to show whether children in the class have packed lunches or school dinners.

Vocabulary

block graph, common/popular, count, label, list, most/least, pictogram, represent, set, sort, table

Curriculum objectives
● To interpret and construct simple tables.
● To ask and answer simple questions by counting the number of objects in each category and sorting the categories by quantity.
● To ask and answer questions about totalling and comparing categorical data.

Success criteria
● I can make lists and tables.
● I can tell you information from lists and tables.

You will need
Photocopiable sheets
'Sports block graph'; 'Lists and tables'; 'Pictograms'

General resources
'Organising data vocabulary cards'; 'Ways to organise data'

Equipment
Individual whiteboards

Differentiation
Less confident learners
Adapt photocopiable page 'Lists and tables' so the children have three items to list and put into a table.

More confident learners
When children have completed the activity they make up a table of other things that they like and dislike and write some questions about the table.

Lesson 1 — Oral and mental starter 38

Main teaching activities

Whole-class work: Remind the children of last term's work on organising and using data. Ask: *Can you remember what we mean by 'data' and 'organising and using data'? What words can you think of about this topic?* Write any words that they say on the board and use the cards from photocopiable page 'Organising data vocabulary cards' from the CD-ROM to prompt when necessary. Discuss the meanings of these words. Ask them to tell you the ways they have used to organise data and make a list on the board: counting, tallying, sorting, voting, making block graphs and pictograms. Explain that these are ways we can represent, group or list information. This saves us having to write lots of words and helps us to see information easily. It also helps us to see what things are most or least popular and common.

Display and discuss the photocopiable pages 'Ways to organise data', 'Sports block graph' and 'Pictograms' from the CD-ROM to revise the ways of organising information. For each of these (list, table, block graph and pictogram) ask questions such as: *How is the information shown here? What four things can you tell me from this table? Which is the most popular? Which is the least common? How many people were asked?* Together make a tally of the children who have school dinners, packed lunches or, if appropriate, go home at lunch time. Turn this into a list and then a table. Discuss what is the same and what is different about each representation.

Paired work: Ask the children to work in pairs, making a list and a table and answering some questions about them. Distribute photocopiable page 'Lists and tables' from the CD-ROM. Demonstrate how to answer the questions using the examples provided.

Progress check: As the children are working on their activity ask questions such as:

● *What does that list tell you? How many people were asked?*
● *What is the same about a list and table? What is different?*

Review

Ask a few pairs to share their work from the task. They need to explain how they decided which numbers and words to put in their list and table and how they found the answers to the questions. Ask other children to show their own lists, tables and questions. Can the rest of the class answer their questions?

Curriculum objectives
- To interpret and construct tables.
- To ask and answer simple questions by counting the number of objects in each category and sorting the categories by quantity.
- To ask and answer questions about totalling and comparing categorical data.

Success criteria
- I can make and interpret a pictogram.

You will need
Photocopiable sheets
'Pictograms'
Equipment
Sticky notes; A1 paper

Differentiation
The children should work in mixed attainment groups. Check that less confident learners have the opportunity to take part and that the more confident learners don't dominate.

Lesson 2
Oral and mental starter 40

Main teaching activities

Whole-class work: The whole-class work will take up this lesson and the group work will take place in the next lesson. Display photocopiable page 'Pictograms' from the CD-ROM. Ask: *What is this called? Give me as much information as you can from it.* Tell the children that they are going to solve this problem using a pictogram: *The school caretaker needs to paint the door of our classroom. He has some paints in his shed, but doesn't know which colour to use. He wants your advice. He wants to find out which is the most popular colour. Here are the colour choices: red, yellow, blue, brown and orange.* Give the children some time to talk to a friend and discuss their favourite colour. Make a tally of their choices on the board. Give each child a sticky note and ask them to draw a smiley face in the colour they have chosen. Say: *Each smiley face represents one child. How many do we need for red paint?* Invite the children who have drawn red smiley faces to stick their sticky note onto the prepared A1 skeleton pictogram. Repeat for the other four colours.

Progress check: As you work through the activity ask questions such as:
- *How many of you want yellow paint?*
- *How many more voted for x paint than y?*
- *How many smiley faces should be on our pictogram at the end?*

Review

Analyse the class pictogram with the children, asking them to tell you as many facts about it as possible. Ask each other questions and come to a conclusion about which paint the caretaker should use.

Curriculum objectives
- To interpret and construct simple pictograms.
- To ask and answer questions about totalling and comparing categorical data.

Success criteria
- I can make and interpret a pictogram.

You will need
Photocopiable sheets
'Which colour?'

Differentiation
Less confident learners
Provide adult help to encourage children to talk about the graph.
More confident learners
Encourage children to make up their own questions for the class to answer.

Lesson 3
Oral and mental starter 43

Main teaching activities

Whole-class work: Discuss and review the pictogram work the class did in lesson 2. Explain that today they will be answering questions from a pictogram and then making up their own.

Paired work: Distribute and model photocopiable page 'Which colour?' from the CD-ROM. The children work in mixed-ability pairs.

Progress check: Spend a few minutes with pairs of children as they work and ask such questions as:
- *What is a pictogram?*
- *What do the symbols represent? Can you explain this in a different way?*

Review

Work through the questions on 'Which colour?'. Invite a few pairs to share the pictograms they made up. Invite more confident children to ask the class their questions. Finally ask the class to make up other questions. Assess how confidently they give correct answers.

Curriculum objectives
- To interpret and construct block diagrams.
- To ask and answer simple questions by counting the number of objects in each category and sorting the categories by quantity.
- To ask and answer questions about totalling and comparing categorical data.

Success criteria
- I can find information from a block graph.

You will need
Photocopiable sheets
'Sports block graph'

General resources
Interactive activity 'Sorting it out'

Equipment
Sticky notes; A1 paper

Differentiation
The children should work in mixed-attainment groups.

Lesson 4
Oral and mental starter 45

Main teaching activities

Whole-class work: Explain that the children are now going to look at block graphs. Ask: *Who can remember this?* Show photocopiable page 'Sports block graph' from the CD-ROM. Ask the children to tell you as much as they can about it and to state all the possible facts. Ask the children who may find this difficult first, when the more obvious facts have not already been said. Then ask them to give you information that requires them to work out how many more and how many altogether.

Now say: *We are going to make our own block graph to show our favourite sports.* Collect about six examples of sports that the children like. Ask them to choose their favourite one. Ask them to draw a stick picture of themselves playing the sport on a sticky note. Write the sport names on sticky notes to label the axis.

Review

Show the class your labels and numbers and invite children to stick them onto the prepared A1 skeleton graph, explaining why. Do the other children agree? Invite everyone to add their sticky note pictures to the correct column. Discuss what this graph shows and ask questions, particularly: *How many more/less/ altogether?* Encourage the class to ask similar questions. Finally ask: *Which is the most popular sport for this class?*

Interactive activity 'Sorting it out' on the CD-ROM offers further practice of representing data in a block graph.

Curriculum objectives
- To interpret and construct block diagrams.
- To ask and answer questions about totalling and comparing categorical data.

Success criteria
- I can make and interpret a block graph.

You will need
Photocopiable sheets
'Our sports graph'

General resources
'0–100 number cards'

Equipment
Block graph from lesson 4; large squared paper

Differentiation
Less confident learners
Adapt the photocopiable sheet so the axes are labelled and five numbers used.

More confident learners
Adapt the photocopiable sheet so there are no numbers on the graph.

Lesson 5
Oral and mental starter 46

Main teaching activities

Whole-class work: Show the class the block graph from lesson 4. Say: *Today you are going to make your own block graph. You need to help* (name the PE coordinator) *decide what things to buy for the sports cupboard.* Model what the children need to do using large squared paper: *With your partner you need to choose five sports that we play – or you'd like to play – at school. You need to finish a skeleton graph like the one we used yesterday. You need to finish it by adding labels.* The children use a pack of shuffled number cards 1–9 and they pick one at a time. Once they have picked a card they cannot use it again. These represent the number of children who choose each sport. They then draw blocks of the right height, for example, if they pick 5, they colour five squares above that sport.

Paired work: Distribute photocopiable page 'Our sports graph' from the CD-ROM for the children to use. They follow the instructions as in teaching.

Progress check: During the activity visit pairs of children to check that they understand what they need to do.

Review

Ask each pair to join with another pair, share their graphs and say four facts that their graph shows. They then share their graphs and facts with the class. Invite children to ask the class a few of their questions. Recap by asking questions such as: *Why are lists, tables, pictograms and block graphs useful for showing information? What is the difference between a list and a table? What is the same? What does a pictogram look like? What about a block graph?*

Counting in steps of different sizes

Most children should be able to link counting in, for example, twos to their two times table.

Some children will require additional practice so provide them with a strip of paper which shows the sequence and gradually cover the numbers in order.

1. Check
39 Counting in steps

Children count forwards and backwards in steps of two, three, five and ten. Ask them to write down multiplication facts, e.g. if counting in threes, when they say 18, they write $3 \times 6 = 18$. Observe which children are confident and which need further practice.

- *What is eight lots of two? Can you write that as a number sentence?*
- *If we count in fives what number will we say on the sixth count? How do you know?*

2. Assess

Show the counting stick. Tell the children that at one end is zero and the other is 50. Ask them what steps they need to count in to get from one end to the other (fives). Point to various divisions and ask them to tell you what number would be there and then to write the appropriate number sentence. Point to the fifth division and ask them how many lots of five make 25. Repeat for counting in steps of two, three and ten. Record the outcomes.

3. Further practice

Photocopiable page 169 'Counting in steps' provides practice in counting in steps of two, three, five and ten. They should work on this independently.

Addition and subtraction

Most children should be able to partition to add two-digit numbers and will have other mental calculation methods that they can use.

Some children will not have made such progress and will need to focus on partitioning for addition.

1. Check
44 Adding

Use the oral and mental starter to check which children can confidently add numbers together using partitioning. Encourage them to add this way first and then think of another strategy they could have used. Ask: *How can you add 23 and 29? Is there another way?*

2. Assess

Ask the children to pick two number cards 10–40. When they have, they add them together using partitioning. Then ask them to use another method, (this could be sequencing, bridging ten or adding a multiple of ten and adjusting depending on the numbers chosen). Observe how confident they are at doing this. Record the outcomes.

3. Further practice

Photocopiable page 170 'Adding problems (2)' is designed as an activity to practise addition using two different strategies. The children use partitioning as one method and then check using another strategy. Expect most children to be able to do this. Some children may only be able to partition. Make a note of these children.

Curriculum objectives
● To calculate mathematical statements for multiplication and division.

You will need
1. Check
Oral and mental starter
[41] Spider charts

2. Assess
'0–100 number cards'; interlocking cubes

3. Further practice
Oral and mental starters
[29] Counting in steps of two, five and ten
[39] Counting in steps
[15] Multiples

Photocopiable sheets
'Grouping (2)'

Curriculum objectives
● To recognise, find, name and write fractions ⅓, ¼, ⅔ and ¾.

You will need
1. Check
Oral and mental starter
[26] Finding fractions

2. Assess
Counters

3. Further practice
Oral and mental starter
[43] Counting in fractions

Photocopiables sheets
'Finding fractions'

Division by grouping

Most children should be able to use their fingers or a number line to count on in steps of 2, 3, 5 and 10 to group.

Some children will not have made such progress and will require concrete apparatus to assist them.

1. Check
[41] Spider charts

Use the oral and mental starter 'Spider charts' with the answers to check which children can now tell you how many groups of the divisor can be made from the numbers that you point to. Ask: *How many fives are there in 30? How can you check? How many twos are there in 24? How can you check?*

2. Assess

Give each child a number card 1–50. Ask them to find out how many groups of ten can be made from their number and how many, if any, will be left. Ask them to show you by counting on in tens using their fingers and then draw a number line and mark on the jumps. Some children may find this difficult. If they do, give them a number card below 20 and some interlocking cubes. They find out how many groups of two can be made from their number. Record the outcomes.

3. Further practice

Expect most children to complete photocopiable page 170 'Grouping (2)' successfully using their fingers and a number line. Some children may need concrete apparatus, so make sure this is available in the form of counters or interlocking cubes.

Fractions

Most children should be able to successfully find fractions for numbers to 30. Some children will require concrete apparatus to assist them.

1. Check
[26] Finding fractions

As you work on the activities suggested in the oral and mental starter 'Finding fractions', observe the children to assess their confidence in finding halves and quarters of even numbers. Observe the strategies they use, for example, halving and halving again for quarters. Give the less confident learners counters to help them. Ask: *What is a fraction? Can you explain in a different way? What can you tell me about a half? What about a quarter? How many quarters are the same as a half?*

2. Assess

Give each child 20 counters. Ask them to show you one half and to tell you how many halves make a whole. Observe how they do this. Do they share the counters into two groups or can they show you straight away? Repeat this for quarters and three quarters. Then repeat for other multiples of four. Record the outcomes.

3. Further practice

Photocopiable page 'Finding fractions' from the CD-ROM asks the children to find halves, quarters and three quarters of numbers. Provide counters in case they are needed. Expect the children to draw pictures to show their thinking and to write the number sentence in the space provided.

Oral and mental starters

Number and place value

38 More doubling and halving

Show the children a numeral card from 10 to 20. Ask the children to double it by partitioning. You may need to remind them how to do this, so demonstrate on the board for double 13:

39 Counting in steps

As you swing the pendulum from side to side, ask the children to count in twos from zero to 24 and back. Repeat with threes to 36, fives to 60 and tens to 120. Divide the class in half. Swing the pendulum; as it swings towards one half of the children they count in tens to 120 and back. As it swings towards the other group they should count in fives to 60 and back. Repeat for different combinations of steps, for example, twos and fives, twos and threes.

Addition and subtraction

40 Taking away

Tell the children that they will be practising taking single digits away from two-digit numbers. Write 20 on the board. Hold up a number card 1–9 (say, 3). The children take 3 away from 20. Do this until you use all the cards. Invite children to explain how they worked out the answer. Repeat for other two-digit numbers less than 30.

44 Adding

Tell the children that they will be practising adding pairs of two-digit numbers. Show pairs of number cards between 10–40. The children add these using one of the mental calculation strategies they have been practising. They write their strategy and answer on whiteboards. Compare solutions.

Multiplication and division

41 Spider charts

Count together in multiples, using fingers. Stop at various points, such as the seventh finger and ask: *How many lots of two make 14? So we can say 2 × 7 = 14.* Give the children challenges to complete in pairs, using the small spider charts. They take turns to point at the numbers around whichever chart you say and then give the answers. Time them for two minutes. How many times can they go round the chart?

42 More multiples

Tell the children that they will rehearse multiples of two, five and ten. Call out numbers, for example 150, 48, 75. The children consider the last number that you say. They clap if it is a multiple of two, jump once if a multiple of five and do both actions for a multiple of ten.

Fractions

43 Counting in fractions

Show a counting stick and say: *Zero is at one end and five is at the other. What size steps do you think we need to count in?* Try out all the ideas the children say. Then agree that you need to count in halves. Do this from 0 to 5 and back again. Repeat, but this time move your finger in different directions so that they really need to focus on where it is, for example, 0, ½, 1, ½, 1, 1½, 2, 1½, ½.

Extension
Over time, build in counting in quarters.

Measurement: time

45 Day of the week, months of the year

Tell the children they will practise the days of the week and months of the year. Begin by reciting both in order. Give groups of children a selection of cards showing the days of the week and months of the year. Give them clues, such as the day before Sunday, the month after September. The children in the group with the appropriate card stand up.

46 Time differences

Give the children a small clock each. Ask them to find different o'clock, quarter past, half past and quarter to times on their clocks. Next ask them to use a number line to find time differences, for example, half past 3 to quarter past 5. You could put these into problem scenarios such as: *Demi went for a bike ride. She left home at quarter to 10 in the morning and arrived back at quarter past 1 in the afternoon. How long was her bike ride?*

Name: _____   Date: _____

What shape could it be?

■ Look at these 2D shapes. Write their names inside each one.
■ They are the faces of some 3D shapes. Which 3D shapes could they be? Write down all the ones you can think of.

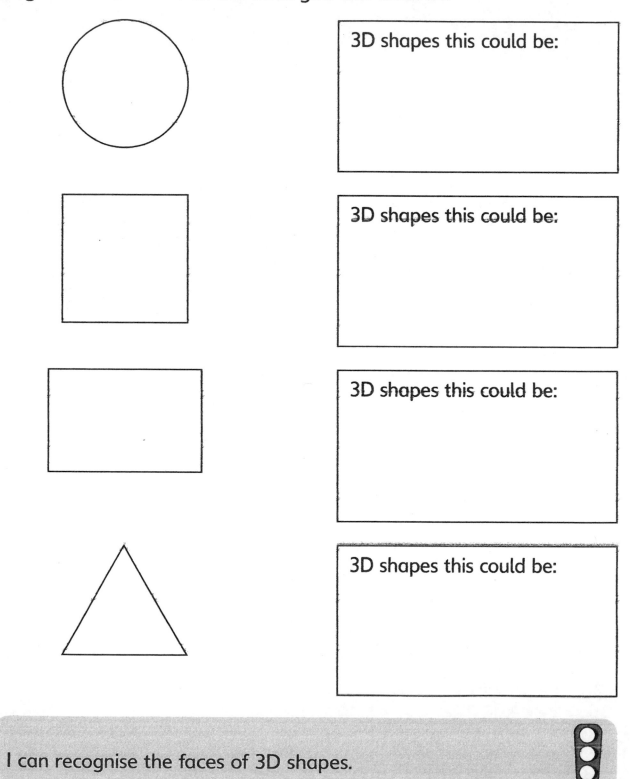

3D shapes this could be:

3D shapes this could be:

3D shapes this could be:

3D shapes this could be:

I can recognise the faces of 3D shapes.

How did you do?

What shape could it be?

■ Look at these 2D shapes. Write their names inside each one.
■ They are the faces of some 3D shapes. Which 3D shapes could they be? Write down all the ones you can think of.

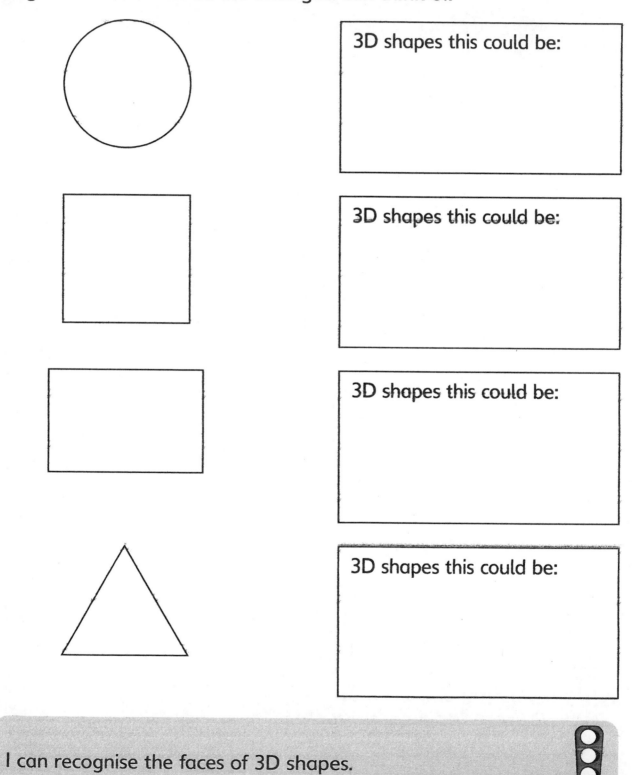

3D shapes this could be:

3D shapes this could be:

3D shapes this could be:

3D shapes this could be:

I can recognise the faces of 3D shapes.

How did you do?

Name: _____   Date: _____

Counting in steps

- Starting at zero, count in steps of each number to the 12th step.

Count in twos

Count in threes

Count in fives

Count in tens

I can count in 2s, 3s, 5s and 10s.

How did you do?

Adding problems (2)

- Answer these calculations using partitioning.
- Check them using a different strategy.

1. 36 + 25

Partitioning	Another strategy

2. 42 + 34

Partitioning	Another strategy

3. 28 + 32

Partitioning	Another strategy

4. 43 + 29

Partitioning	Another strategy

I can solve problems using addition.

How did you do?

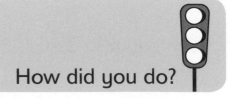

PHOTOCOPIABLE   ■SCHOLASTIC www.scholastic.co.uk

Grouping (2)

- Work out the answers to these by grouping.
- Draw a number line to show what you have done.

1. | $12 \div 3 =$

Draw your number line here:

2. | $16 \div 2 =$

Draw your number line here:

3. | $25 \div 5 =$

Draw your number line here:

4. | $30 \div 10 =$

Draw your number line here:

5. | $15 \div 3 =$

Draw your number line here:

I can group in 2s, 3s, 5s, and 10s.

How did you do?

Number and place value: estimating, counting, comparing and ordering

Expected prior learning

Children should be able to:

- count forwards or backwards in steps of two, five and ten
- partition two-digit numbers into tens and ones in different ways
- begin to partition numbers to 100 in different ways.

Topic	Curriculum objectives	Expected outcomes
Number and place value	**Lesson 1**	
	To recognise the place value of each digit in a two-digit number (tens, ones).	Partition numbers in different ways.
	To identify, represent and estimate numbers using different representations, including the number line.	Estimate quantities and count to check.
	To read and write numbers to at least 100 in numerals and in words.	Begin to write numbers to 100 in words.
	Lesson 2	
	To recognise the place value of each digit in a two-digit number (tens, ones).	Understand the job of zero and the equals sign.
	To identify, represent and estimate numbers using different representations, including the number line.	
	Lesson 3	
	To identify, represent and estimate numbers using different representations, including the number line.	Rounding numbers to the nearest ten.
	Lesson 4	
	To recognise the place value of each digit in a two-digit number (tens, ones).	Order and compare numbers.
	To identify, represent and estimate numbers using different representations, including the number line.	Round numbers. Partition.
	Lesson 5	
	To identify, represent and estimate numbers using different representations, including the number line.	Use rounding to solve simple oral problems.
	To use place value and number facts to solve problems.	

Preparation

Lesson 4: enlarge a 100 square on to A3 paper

You will need

Photocopiable sheets

'Which number am I?'; 'Round it!' instructions; 'Round it! gameboard' (1) and (2); 'In the balance'; 'Lunch money'

General resources

'Which number am I? template'; 'Arrow cards'; 'Hundred square'; '0–100 number cards'

Equipment

1p, 10p, 5p and 2p coins; bead string; individual whiteboards; balance scales; 100g and two 50g weights; counters

Further practice

Use the 'Which number am I? template' to offer further practice of identifying two-digit numbers.

Oral and mental starters for week 1

See bank of starters on page 209. Oral and mental starters are also on the CD-ROM.

47 Adding 9 and 11

48 Doubling and near doubling

Overview of progression

During this week the children will continue to practise their counting skills by counting in steps of two, three, five and ten from and to zero. They will extend and develop their understanding of rounding and use this to estimate answers to problems. They will be looking closely at the role of zero and the equals sign. They will reinforce and continue to consolidate partitioning numbers in different ways and comparing and ordering them.

Watch out for

Some children may have difficulty counting in steps of different sizes. Give them written prompts such as number cards with sequences counting in steps of, for example, two from 0 to 20. Ask them to practise using the card and then only refer to it when they get stuck.

Creative context

Ask the children to look out for times when they say or see numbers in other contexts. They could make a note of these in words or pictures.

Vocabulary

count in twos, count in fives, count in tens, continue, **multiple of**, nearest ten, one-digit number, place, place holder, **place value**, predict, represents, sequence, stands for, tens, tens digit, two-digit number, 'teens' number

Curriculum objectives

- To recognise the place value of each digit in a two-digit number (tens, ones).
- To identify, represent and estimate numbers using different representations, including the number line.
- To read and write numbers to at least 100 in numerals and in words.

Success criteria

- I can partition numbers in different ways.
- I can estimate quantities.
- I can write numbers to 100 in words.

You will need

Photocopiable sheets

'Which number am I?'

General resources

'Which number am I? template'

Equipment

1p, 10p, 5p and 2p coins; individual whiteboards

Differentiation

Less confident learners

Adapt photocopiable page 'Which number am I' so the children are working with amounts to 20p.

More confident learners

Adapt photocopiable page 'Which number am I' so the children are working with amounts to £1. Once they have completed the activity, ask them to make up some problems of their own.

Main teaching activities

Whole-class work: Explain that in this lesson the children will be recapping their knowledge of writing numbers, odd and even numbers, place value and counting by grouping objects. Call out five or six two-digit and three-digit numbers for the children to write on their whiteboards. Pick one or two of the two-digit numbers and ask them to try writing these in words. Invite volunteers to write the words on the board and the class see if they agree. For each number ask: *Put your thumbs up if you think this is an odd number, put them down if you think it is even. How do you know? What do odd numbers end with? How about even? Why?* Discuss the place value of each number and ask the children to partition them in at least two different ways. Next ask them to count on from that number in ones and then tens, fives and twos. Discuss the patterns seen.

Show 57 1p coins. Ask: *How can we count them?* Ask the children to estimate how many there are and write their estimate on their whiteboards. Then change groups of ten pennies to 10p coins, five to a 5p coin and the remaining two for a 2p coin. Discuss how close the children's estimates were. Ask: *If I had 105 pennies, how many 10p coins could I make?* (10) *What could I change those for?* (£1 coin) Repeat with similar examples.

Paired work: The children should work in ability pairs. Tell them that they will be working on some problems that involve finding amounts of money that fit certain criteria. Demonstrate using the two puzzles on photocopiable page 'Which number am I?' from the CD-ROM. Work through each clue, eliminating numbers as you do, completing the 'I can't be...' statements.

Progress check: Check the class are on track by asking:

- *How do you know that it can't be this number?*
- *Is there another number it can't be? Why?*

Review

Take feedback from the activity, asking the children to share their clues with the class and ask the class to work out which numbers they could be thinking of. Write some missing number sentences on the board, such as 53 + 50 = ☐, 67 = ☐ + 27, 49 = 19 + ☐, 98 = ☐ + 38. Ask the children to complete them, explaining how they know.

For further practice, a template of 'Which number am I?' has been provided.

SUMMER 1

WEEK 1

Curriculum objectives
● To recognise the place value of each digit in a two-digit number (tens, ones).
● To identify, represent and estimate numbers using different representations, including the number line.

Success criteria
● I can tell you about a zero.
● I can tell you about the equals.

You will need
Photocopiable sheets
'In the balance'
General resources
'Arrow cards'
Equipment
Individual whiteboards; balance scales; 100g and 2×50g weights

Differentiation
Less confident learners
Adapt photocopiable page 'In the balance' so children work with simpler calculations.

More confident learners
Adapt photocopiable page 'In the balance' so children work with more complex calculations.

Lesson 2 — Oral and mental starter 48

Main teaching activities

Whole-class work: Tell the children that today they will be thinking about the special jobs of zero and the equals sign. Write the number 25 on the board. Ask the children to partition it into tens and ones on their whiteboards in as many ways as they can. Write 20 + 5 = 25 and 10 + 15 = 25 on the board and ask the children to check that they have written those. Make 25 using arrow cards. Invite two children to help you. Ask the child with the 5 to move away. Say: *What is left in the place of the five? What would the number say if the zero wasn't there? The zero holds the place of the ones number. We call it a place holder.* Repeat this with 49, 18, 67 and 34. Then write 104 on the board. Ask which number the zero is the place holder for. Repeat for 108 and 2045.

Ask the children what the = sign means. Invite a child to draw one on the board. Many children think that the = sign means 'the answer'. It is very important for them to understand that it means that what is on one side of the sign is equal to what is on the other side. Demonstrate this with a balance scales. Put a 100g weight in one side and a 50g weight in the other side and ask whether both sides are equal. Agree that they are not. Add another 50g so that they are equal. Write a number sentence on the board to show this: 100g = 50g + 50g.

Write on the board: 10 + 5 = 11 + ☐. Ask: *What can you put in the square to make the number sentence true? How do you know?* Encourage the children to work out the right side and decide what to do to make the other side the same. Agree the missing number is 4. Repeat for other numbers, for example: 12 − ☐ = 10 − 1, 20 − 6 = ☐ + 4, ☐ + 10 = 10 × 2.

Paired work: Demonstrate the example from photocopiable page 'In the balance' from the CD-ROM. Let the children complete the sheet in pairs.

Progress check: Visit pairs to make sure they understand the task. Ask questions such as:

- *If I have ten and four on this side of the equals sign, what could I have on the other?*
- *Are there any other possibilities? Can you think of more? What are they?*

Review

Invite children to share examples of the number sentences they made during the activity. Write an incorrect number sentence on the board, such as, 11 + 5 = 20 − 10. Ask the children to tell you what is wrong with it and how they can make it correct. Repeat with other examples.

Curriculum objectives
● To identify, represent and estimate numbers using different representations, including the number line.

Success criteria
● I can round numbers to the nearest ten.

You will need
Photocopiable sheets
'Round it! instructions'; 'Round it! gameboard'

General resources
'0–100 number cards'

Equipment
Individual whiteboards; counters; bead string

Differentiation
If the less confident learners find the instructions for the 'Round it' game difficult to understand, let them work with a more confident learner or with adult support.

Lesson 3
Oral and mental starter 47

Main teaching activities

Whole-class work: This lesson is about rounding numbers to the nearest ten. Ask: *Does anyone know what we mean by rounding?* Take suggestions and then explain using a bead string or draw a numbered number line from 0 to 20.

Mark 13 with an arrow. Explain that to round 13 they need to find the multiple of ten that it is closest to. Agree it is closest to ten. Repeat for other numbers from 0 to 20. Explain that numbers ending with 5 are always rounded up, so for example 15 would be rounded to 20. Draw a number line with 11 marks but no numbers. Write 26 on the seventh mark. Ask: *Which two tens numbers should I put on this number line? Which one is 26 closest to?* Repeat with a variety of numbers to 100.

Group work: Tell the children that they are going to practise rounding by playing a game. Demonstrate 'Round it!' Let the children play in pairs or small groups using 'Round it! gameboard'. Encourage them to play twice, the second time recording in the way shown in the instructions.

Progress check: Check that everyone is rounding in the correct way by asking questions such as:

● *What is 13 rounded to the nearest ten? Can you explain why?*
● *Which numbers would I round to 20? How do you know?*

Review

Call out numbers for the children to round to the nearest ten on whiteboards. Ask the children to talk to a partner about occasions when they think rounding might be helpful. Take feedback and try to elicit the idea that rounding can make mental calculation easier. Give the example of adding 9 or 11 by adding 10 and adjusting.

Curriculum objectives

● To recognise the place value of each digit in a two-digit number (tens, ones).
● To identify, represent and estimate numbers.

Success criteria

● I can order and round numbers from 0 up to 100.

You will need

Photocopiable sheets

'Round it! instructions'; 'Round it! gameboard'

General resources

'Hundred square'; 'Arrow cards'; '0–100 number cards'

Equipment

Individual whiteboards

Differentiation

Less confident learners

Give them 'Round it! gameboard (2)' that show numbers 10 and 20 only.

More confident learners

Children work on the challenge.

Lesson 4   Oral and mental starter 48

Main teaching activities

Whole-class work: Explain to the children that this lesson is about ordering numbers to 100 and rounding them to the nearest ten. Place a pile of two-digit number cards on the table in front of you. Invite five children to pick a card and show them to the class. They order them from smallest to largest. Ask the children to tell you how these numbers can be partitioned. Ask them to make a few number sentences that involve < and >. Repeat. Ask the children to find the numbers on the enlarged class 100 square. Mark these numbers and say: *We are going to round these to the nearest ten.* Remind the children that rounding can help when calculating mentally – it is easier to work with multiples of ten. Together round the numbers you marked on the 100 square. Ask: *Is 23 closer to 20 or 30?* On the 100 square count how far 23 is from both numbers. Call out numbers for the children to round on their whiteboards. Include those ending in five.

Paired work: In similar-ability pairs, distribute photocopiable pages 'Round it! instructions' and 'Round it! gameboard' from the CD-ROM. When the children have finished they should play again and record their work.

Progress check: Spend time with those you wish to assess. Ask: *How do you know that number is rounded up? What are the ones digits for numbers that are rounded down?*

Review

Call out numbers for the children to round on their whiteboards. Ask them to talk to a partner about when they think rounding might be helpful.

Curriculum objectives

● To identify, represent and estimate numbers.
● To use rounding to solve problems.

Success criteria

● I can solve word problems involving rounding.

You will need

Photocopiable sheets

'Lunch money'

Equipment

Individual whiteboards

Differentiation

Less confident learners

Adapt photocopiable page 'Lunch money' so children work with smaller amounts for the prices.

More confident learners

Adapt photocopiable page 'Lunch money' so the full calculation is used to check.

Lesson 5   Oral and mental starter 48

Main teaching activities

Whole-class work: Ask the children to tell you what they remember about rounding. Call out some numbers for them to round on their whiteboards, include numbers that end in 5. Recap why rounding can be helpful. Call out numbers such as 24, 37 and 63. The children add 9 and 11 by adding 10 and adjusting. The children show you their answers on their whiteboards. Repeat this for taking away 9 and 11. Move on to estimating the answers to problems through rounding: *Imagine I am in a shop and I have 30p. I would like to buy three chews. They cost 9p each. Do I have enough money? How can I decide quickly?* Ask the children to talk to each other and come up with suggestions. Agree that as 9p is close to 10p and three chews would be 30p, so you do have enough.

Give another problem: *I am in a shop and have 50p. I want to buy a bag of crisps for 32p and a can of cola for 29p. Have I enough money?* Ask the children what they think, then work through the problem on the board: 29p is nearly 30p, 32p and 30p are 62p which is much more than you have.

Independent work: Distribute photocopiable page 'Lunch money' and demonstrate what to do using the first example. Emphasise that the children do not need to calculate the exact answers, only estimate the answers by rounding.

Progress check: Invite volunteers to share examples of the problems they are solving. Do the class agree with their answers?

Review

Invite some children to explain how they made their estimations. Check each estimate by working out the answer. Recap the < and > symbols and ask them to make sentences to compare their estimates with the actual answer.

Addition and subtraction: using mental calculation strategies

Expected prior learning

Children should be able to:

- add and subtract using partitioning and counting on
- use the inverse operation to check additions and subtractions.

Topic	Curriculum objectives	Expected outcomes
Addition and subtraction	**Lesson 1**	
	To recognise and use the inverse relationship between addition and subtraction and use this to check calculations and solve missing number problems.	Use inverse operations to solve missing number problems.
	Lesson 2	
	To recognise and use the inverse relationship between addition and subtraction and use this to check calculations and solve missing number problems.	Use inverse operations to solve missing number problems.
	Lesson 3	
	To add and subtract numbers using concrete objects, pictorial representations, and mentally, including: a two-digit number and ones.	Add and subtract using sequencing (keeping first number whole and partitioning the second).
	To recognise and use the inverse relationship between addition and subtraction and use this to check calculations and solve missing number problems.	
	To show that addition of two numbers can be done in any order (commutative) and subtraction of one number from another cannot.	
	Lesson 4	
	To add and subtract numbers using concrete objects, pictorial representations, and mentally, including: two two-digit numbers.	Add and subtract using sequencing.
	To recognise and use the inverse relationship between addition and subtraction and use this to check calculations and solve missing number problems.	
	Lesson 5	
	To solve problems with addition and subtraction:	Use addition and subtraction strategies to solve simple addition and subtraction problems.
	• using concrete objects and pictorial representations, including those involving numbers, quantities and measures	
	• applying their increasing knowledge of mental and written methods.	

Preparation

Lesson 3: prepare a set of addition and subtraction vocabulary cards; enlarge a 100 square to A3

You will need

Photocopiable sheets

'What's in the box?'; 'Figure it out!'; 'Keeping it whole'; 'Adding and taking away'; 'Problems, problems'

General resources

'0–100 number cards'

Equipment

Individual whiteboards; 100 square

Further practice

Photocopiable sheets

'Ivor Dog's dog and puppy food': the children choose two or three tins to add using sequencing.

Oral and mental starters for week 2

See bank of starters on pages 208 to 209. Oral and mental starters are also on the CD-ROM.

47 Adding 9 and 11

48 Doubling and near doubling

49 Counting in steps of different sizes

51 Make ten

52 Number pairs again

Overview of progression

During this week children will continue to develop their understanding of addition and subtraction. They will be solving missing number sentences using the inverse operation so consolidating their understanding of the relationship between addition and subtraction. There will be a focus on addition and subtraction using sequencing with opportunities for the children to choose their own preferred methods.

Watch out for

Some children may find it difficult solving missing number sentences. Give these children single-digit sentences that involve using number pairs to ten and gradually increase the size of the numbers.

Creative context

Ask the children to look at toy catalogues with whole pounds. Encourage them to add and subtract pairs of prices to find totals and differences using the sequencing strategy.

Vocabulary

add, addition, altogether, **bridging ten**, counting on, difference, **inverse operation**, make, **partitioning**, plus, subtract, sum, take away, **tens boundary**, total

Lesson 1 — Oral and mental starter 47

Main teaching activities

Whole-class work: Ask: *What can you tell me about addition and subtraction?* Establish that numbers can be placed in any order for addition and the answer will be the same, for subtraction the answer will usually be different. Addition and subtraction are inverse operations. Write examples of these on the board to demonstrate.

$$12 \underset{-\ 5}{\overset{+\ 5}{\rightleftarrows}} 17 \qquad 14 \underset{-\ 8}{\overset{+\ 8}{\rightleftarrows}} 22$$

Ask the children what these show. Ask them to write down two number sentences for each diagram on their whiteboards. Use the arrow diagrams to make up questions, such as: $\square + 5 = 17$, $\square - 5 = 12$, $14 + \square = 22$. Ask the children to find the answers using the arrow diagrams. Repeat with several similar examples, including higher two-digit numbers. Discuss strategies for finding the answers reinforcing the aspect of inversion.

Paired work: Distribute photocopiable page 'What's in the box?' from the CD-ROM and model the example, then let the children complete the sheet.

Progress check: Visit pairs of children to make sure they understand what to do. Ask questions such as:

● *How are you going to work out what number goes there?*
● *What will you do to check that you are correct?*

Review

Take feedback about the activity. Invite volunteers to demonstrate what they did on the board. Finish the lesson by recapping the important points about addition and subtraction.

Lesson 2 — Oral and mental starter 48

Main teaching activities

Whole-class work: Remind the children of the problems they solved in lesson 1. Explain that today they will use other symbols for the missing numbers. Pick two number cards to 50 (such as 45 and 23) and make a number sentence with a triangle to represent the first number and the cards as the second and answer numbers. Relate this to the inversion arrow diagram. Ask: *What do we know that can help us?* Write these number sentences on the board: $\triangle + 23 = 45$ and $45 - 23 = \triangle$. *Which number sentence can help us see what the triangle stands for?* Agree the subtraction and work out the answer by sequencing ($45 - 20 - 3 = 22$). Work through five or six similar examples.

Paired work: Distribute photocopiable page 'Figure it out' from the CD-ROM and demonstrate what the children need to do. They should work in similar-ability pairs to complete it.

Progress check: Invite some pairs to describe their work so far. Check that everyone is doing something similar.

Review

Ask some volunteers to share an example of their work and explain what they did. Look at number sentences with symbols in the middle. Write on the board: $23 + \triangle = 45$. Can the children tell you how to solve this? Ask what other number sentences they can make from it. Say that because addition can be done in any order the number sentence could say: $\triangle + 23 = 45$. Use the inversion arrow diagram to show that $\triangle = 22$. Repeat with other examples.

Curriculum objectives
● To add and subtract using concrete objects, pictorial representations, and mentally, including: two two-digit numbers.
● To recognise and use the inverse relationship between addition and subtraction and use this to check calculations and solve missing number problems.
● To show that addition can be done in any order (commutative) and subtraction of one number from another cannot.

Success criteria
● I can add and subtract two-digit numbers by keeping the first number whole and partitioning the second.
● I can check a calculation by doing the opposite operation.

You will need
Photocopiable sheets
'Keeping it whole'
General resources
'Hundred square'
Equipment
Individual whiteboards

Differentiation
Less confident learners
Adapt photocopiable page 'Keeping it whole' with numbers to 30. Allow the children to use 100 squares.
More confident learners
Adapt photocopiable page 'Keeping it whole' with numbers to 100.

Lesson 3
Oral and mental starter 49

Main teaching activities
Whole-class work: Recap what the children did in the previous lesson. Ask them what they can tell you about addition and subtraction. Expect them to include that addition can be done in any order and the answer will be the same but that this is not always the case for subtraction and also that addition and subtraction are inverse operations. Give examples from lesson 2 to illustrate the last point. Revise the appropriate vocabulary using the cards you have prepared; hold up the cards as the children say them and stick them on the board. Add any the children have forgotten.

Say that today they will revisit sequencing (keeping the first number whole and partitioning the second). Demonstrate this using the enlarged 100 square. Write 34 + 25 on the board. Explain that we can keep 34 whole and partition 25 into 20 and 5 to add 20 (54) and then 5 (59). Show these stages on the class 100 square. Record on the board: 34 + 20 + 5 = 54 + 5 = 59. Repeat with four or five additions. Expect the children to work these out on their whiteboards. Check each by subtraction.

Move on to a subtraction, such as 53 − 24. The children keep 53 whole and partition 24 into 20 and 4. They take away 20, then 4. Show the stages on the 100 square and record: 53 − 20 − 4 = 33 − 4 = 29. Repeat with several subtractions. Check by addition.

Group work: Distribute and demonstrate photocopiable page 'Keeping it whole' from the CD-ROM, which gives the children an opportunity to practise what they have learned. They should work in similar-ability groups.

Progress check: Check to make sure everyone has understood what to do by asking two or three children to give examples.

Review
Take feedback about the activity and then link their work to money problems. For example: *Sally had 67p. She spent 23p. How much did she have left?* Ask the children to work this out on their whiteboards using sequencing:
67p − 20p − 3p = 44p. Try a few similar problems. For each, check using the inverse operation.

Curriculum objectives
● To add and subtract using concrete objects, pictorial representations, and mentally, including: two two-digit numbers.
● To recognise and use the inverse relationship between addition and subtraction and use this to check calculations and solve missing number problems.

Success criteria
● I can add by counting on along a number line.
● I can find differences by counting on.

You will need
Photocopiable sheets
'Adding and taking away'
Equipment
Individual whiteboards

Differentiation
Less confident learners
Adapt photocopiable page 'Adding and taking away' so that the children are adding and subtracting numbers to 30.

More confident learners
Adapt photocopiable page 'Adding and taking away' so that the children are adding and subtracting numbers to 100.

Lesson 4 — Oral and mental starter 51

Main teaching activities

Whole-class work: Continue to add and subtract two-digit numbers using the sequencing strategy from lesson 3. Say: *Rachel had a collection of 46 shells. She found 23 more on the beach. How many shells does she have now?* Discuss how to solve the problem. Ask the children to solve this on their whiteboards and invite someone to demonstrate how they found the answer:
46 + 20 + 3 = 66 + 3 = 69.

Repeat with similar problems. Each time check using subtraction.

Say: *Tom had 54 building blocks. He lost 16. How many did he have left?* Discuss how the children can find the answer. Ask the children to solve this problem, on their whiteboards. Invite a volunteer to demonstrate:
54 − 10 − 6 = 44 − 6 = 38.

Repeat for similar problems. Each time check using addition.

Independent work: Distribute photocopiable page 'Adding and taking away' from the CD-ROM and tell the children that this activity will give them some further practice of sequencing. Demonstrate the activity by selecting a number from the boxes at the top of the sheet. This number then should be added to and subtracted from the first number in the left-hand column. Ask the children to repeat for all of the numbers on the sheet.

Progress check: Ask individuals to demonstrate some of their calculations. Check that everyone understands what to do.

Review

Take feedback about the activity. Invite children to share their calculations and how they worked out their answers. Finish the lesson by asking children to quickly work out some calculations that involve adding and subtracting using sequencing, for example, 53 + 14, 68 − 13.

Curriculum objectives
● To solve problems with addition: using concrete objects and pictorial representations, including those involving numbers, quantities and measures: applying their increasing knowledge of mental and written methods.

Success criteria
● I can solve word problems using different strategies.
● I can check my answers using the opposite operation.

You will need
Photocopiable sheets
'Problems, problems'
General resources
'0–100 number cards'
Equipment
Individual whiteboards

Differentiation
Less confident learners
Adapt photocopiable page 'Problems, problems' so that the children are adding and subtracting numbers to 30.
More confident learners
Adapt photocopiable page 'Problems, problems' so that the children are adding and subtracting three-digit numbers.

Lesson 5
Oral and mental starter 52

Main teaching activities

Whole-class work: Explain that the children are going to use the strategies they have been learning about so far to answers problems involving addition and subtraction. Say: *Waleed counted £34 in his money box. His brother Samir counted £29 in his. How much did they have altogether?* Ask for suggestions as to how to answer the problem. Agree they need to add the two amounts. Invite the children to share the strategies they could use.

- Look for partitioning (30 + 20 + 4 + 9 = 50 + 13 = 63)
- Sequencing (34 + 20 + 9 = 54 + 9 = 63)
- Rounding and adjusting (34 + 30 − 1 = 64 − 1 = 63).

Invite them to demonstrate any suggested strategies *How can we check that we are correct?* Establish that they could add the numbers in a different order, use a different strategy or the inverse operation. Now, ask them to work out the difference in the amounts of money the boys have. Share different strategies. Look for sequencing, counting on and rounding and adjusting. Invite volunteers to demonstrate these strategies.

Work through examples of each of these using a problem within a context that you think will interest your class. *Can you make up a problem for adding and subtracting 42 and 28? Talk to your partner.* Invite pairs of children to share their problems. Together find the solution and then check using a different strategy.

Independent work: Distribute photocopiable page 'Problems, problems' from the CD-ROM and explain what the children need to do.

Progress check: Ask different children who you wish to assess these questions:
- *Which is the best strategy to use to solve this? Is there another you can use?*
- *How could you check that you are correct? Is there another way?*

Review
Take feedback about the activity. Invite children to share their strategies for finding the solutions. They should also share the problems they made up. The class finds the solutions and checks using a different strategy.

Multiplication and division: times tables and problem-solving

Expected prior learning

Children should be able to:

- answer multiplication calculations by counting up along a number line
- answer division calculations by grouping
- recognise that multiplication and division are inverse operations.

Topic	Curriculum objectives	Expected outcomes
Multiplication and division	**Lesson 1**	
	To calculate mathematical statements for multiplication and division within the multiplication tables and write them using the multiplication (×), division (÷) and equals (=) signs.	Use number lines and arrays to explore the relationship between multiplication and division.
	Lesson 2	
	To calculate mathematical statements for multiplication and division within the multiplication tables and write them using the multiplication (×), division (÷) and equals (=) signs. To recall and use multiplication and division facts for the 2, 5 and 10 multiplication tables, including recognising odd and even numbers.	Understand multiplication and division are inverse operations. Use times tables facts to answer division calculations. Complete missing number sentences.
	Lesson 3	
	To calculate mathematical statements for multiplication and division within the multiplication tables and write them using the multiplication (×), division (÷) and equals (=) signs. To recall and use multiplication and division facts for the 2, 5 and 10 multiplication tables, including recognising odd and even numbers.	Understand multiplication as repeated addition. Complete number patterns. Use multiplication facts.
	Lesson 4	
	To calculate mathematical statements for multiplication and division within the multiplication tables and write them using the multiplication (×), division (÷) and equals (=) signs.	Understand division as grouping. Understand that there might be a remainder when dividing.
	Lesson 5	
	To solve problems involving multiplication and division, using materials, arrays, repeated addition, mental methods and multiplication and division facts, including problems in contexts..	Use multiplication and division to solve and check simple problems. Make up multiplication problems.

■SCHOLASTIC

Oral and mental starters for week 3

See bank of starters on pages 208 to 209. Oral and mental starters are also on the CD-ROM.

41 Spider charts

49 Counting in steps of different sizes

61 Double that number

50 Missing numbers

53 Finding fractions again

Overview of progression

During this week children will consolidate and extend their knowledge of multiplication and division. They will continue to develop the idea that multiplication is repeated addition and division is repeated subtraction. They will check answers by using the inverse operation. They will explore arrays for both operations and link to number lines. They will reinforce repeated subtraction as grouping. They will make use of their multiplication table facts to solve problems.

Watch out for

Some children may have difficulty with the concept of grouping. Give them simple number problems and practical apparatus so that they can practise taking groups of the divisor away.

Creative context

You could ask the children to look for times in other subject areas or times during the day when they may use their multiplication tables.

Vocabulary

Divide, divided by, equal groups of, grouping, groups of, **inverse operation**, lots of, multiplied by, multiple of, multiply, **remainder**, repeated addition, repeated subtraction, times

Curriculum objectives

Curriculum objectives
- To calculate mathematical statements for multiplication and division within the multiplication tables and write them using the multiplication (×), division (÷) and equals (=) signs.

Success criteria
- I can use my times tables facts to help me solve problems.
- I can explain the relationship between multiplication and division.

You will need

Photocopiable sheets
'Array for maths! (3)'

General resources
'Multiplication and division vocabulary'

Equipment
Individual whiteboards

Differentiation

Less confident learners
Let children make the arrays with counters before drawing them.

More confident learners
When the children have finished ask them to find different arrays for the number 36.

Lesson I
Oral and mental starter 49

Main teaching activities

Whole-class work: Explain that over the next few lessons the children will be learning more about multiplication and division. Revise the meaning of *multiply* and *divide* and ask for related vocabulary. Use the cards from photocopiable page 'Multiplication and division vocabulary' from the CD-ROM and sort them into two groups: multiplication and division. Discuss any words that could be placed in both groups. Say: *Today we will focus on division and multiplication as inverse operations.* Explain this by linking to work the children did in week 2 on this for addition and subtraction as inverse operations. Demonstrate using a number line for repeated addition and repeated subtraction. Follow this by demonstrating using arrays. Draw an array of eight dots arranged in two rows of four dots. Ask volunteers to loop dots to show possible multiplications: 2 × 4 and 4 × 2. Draw it again and demonstrate eight divided into groups of two and then four and then write the division sentences: 8 ÷ 2 and 8 ÷ 4. As part of this write the repeated additions and subtractions. Ask the children to draw as many arrays as they can for 12 and to write the appropriate multiplications. Take feedback and then go through each to show the division.

Paired work: Ask the children to work in similar-ability pairs to make arrays and derive four number sentences for each: two multiplications and two divisions. Model the example from photocopiable page 'Array for maths! (3)' from the CD-ROM.

Progress check: Focus on pairs that you wish to assess. Watch how they find the answers. Can they draw arrays, make their number sentences correctly and explain what each array means?

Review

Invite pairs to draw and explain one of their arrays. Discuss what is helpful in order to do this quickly. Establish that knowledge of their tables facts will help. Go through a couple of examples. *If you take 12, a multiplication could be 2 × 6, another could be 6 × 2 because they both total 12. The divisions would be the opposite: 12 ÷ 2 = 6, 12 ÷ 6 = 2.*

Lesson 2

Curriculum objectives
● To recall and use multiplication and division facts for the 2, 5 and 10 multiplication tables.
● To calculate mathematical statements for multiplication and division.

Success criteria
● I can use my times tables to multiply and divide.

You will need
Photocopiable sheets
'Table facts'
Equipment
Individual whiteboards

Differentiation
Less confident learners
Children focus on two-times table facts.
More confident learners
Encourage children to include 3- and 4-times table facts.

Main teaching activities

Whole-class work: Repeat the inversion aspect of lesson 1 in detail. Then discuss how multiplication facts can help as in the review for lesson 1, using plenty of examples such as: *If I know that 2 x 8 = 16, I also know that 8 x 2 = 16, 16 ÷ 8 = 2 and 16 ÷ 2 = 8.* Write 8 on the board and ask the children to use their times tables knowledge to make up as many sentences as they can with 8 as the answer on their whiteboards. Ask children to draw an array to explain one of their sentences. Ask them to make up division facts in the same way. Repeat for other numbers, for example, 12, 16 and 20.

Paired work: The children should work through photocopiable page 'Table facts' from the CD-ROM in similar-ability pairs. The activity gives them a number and asks them to think of multiplication and division facts to go with it and to draw arrays to show their thinking. Encourage them to think of facts to do with their two-, five- and ten-times tables.

Progress check: To check their understanding, ask the children:
● *Can you give me a multiplication sentence for this number? Is there another?*
● *How can you check using division to make sure you are correct?*

Review

Invite pairs to explain their work. Write ☐ × ☐ = 30 on the board and ask them to think of as many ways as they can to complete the missing number sentences. Then write up 30 ÷ ☐ = ☐ and ask them to use the previous task to help them make up as many division sentences as they can.

Lesson 3

Curriculum objectives
● To calculate mathematical statements for multiplication and division.
● To recall and use multiplication and division facts for the 2, 5 and 10 multiplication tables.

Success criteria
● I can multiply using repeated addition.
● I can multiply using arrays.

You will need
Photocopiable sheets
'Number patterns'
Equipment
Individual whiteboards; interlocking cubes

Differentiation
Less confident learners
Adapt 'Number patterns' to focus on counting in twos, fives and tens.
More confident learners
Adapt 'Number patterns' to focus on counting in steps of three and four.

Main teaching activities

Whole-class work: Ask: *What can you tell me about multiplication?* Agree that it is finding the total of groups of the same number. It is also repeated addition. Write 2 × 6 on the board. Tell the children this means six lots of two. Demonstrate this by giving six children two cubes each. Together count in twos pointing at the children one at a time to give 12. Show as:
2 + 2 + 2 + 2 + 2 + 2 = 12. Agree that they could also count in twos six times using their fingers.

Repeat for other multiplication facts that involve two-, three-, five- and ten-times tables.

Say: *Tammy has seven pairs of shoes. How many shoes does she have altogether?* The children use one of the methods discussed to work out the answer. Invite them to explain how they worked out the answer. Ask other similar problems to Tammy's.

Independent work: Ask children to complete photocopiable page 'Number patterns' from the CD-ROM.

Progress check: During the activity visit groups of individuals and ask:
● *What is 3 × 6? How did you work that out?*
● *Sam had five plates. On each plate there were ten cakes. How many cakes were there altogether? What strategy did you use to work that out?*

Review

Take feedback from the activity. Invite the children to share their missing number sentences. The class work out the missing numbers. Recap the key points about multiplication.

Curriculum objectives
● To calculate mathematical statements for multiplication and division within the multiplication tables and write them using the multiplication (×), division (÷) and equals (=) signs.

Success criteria
● I can divide by grouping.
● I can tell you if there will be a remainder when I group.

You will need
General resources
'Home we go!'; 'Home we go! gameboard'; 'Number lines 0–20 and 0–30'

Equipment
Interlocking cubes; bags; individual whiteboards

Differentiation
Less confident learners
Give children number lines, counters or 1p coins to help them group.

More confident learners
Encourage children to record their work as a remainder, for example 16 ÷ 3 = 5 remainder 1.

Lesson 4
Oral and mental starter 50

Main teaching activities

Whole-class work: Explain that today the children will focus on division. Find out what they can remember about this area of maths. Focus on the two aspects: sharing and grouping. Briefly explain the difference, using word problems as follows:

● I have 16 sweets and I am going to share them equally between my four friends. How many will they each get?
● I have 16 sweets and I am going to put them in bags, four to a bag. How many bags do I need?

Demonstrate sharing by involving four children to act as friends and share 16 sweets (or cubes) between them (one for you, one for you, and so on). Next demonstrate grouping by taking groups of four cubes away from the sixteen and placing them in bags.

Focus on grouping for the rest of the lesson (sharing will be a focus of the next lesson about fractions). Demonstrate grouping practically, on a number line and as arrays. Ask the children to take, for example, three groups of five from 15 cubes and draw what they have done using symbols on their whiteboards. Repeat this a few times. For each selection, ask the children to write the appropriate number sentence. Where appropriate, include numbers with remainders and ask them to record, for example:

13 ÷ 2 = 6 remainder 1.

Group work: Ask the children to practise this by playing 'Home we go!'. Model the game according to the instructions outlined for this lesson.

Progress check: Check that the groups are all on task and playing fairly. Ask questions such as:

● *If I have 20 toys and I group them into fives, how many groups will I have? How did you work that out?*
● *If I did the same for 23 toys, would I have a remainder? How do you know?*

Review

Play 'Home we go!' in two teams. Make sure everyone counts. Recap the main points of this lesson: division can be grouping which is repeated subtraction and there can be remainders.

Curriculum objectives
● To solve problems involving multiplication and division, using materials, arrays, repeated addition, mental methods and multiplication and division facts, including problems in contexts.

Success criteria
● I can solve simple problems involving multiplication and division.

You will need

Photocopiable sheets
'Multiplication and division problems'

Equipment
Playing cards; individual whiteboards; interlocking cubes

Differentiation

Less confident learners
Adapt photocopiable page 'Multiplication and division problems' so that children focus on multiplying by two and ten.

More confident learners
Adapt photocopiable page 'Multiplication and division problems' so that children focus on multiplying by three and four.

Lesson 5 — Oral and mental starter 53

Main teaching activities

Whole-class work: Recap the important things to remember about multiplication and division: multiplication is repeated addition, division is repeated subtraction or grouping and also sharing, you can solve these using tables facts, number lines and arrays, they are inverse operations, it does not matter which way round you multiply the answer will be the same, this is not so for division because the answer is usually different.

Explain that today the children will make up and solve problems involving multiplication and division. Say: *Barney had a collection of 30 football cards. He put them into piles of five. How many piles did he make?* Ask the children what they need to do to find the answer. Agree take groups of five cards away from the 30. Demonstrate using cards and then show as repeated subtraction on a number line and write the appropriate number sentence. *How can we check?* Agree they can count in fives six times to see if they get 30. Again demonstrate this. Repeat for other examples.

Say: *Jayne baked five cakes. Her friend baked three times as many. How many did her friend bake?* Again, discuss what the children need to do to find the answer. Agree multiply five by three. Demonstrate with cubes and then show as repeated addition on a number line and write the appropriate number sentence. Discuss how to check using grouping. Repeat with other problems.

Independent work: Distribute photocopiable page 'Multiplication and division problems' from the CD-ROM. Explain that the children need to solve problems like those they have just been working on and then to make some up of their own.

Progress check: Ask the children who you might want to assess to show you how they solved one of their problems.

Review

Invite a few children to share how they solved one of their problems. Ask them how they knew whether to multiply or divide. Ask the class how they could check that the answer is correct and invite someone to do this.

Fractions: finding fractions of quantities, shapes and sets of objects

Expected prior learning

Children should be able to:

- find halves and quarters of simple shapes
- find halves and quarters of small numbers.

Topic	Curriculum objectives	Expected outcomes
Fractions	**Lesson 1**	
	To recognise, find, name and write fractions $\frac{1}{3}$, $\frac{1}{4}$, $\frac{2}{4}$ and $\frac{3}{4}$. To write simple fractions such as $\frac{1}{2}$ of 6 = 3 and recognise the equivalence of $\frac{2}{4}$ and $\frac{1}{2}$.	Understand simple equivalences. Find halves and quarters. Explain that finding quarters is the same as halving and halving again.
	Lesson 2	
	To recognise, find, name and write fractions $\frac{1}{3}$, $\frac{1}{4}$, $\frac{2}{4}$ and $\frac{3}{4}$. To write simple fractions such as $\frac{1}{2}$ of 6 = 3 and recognise the equivalence of $\frac{2}{4}$ and $\frac{1}{2}$.	Find fractions of a circle. Link fractions to time.
	Lesson 3	
	To recognise, find, name and write fractions $\frac{1}{3}$, $\frac{1}{4}$, $\frac{2}{4}$ and $\frac{3}{4}$. To write simple fractions such as $\frac{1}{2}$ of 6 = 3 and recognise the equivalence of $\frac{2}{4}$ and $\frac{1}{2}$.	Find fractions of a circle. Link fractions to time.
	Lesson 4	
	To recognise, find, name and write fractions $\frac{1}{3}$, $\frac{1}{4}$, $\frac{2}{4}$ and $\frac{3}{4}$.	Find different ways to show halves and quarters of shapes. Understand that if something is shared between three, each is a third.
	Lesson 5	
	To recognise, find, name and write fractions $\frac{1}{3}$, $\frac{1}{4}$, $\frac{2}{4}$ and $\frac{3}{4}$. To write simple fractions such as $\frac{1}{2}$ of 6 = 3 and recognise the equivalence of $\frac{2}{4}$ and $\frac{1}{2}$.	Use concrete and pictorial representations to solve simple problems.

Preparation

Lesson 1: prepare three strips from A3 paper: one whole; one folded in half and each half labelled ½; one folded into quarters and each part labelled ¼. Make towers using interlocking cubes: 5 red, 5 green; 3 red, 3 yellow, 3 blue, 3 green; 6 red, 3 yellow, 3 green; 4 red, 4 yellow, 4 blue, 4 green; 8 red, 4 yellow, 4 green

Lesson 2: make half and quarter clock size circles by drawing round a large class clock on card and cutting the card in half and repeat for quarters; copy photocopiable page 'Clock fractions' onto A3 paper for demonstration purposes

Lesson 3: adapt photocopiable page 'Number spinner' to larger even numbers to 50 and adapt photocopiable page 'Fraction spinner' to include ¾

Lesson 4: make three sandwiches with a filling that makes for easy cutting

You will need

Photocopiable sheets

'Clock fractions'; 'Shading fractions'; 'Fraction problems (1)'; 'Pennies game'; 'Pennies game recording sheet'; 'Number spinner'; 'Fraction spinner'

General resources

'0–100 number cards'; interactive activity 'Finding fractions'

Equipment

Individual whiteboards; A3 paper; card; interlocking cubes (red, green, yellow and blue); individual clocks; three sandwiches; knife; counters; 1p coins; class clock

Further practice

Interactive activity 'Finding fractions' offers further practice of finding simple fractions in a problem solving context.

Oral and mental starters for week 4

See bank of starters on pages 208 to 209. Oral and mental starters are also on the CD-ROM.

49 Counting in steps of different sizes

51 Make ten

52 Number pairs again

53 Finding fractions again

Overview of progression

During this week children will extend and consolidate their knowledge of fractions. They will recap the key ideas that they have learned so far. They will link finding fractions to division, particularly sharing, and use this knowledge to find fractions of shapes and small numbers. They will explore different ways of making halves and quarters and also link to time. They will use their understanding gained during the week to solve simple problems in familiar contexts.

Watch out for

Some children may still think a quarter is bigger than a half because four is bigger than two. Give them plenty of practice at making halves and quarters of identical shapes so that they can 'see' that a quarter is a smaller amount because it has been shared into more groups.

Creative context

You could ask the children to make paintings or drawings out of squares and rectangles and then spot and name the fractions they can see in each other's work.

Vocabulary

divide, equal parts, **equivalent**, four quarters, fraction, group, one half, one quarter, one whole, part, share, **third**, three quarters, two halves, two quarters

Curriculum objectives

• To recognise, find, name and write fractions ⅓, ¼, ¾ and ¾.
• To write simple fractions such as ½ of 6 = 3 and recognise the equivalence of ¾ and ½.

Success criteria

• I can explain what halves and quarters are.
• I can find halves and quarters of numbers.

You will need

Photocopiable sheets
'Pennies game'; 'Pennies game recording sheet'

General resources
'0–100 number cards'

Equipment
A3 paper; interlocking cubes; 1p coins

Differentiation

Less confident learners

Work with this group and encourage them to find quarters as well as halves, using up to 30 counters.

More confident learners

Children use number cards to generate numbers from 30 to 100.

Lesson 1 — Oral and mental starter 49

Main teaching activities

Whole-class work: Ask: *Who can tell me something about a fraction?* Write down responses on the board. As in Spring Term 2 aim for these statements, prompting if necessary: *A fraction is part of a whole; A half is when you divide something into two equal parts; A quarter is when you divide something into four equal parts; Two halves make a whole; Four quarters make a whole; Two quarters make a half; A half and a quarter makes three quarters; You can find a quarter by halving and halving again.* Remind the children that finding a fraction is the same as sharing which is a type of grouping which is the same as division. It is sharing amounts from a whole group equally into smaller groups. Give a volunteer ten cubes and ask them to share these equally between two other volunteers. Each volunteer will have a group of five.

Show the A3 fraction strips and ask the children if they remember making them. Ask what they demonstrate: one whole is equal to two halves and four quarters, two quarters is equal to one half and three quarters can be made from one half and one quarter and also three single quarters.

Give a volunteer 12 cubes and ask them to share them equally into half on the half strip. *How many groups are we sharing into? What number on the fraction tells us?* Agree the bottom number or denominator. Repeat this for quarters. *What is half of 12? What is a quarter? Which is the bigger fraction?* Agree half because the number of groups to be made is smaller and therefore the amount is going to be larger. It is important that the children recognise this. Repeat this for 16 cubes, 20 and then 24. Say: *I love chocolate! If someone offered me half a bar or a quarter of the same bar and I wanted the bigger bit, which should I pick? Why?*

Group work: Ask the children to practise finding fractions of numbers by playing the game on the photocopiable page 'Pennies game' on the CD-ROM. Ask whether they remember the game. Briefly model the instructions using up to 50 1p coins. They should record their results on the photocopiable page 'Pennies game recording sheet'.

Progress check: Visit the groups to ensure everyone is playing the game and recording their work as you demonstrated.

Review

Show the towers of different-coloured interlocking cubes and say true and false statements (similar to Spring term 2 lesson 2). Ask the children to respond by holding their thumbs up/down. Statements you could ask:

- Make a tower of 10 cubes, 6 red, 4 of another colour and say: *Half of this tower is red. (T) You can find a quarter of ten. (F) Why not?*
- Make a tower of 4 cubes, 1 red, 1 green, 1 yellow, 1 another colour and say: *Half of this tower is red. (F) The red and the green make up half. (T) If I add the yellow to the red and green I will have three. (T)*
- Make a tower of 12 cubes, 3 yellow, 3 green, 6 of another colour and say: *Half of this tower is yellow. (F) A quarter is green. (T) The green and the yellow make half. (T)*

Curriculum objectives
● To recognise, find, name and write fractions ⅓, ¼, ¾ and ¾.
● To write simple fractions such as ½ of 6 = 3 and recognise the equivalence of ¾ and ½.

Success criteria
● I can find halves and quarters of a circle.
● I can link fractions to time.

You will need
Photocopiable sheets
'Clock fractions'
Equipment
Class clock; card

Differentiation
Less confident learners
Provide pre-cut half and quarter circle shapes. Ask the children to find up to four different ways of making half and then a quarter.

More confident learners
Ask the group to find three-quarters as well as halves and quarters.

Main teaching activities

Whole-class work: Ask the children to tell you some fraction facts that they learned in the previous lesson. Say that today they will be linking fractions with time. Ask: *Can anyone tell me when we use fractions to talk about time?* Agree quarter past, half past and quarter to. Show a large class clock. *How many minutes are there all the way round it? So how many minutes are there in a whole hour?* Cover half the clock with the half card circle. *How many minutes are showing? How did you work that out? Did anyone halve 60? What fraction of the clock is showing? What fraction is hidden?* Put the other half card circle on the clock. *How much is covered now?* Take off the card halves and cover the first quarter (from 12 to 3) and ask similar questions including how many minutes in a quarter. Invite children to come and cover different quarters: 3 to 6, 6 to 9, 2 to 5, and so on. Establish that each time a quarter has been covered and that 15 minutes is hidden. Ask for a volunteer to cover three quarters. *How many minutes are covered now? How did you work that out?*

Paired work: Distribute photocopiable page 'Clock fractions' from the CD-ROM and encourage the children to make halves and quarters in different ways.

Progress check: Check that the class is following your instructions by asking questions such as:

● *Can you describe how you have coloured your quarter?*
● *Has anyone done this in a different way?*

Review

Ask a few pairs to show some of the ways they covered fractions of their clocks. Cover from 4 to 10 on the class clock. *How do we know this is half? Is there another way we can tell?* Cover from 2 to 5 and 8 to 11 with two of the quarter cards. *What fraction have I covered now? How do you know?* Agree half and that they know this because two quarters are the same as a half.

Curriculum objectives

- To recognise, find, name and write fractions ⅓, ¼, ²⁄₄ and ¾.
- To write simple fractions such as ½ of 6 = 3 and recognise the equivalence of ²⁄₄ and ½.

Success criteria

- I can find halves and quarters of a circle.
- I can link fractions to time.

You will need

Photocopiable sheets

'Clock fractions'; 'Fraction spinner'; 'Number spinner'

Equipment

Individual clocks

Differentiation

Less confident learners

Ask children to make quarters and halves using the quarter pieces.

More confident learners

Ask the group to look for other fractions such as thirds.

Lesson 3

Oral and mental starter 52

Main teaching activities

Whole-class work: The children will need a small clock each. Ask them to find 12 o'clock. Now ask them to move the minute hand around in fractions of an hour and to tell you the new time. For example: *Move clockwise a quarter of an hour; Clockwise half an hour; Anticlockwise a quarter of an hour.* If necessary, tell them to move the hour hand as well. Spend five minutes or so doing this.

Group work: Remind the children of the task they did in lesson 2. Give them another copy of 'Clock fractions' and ask them to find different ways of making half and three quarters, using quarter pieces only. The halves should be different from those they made the day before.

Progress check: Ask the children to give examples of the halves and quarters they have made. You could ask questions such as:

- *Which is smaller, a half or a quarter?*
- *If I covered from 1 to 10, what fraction is that?*

Review

Play a class team game. Adapt the 'Number spinner' to give six larger even numbers to 50 and the fraction spinner to include ¾. When ¾ comes up, ask the children how they can find three quarters of the amount of the number on the number spinner. If necessary, prompt them by saying: *If we know a quarter is... then three quarters is three times...*

Curriculum objectives

- To recognise, find, name and write fractions ⅓, ¼, ²⁄₄ and ¾.
- To write simple fractions and recognise the equivalence of ²⁄₄ and ½.

Success criteria

- I can find halves of shapes.
- I can find quarters of shapes.

You will need

Photocopiable sheets

'Shading fractions'

Equipment

Three sandwiches; knife

Differentiation

Less confident learners

Children focus on finding halves of the shapes on the photocopiable sheet.

More confident learners

Children complete the activity then draw their own shapes and find halves and quarters of these.

Lesson 4

Oral and mental starter 53

Main teaching activities

Whole-class work: Recap on finding fractions of clocks. Call out some multiples of four and ask the children to find a half and a quarter. Show a sandwich and ask the children if they remember finding out how they could divide Harry's sandwich into quarters (Autumn term 2 week 4 lesson 1). Tell them that they are going to explore fractions of sandwiches again. Ask: *How can I share my sandwich between two?* Draw some rectangles on the board and invite volunteers to show how they could make two halves and to shade one of them in. Encourage them to think of as many different ways as possible, including dividing into four and shading two. Take a vote as to which way you should cut the sandwich and do this. *How do we know that we need to make two equal amounts?* Establish that the denominator of the fraction tells them. Repeat for quarters using another sandwich.

Independent work: Distribute 'Shading fractions' from the CD-ROM and demonstrate what to do, linking to cutting halves and quarters of the sandwiches.

Progress check: Invite children to demonstrate how they find halves and quarters of the shapes so that the class can check that they are working correctly.

Review

Take feedback about the activity. How many different ways did the class find to shade halves and quarter? Show the third sandwich. *I'm going to share this sandwich between three. Can you work out what fraction each will have?* Write ½ (2) and ¼ (4) on the board as a clue. Establish that the fraction would be ⅓. Draw rectangles on the board and ask the children to make thirds (and cut the sandwich!).

Curriculum objectives

• To recognise, find, name and write fractions ⅓, ¼, ⅔ and ¾.
• To write simple fractions such as ½ of 6 = 3 and recognise the equivalence of ¾ and ½.

Success criteria

• I can solve simple problems involving fractions.

You will need

Photocopiable sheets
'Fraction problems (1)'

General resources
Interactive activity 'Finding fractions'

Equipment
Counters

Differentiation

Less confident learners

Edit photocopiable page 'Fraction problems (1)' so the children are focusing on halves. Give them help with reading. Let them use counters to help if required.

More confident learners

Edit photocopiable page 'Fraction problems (1)' so that they are finding more complex fractions, for example thirds, eighths.

Lesson 5
Oral and mental starter 53

Main teaching activities

Whole-class work: Recap on what the children have done during the week. Ensure you reinforce that: the bottom number of the fraction (denominator) tells them how many to share into; fractions are equal amounts but do not necessarily look the same. Talk through the equivalences for halves and quarters and discuss thirds. *How many thirds will make a whole? Is a third bigger or smaller than half? ...quarter?* Demonstrate all points on the board using the children to help you. Thirds will be a focus of fractions in Summer Term 2. The purpose of mentioning these in Lessons 4 and 5 is to familiarise the children with this new fraction.

Set this problem: *Milly had 20 sweets, she gave a quarter to her friend. How many did she have left?* Give the children a few minutes to work out how they could find the answer. Take feedback and establish that they need to find a quarter of 20 and take that away because she gave those to her friend. Do this using counters and agree that she will have 15 left. Ask similar problems. Tell the children that they will now use their knowledge of fractions to solve problems.

Paired work: Distribute photocopiable page 'Fraction problems (1)' from the CD-ROM. Demonstrate an example of a problem that the less confident learners will be working from.

Progress check: Visit the pairs to find out how they are getting on. Resolve any issues. If there are any common issues, stop the class to address these.

Review

Go through some examples of the children's problems. Write ½, ¼ and ¾ on the board. Ask the children to work with a partner to make up a problem using one of the fractions. Listen to some of the problems and as a class answer them. For further practice of finding simple fractions, give the children interactive activity 'Finding fractions' on the CD-ROM to complete.

Geometry: properties of 3D and 2D shapes

Expected prior learning

Children should be able to:

- identify and describe the properties of 3D shapes including edges, vertices and faces (including the names and lines of symmetry)
- identify and describe the properties of 2D shapes.

Topic	Curriculum objectives	Expected outcomes
Geometry: 3D and 2D shapes	**Lesson 1**	
	To identify and describe the properties of 3D shapes, including the number of edges, vertices and faces.	Identify and describe the properties of spheres, cones, cylinders, cubes, cuboids, square-based pyramids.
	To identify and describe the properties of 2D shapes, including the number of sides and line symmetry in a vertical line.	Identify and describe the properties of 2D shapes.
	To compare and sort common 2D and 3D shapes and everyday objects.	Sort 3D and 2D shapes.
	Lesson 2	
	To identify and describe the properties of 3D shapes, including the number of edges, vertices and faces.	Recognise 3D shapes from 2D pictures of them.
	To identify 2D shapes on the surface of 3D shapes [for example, a circle on a cylinder and a triangle on a pyramid].	Recognise 3D shapes in the classroom and real life.
	To compare and sort common 2D and 3D shapes and everyday objects.	
	Lesson 3	
	To identify and describe the properties of 2D shapes, including the number of sides and line symmetry in a vertical line.	Identify 2D shapes.
	Lesson 4	
	To identify and describe the properties of 2D shapes, including the number of sides and line symmetry in a vertical line.	Recognise symmetry in 2D shapes. Make symmetrical patterns.
	Lesson 5	
	To identify 2D shapes on the surface of 3D shapes [for example, a circle on a cylinder and a triangle on a pyramid].	Make a cube or cuboid.

Preparation

Lesson 1: copy, cut up and laminate the shape names from the photocopiable sheets '2D shape vocabulary' and '3D shape vocabulary'

Lesson 2: prepare a small amount of Plasticine® for each child to use during the lesson; make up a collection of 3D shapes: sphere, cone, cylinder, cube, cuboid, pyramid, triangular prism; make an A3 copy of photocopiable page 'Treasure shapes' and copy enough on A4 for pairs or groups to use

You will need

Photocopiable sheets

'Treasure shapes'; 'Treasure shapes recording sheet'; 'Name the shape'; 'Symmetrical patterns'

General resources

'2D shape vocabulary'; '3D shape vocabulary'; 'Templates for regular shapes'

Equipment

Individual whiteboards; 3D shapes: spheres, cones, cylinders, cubes, cuboids, square-based pyramids, triangular prism; Plasticine®; string; counters; card; scissors; glue; sticky tape; feely bag

Further practice

Photocopiable sheets
'From 3D to 2D'

Oral and mental starters for week 5

See bank of starters on pages 208 to 209. Oral and mental starters are also on the CD-ROM.

52 Number pairs again

54 Odd and even

61 Double that number

53 Finding fractions again

Overview of progression

During this week children will extend their knowledge of 3D and 2D shape. They will begin by identifying and describing familiar 3D and 2D shapes. They will describe their properties in terms of faces, edges and vertices, sides, corners and symmetry as appropriate. They will identify the properties of the 2D shapes that make up the faces of 3D shapes. They will explore symmetry. From their explorations of 3D shapes and their 2D faces, they will begin to visualise how these can be made and make a cube or cuboid.

Watch out for

Some children will find it difficult to visualise. Provide them with real shapes for the activities that they carry out and interlocking shapes to explore how 3D shapes are made.

Creative context

Encourage the children to use their knowledge of shape in art and topic work, for example in designing patterns and model making.

Vocabulary

angle, circle, cone, corner, cube, cuboid, cylinder, edge, face, hexagon, octagon, pentagon, pyramid, rectangle, side, sphere, square, symmetry, triangle, **triangular prism**, **vertex**

Curriculum objectives

● To identify and describe the properties of 3D shapes, including the number of edges, vertices and faces.
● To identify and describe the properties of 2D shapes, including the number of sides and line symmetry in a vertical line.
● To compare and sort common 2D and 3D shapes and everyday objects.

Success criteria

● I can name and describe the properties of 3D shapes.
● I can name and describe the properties of 2D shapes.

You will need

General resources

'2D shape vocabulary'; '3D shape vocabulary'; 'Templates for regular shapes'

Equipment

3D shapes: sphere, cone, cylinder, cube, cuboid, pyramid, triangular prism; feely bag

Differentiation

Less confident learners

Encourage children to focus on simpler sorting, such as 2D/3D, straight/curved.

More confident learners

Encourage children to think about more complex sorting, for example, 'has at least one triangular face', 'has at least one right angle' or 'has at least one curved surface' and to make a table to record their work.

Lesson I

Oral and mental starter **52**

Main teaching activities

Whole-class work: Tell the children that they will spend the next few lessons thinking about 3D and 2D shapes. Ask them to turn to a partner and think of all the names of shapes that they can think of. Take feedback, asking them to describe the shapes in terms of their specific properties, for example, curved surfaces, faces, sides, vertices, corners. Give each child a 3D shape or a 2D shape. Hold up a shape vocabulary card and ask children holding a shape that links to it in some way to stand up. Ask a few children to explain why they are standing. Repeat for as many vocabulary cards as possible.

Ask the children to stand up if their shape has any right angles. Use this as an opportunity to revise right angles and look for examples around the classroom. Ask them to make right angles using their thumbs and forefingers. Repeat this for lines of symmetry. Encourage children holding 3D shape cards to think about the right angles and symmetry of the faces of these shapes. Discuss shapes around the classroom. Can any children see any 3D or 2D shapes? Ask them to describe them without saying what they are and for the rest of the class to identify them.

Group work: The children will need a selection of 3D and 2D shapes. Use photocopiable page 'Templates for regular shapes' for the 2D shapes. First they sort the shapes into 3D and 2D shapes. Then they sort each group according to their own criteria and record in their own way. Model an example, such as flat faces/not flat faces, in a table.

Progress check: Visit each group in turn to make sure everyone is on task. Ask questions such as:

- *Why have you chosen these criteria?*
- *Is there another way you could have sorted your shapes?*

Review

Take feedback from the group activities and ask the children to evaluate the way their peers have sorted their shapes. Look at two shapes and ask: *What is the same about them? What is different?* Reveal a shape in parts from behind your back or out of a feely bag and ask: *What could it be? How do you know? What could it not be? Why?*

MSCHOLASTIC

Curriculum objectives
- To identify and describe the properties of 3D shapes.
- To identify and describe the properties of 2D shapes.
- To compare and sort common 2D and 3D shapes.

Success criteria
- I can name 3D shapes from 2D pictures.
- I can recognise 3D shapes in the classroom.

You will need

Photocopiable sheets
'Treasure shapes'; 'Treasure shapes recording sheet'

Equipment
3D shapes: sphere, cone, cylinder, cube, cuboid, square-based pyramid, triangular prism; Plasticine®

Differentiation
Let the children work together in mixed-ability groups.

Lesson 2   Oral and mental starter 54

Main teaching activities

Whole-class work: Recap the work from lesson 1. Say: *This lesson is about recognising 3D shapes from 2D pictures.* Go over the vocabulary of 3D shapes, using the vocabulary cards from lesson 1. Hold up a sphere and ask the children to describe it. Hold up the large version of photocopiable page 'Treasure shapes' from the CD-ROM and ask children whether they can see any spheres in the picture. Discuss how they recognised the spheres: round, no edges and so on. *What shape does the sphere look similar to?* Refer to circles. Where in real life would they see spheres? Repeat with cones, cylinders, cubes, cuboids, square-based pyramids and triangular prisms. Compare and sort according to different criteria, for example, curved surfaces/not curved surfaces.

Group work: The children work in mixed-ability small groups. Give them photocopiable page 'Treasure shapes' and some Plasticine®. Between them they make each of the 3D shapes they have seen in the main teaching activity and use these to identify the shapes in the picture. They colour each shape with a different-coloured pencil and record on photocopiable page 'Treasure shapes recording sheet'.

Progress check: Visit each group and ask questions such as: *How do you know this is a cube? What clues did you look for?*

Review

Discuss how many of each shape the children found and how they recognised them. Write: *All 3D shapes have faces.* Ask the children to say whether this is true and explain how they know. Expect them to give responses such as: *All shapes have surfaces, some are curved, some are flat. Faces are flat so a sphere doesn't have faces but other shapes have at least one.*

Curriculum objectives
- To identify and describe the properties of 2D shapes.

Success criteria
- I can name 2D shapes.
- I can explain the difference between regular and irregular shapes.

You will need

Photocopiable sheets
'Name the shape'

Equipment
Individual whiteboards; gluestick

Differentiation

Less confident learners
Give the children pre-written shape names to stick in the appropriate place.

More confident learners
Ask children to draw other irregular shapes for each named shape.

Lesson 3   Oral and mental starter 61

Main teaching activities

Group work: Ask: *What do we mean by 2D shapes?* Agree that 2D shapes are not solid and cannot be held. *Can you give me the names of some 2D shapes?* Expect: circle, triangle, square, rectangle, pentagon, hexagon and octagon. They draw one of each on their whiteboards and describe their properties to a partner (number of sides, angles, lines of symmetry). Establish that a regular shape has sides and angles that are the same size, an irregular one has sides and angles that are not the same. Demonstrate by drawing a regular and irregular triangle and pentagon on the board. Ask the children to draw three different hexagons and octagons. Focus on rectangles: a shape with four sides and four right angles is a rectangle. A square is a rectangle. It is a regular rectangle because all sides are the same length. Discuss where these shapes can be seen.

Independent work: Distribute photocopiable page 'Name the shape' from the CD-ROM. Explain that the task is to name and label the shapes and then colour those that are regular.

Progress check: Ask questions such as: *What shape is this one? How do you know whether it is regular or irregular? Is there another way to find out?*

Review

Invite the children to share the names they labelled and whether they thought that the shapes were regular or irregular. Recap the shapes covered during this lesson and their properties.

Curriculum objectives
● To identify and describe the properties of 2D shapes.
Success criteria
● I can recognise symmetry in 2D shapes.

You will need
Photocopiable sheets
'Symmetrical patterns'
Equipment
Individual whiteboards; string; counters

Differentiation
Less confident learners
Colour some rectangles on one side of the grid on the photocopiable sheet for the children to match their positions on the other side.
More confident learners
Ask children to create their own pattern with a horizontal line of symmetry.

Lesson 4   Oral and mental starter 53

Main teaching activities
Whole-class work: Ask: *What do we mean if something is symmetrical?* Agree that a symmetrical shape or pattern has two halves that look exactly the same. Draw a square, rectangle and regular triangle. Invite children to draw the lines of symmetry onto them. The rest of the class decides if they are correct. Agree that a square has four lines of symmetry, rectangle two and regular triangle three. Ask them to estimate how many lines of symmetry a regular pentagon might have. Draw one and prove that it has five. Repeat for a hexagon. Agree a circle has many lines of symmetry.

Give pairs of children a piece of string and 14 counters in the same colour. They place the string on the table. One of the pair places a counter on one side of the string. Their partner matches it on the other side of the string. They do this until all the counters have been used. They draw the pattern on paper.

Independent work: Distribute photocopiable page 'Symmetrical patterns' on the CD-ROM for the children to complete.

Progress check: Ask questions such as: *What is meant by the word symmetry? Is this shape symmetrical? How do you know?*

Review
Invite children to share their patterns. Ask others to check to make sure the patterns are symmetrical. Draw a horizontal line on the board with coloured dots on one side. Invite individuals to draw coloured dots on the other to make it symmetrical. Establish that symmetrical patterns can be horizontal as well as vertical.

Curriculum objectives
● To identify 2D shapes on the surface of 3D shapes.
Success criteria
● I can solve simple problems involving 3D shape.
● I can make a 3D shape.

You will need
Equipment
A4 card; scissors; glue; sticky tape; 3D shapes: spheres, cones, cylinders, cubes, cuboids, square-based pyramid, triangular prism

Differentiation
Organise the children in mixed-ability pairs so that they can talk about what they are doing and support each other if necessary. Ensure that each child makes their own shape.

Lesson 5   Oral and mental starter 53

Main teaching activities
Whole-class work: Recap the work over the previous four lessons. Hold different 3D shapes up and ask the children to name them and describe their properties including the shapes of their faces and the lines of symmetry. Draw a square on the board and ask the children to tell you what 3D shape it might be (cube, cuboid, square-based triangle). Repeat for circle, rectangle and triangle. Say: *Janey has lost her collection of cubes and cuboids. She has asked us to make her some more.* Give pairs of children a cube and a cuboid. Ask them to examine them and talk to each other discussing how they think they might be able to make one. Take feedback. Try to elicit from them that they could draw around the faces, cut them out and stick them together.

Paired work: Children work in pairs to support each other – one makes a cube, the other a cuboid. Give each a piece of card, a pair of scissors, glue and some sticky tape and ask them to make their shape.

Progress check: Check to make sure the children are thinking about the number of faces they need to create. Watch out for children who are drawing the squares or rectangles side by side and cutting them as one piece.

Review
Discuss how the children made their shapes. Did any draw the faces side by side? For example:

If so, discuss how they could have added the other parts instead of cutting them out separately.

▰SCHOLASTIC

Measures and money

Expected prior learning

Children should be able to:

- estimate, measure and compare lengths, masses (weights) and capacities
- recognise that a thermometer measures temperature.

Topic	Curriculum objectives	Expected outcomes
Measurement	**Lesson 1** To choose and use appropriate standard units to estimate and measure length/height in any direction (m/cm); mass (kg/g); temperature (°C); capacity (litres/ml) to the nearest appropriate unit using rulers, scales, thermometers and measuring vessels. To compare and order lengths, mass, volume/capacity and record the results using >, < and =.	Use standard units of measurement. Use the appropriate language and abbreviations. Compare using >, <, = and order lengths. Read scales to the nearest sensible division.
	Lesson 2 To choose and use appropriate standard units to estimate and measure length/height in any direction (m/cm/mm); mass (kg/g); temperature (°C); capacity (litres/ml) to the nearest appropriate unit using rulers, scales, thermometers and measuring vessels. To compare and order lengths, mass, volume/capacity and record the results using >, < and =.	Use standard units of measurement. Use the appropriate language and abbreviations. Compare using >, <, = and order masses. Read scales to the nearest sensible division.
	Lesson 3 To choose and use appropriate standard units to estimate and measure length/height in any direction (m/cm/mm); mass (kg/g); temperature (°C); capacity (litres/ml) to the nearest appropriate unit using rulers, scales, thermometers and measuring vessels.	Use standard units of measurement. Use the appropriate language and abbreviations. Read scales to the nearest sensible division.
	Lesson 4 To recognise and use symbols for pounds (£) and pence (p); combine amounts to make a particular value. To find different combinations of coins that equal the same amounts of money.	Know the coins we use in our monetary system and their equivalences. Find totals and give change.
	Lesson 5 To solve simple problems in a practical context involving addition and subtraction of money of the same unit, including giving change. To recognise and use symbols for pounds (£) and pence (p); combine amounts to make a particular value. To find different combinations of coins that equal the same amounts of money.	Solve problems involving the addition and subtraction of money.

Preparation

Lesson 1: enlarge the cards from photocopiable page 'Measures vocabulary' to A3, cut out and laminate; prepare three sheets of A3 paper with the headings 'length' 'weight' and 'capacity'; adapt photocopiable page 'Lengths' so that all measurements are less than 30cm

Lesson 2: ensure that the weight vocabulary words from lesson 1 are available for the children to see; have available a 5kg bag of potatoes, 1kg bag of sugar and packet of crisps

Lesson 3: ensure that the volume and capacity vocabulary words from lesson 1 are available for the children to see; make a collection of different-sized bottles and containers for the activity

Lesson 4: prepare appropriate price labels, showing pence as well as pounds and pence amounts; prepare containers with a selection of all the coins we use

You will need

Photocopiable sheets

'Weight cards'; 'Capacity cards'; 'How much change?'

General resources

'Lengths'; 'Measures vocabulary'; interactive teaching resource 'Weighing scales'; interactive teaching resource 'Measuring jug'

Equipment

Rulers; metre stick; A3 paper; 5kg bag of potatoes; 1kg bag of sugar; packet of crisps; kitchen weighing scales; litre bottles; containers; small tubs measuring jugs; water; coins: 1p, 2p, 5p, 10p, 20p, 50p, £1, £2

Further practice

Photocopiable sheets

'Reading scales'

Oral and mental starters for week 6

See bank of starters on pages 208 to 209. Oral and mental starters are also on the CD-ROM.

47 Adding 9 and 11

48 Doubling and near doubling

53 Finding fractions again

62 Making numbers again

Overview of progression

During this week children will extend their knowledge of measures. They will practically estimate, measure and compare lengths, masses, capacities and volumes and look at the units used to describe them and their equivalences and abbreviations. They will also explore money by finding way to make amounts, working out change and answering real-life problems.

Watch out for

Some children may find it difficult to make amounts of money using coins other than 1p coins. First encourage them to exchange ten 1p coins for 10p coins, then move on to matching the correct numbers of pennies with 2p, 5p and 10p coins.

Creative context

Encourage the children to use their knowledge of money at other times during the day, for example, in the role-play area.

Vocabulary

capacity, centimetre, empty, full, gram, heavy, kilogram, length, light, litre, long, mass, measure, measuring jug, metre, millilitre, short, **temperature**, **thermometer**, volume, weigh

■ SCHOLASTIC

Curriculum objectives
- To choose and use appropriate standard units to estimate and measure length/height in any direction (m/cm) to the nearest. appropriate unit using rulers.
- To compare and order lengths and record the results using >, < and =.

Success criteria
- I can measure in centimetres.
- I can estimate lengths.

You will need
General resources
'Measures vocabulary'; 'Lengths'
Equipment
Rulers; metre stick; A3 paper

Differentiation
This is a mixed-ability pair activity. Ensure all the children take an active part.

Lesson 1   Oral and mental starter 47

Main teaching activities

Whole-class work: Say: *Today we are going to begin a series of lessons on measures. What do I mean by measures?* Stick three A3 sheets of paper with the headings 'length', 'weight' and 'capacity' on the board. *Tell me the words you know that can be put under these headings.* Add the measures vocabulary cards they say to the appropriate sheets. Expect the children to tell you what the words they say mean. Ensure the descriptive words, units and equipment are included. Show any words that they don't say and ask them to tell you what they are and where you should put them. Ask questions such as: *What would we measure in this unit? What would we measure using a metre stick? Is there anything else?*

Say that today they will focus on measuring small lengths. *What can you tell me about length?* Take feedback. Discuss the different lengths that we measure, asking the children to give examples, for example length of string, width of a book, height of a child. *In what units do we measure length?* Agree centimetres and metres. If any say millilitres and kilometres or miles, feet and inches celebrate this. Show a ruler and metre stick. *How many centimetres are the same as one/two/three metres?* Ask the children to show you a centimetre with their fingers. They check with their ruler and practise counting forwards and backwards along the ruler in centimetres as if it was a number line.

Ask them to work with a partner to find some items that are longer and shorter than 1cm, 10cm, 20cm, 1m and ½m. Once they have, invite pairs to bring some of their items to the front of the class. The rest of the children tell them where to place them so that they are in order from shortest to longest.

Paired work: The children work in mixed-ability pairs. Give each pair a selection of lengths from photocopiable page 'Lengths' from the CD-ROM and ask them to estimate how long a line would be of the length shown on the card. Ask them to draw their estimates on paper without using a ruler. They then measure the lines to see who was the closest. Ask them to draw the line with a ruler to the correct length beside their estimate.

Progress check: Visit pairs of children as they work to check that they are using their rulers correctly. Ask questions such as:
- *How long do you think that length is?*
- *Can you show me how you measured your line?*
- *Which part of your ruler did you start measuring from?*

Review

Take feedback from the activity. Compare the different lines they estimated and measured. Hold up two 'Length' cards and draw > on the board. Ask the children where you should put the cards. Repeat for the < symbol.

Curriculum objectives
● To choose and use appropriate standard units to estimate and measure mass (kg/g) to the most appropriate unit using scales.
● To compare and order mass and record the results.

Success criteria
● I can estimate and measure in kilograms and grams.

You will need
Photocopiable sheets
'Weight cards'

General resources
'Measures vocabulary'; interactive teaching resource 'Weighing scales'

Equipment
5kg bag of potatoes; 1kg bag of sugar; bag of crisps; kitchen weighing scales

Differentiation
Ask more confident learners to help the less confident learners in their group.

Curriculum objectives
● To choose and use appropriate standard units to estimate and measure capacity (litres/ml).
● To compare and order volume/capacity and record the results using >, < and =.

Success criteria
● I can estimate and measure in litres and millilitres.

You will need
Photocopiable sheets
'Capacity cards'

General resources
'Measures vocabulary'; interactive teaching resource 'Measuring jug'

Equipment
Litre bottles; containers; small tubs; water; measuring jugs

Differentiation
Ask more confident children to help the less confident learners in their group.

Lesson 2 — Oral and mental starter 48

Main teaching activities

Whole-class work: Show the weight vocabulary from lesson 1. Discuss each word and ask the children to say them in a sentence. Sort the words according to type: descriptive, units, measuring equipment, using the vocabulary cards to help. Ask which units would be used to measure small items/heavy ones. On the board write 1kg = 1000g and ask the children to give you other equivalences, for example ½kg, 2kg, 1500g.

Use the interactive teaching resource 'Weighing scales' on the CD-ROM to demonstrate weighing some items on the screen and asking appropriate questions. Show the potatoes, sugar and crisps and ask: *Which is the heaviest? Which is the lightest? Why do you think that? What do you think they each weigh? How can you check your estimate?* Establish that the children would need some form of weighing scale. Show the scales and invite children to check the weight of each item using them.

Group work: The children work in mixed-ability groups of four. Ask each group to tackle one of the activities on photocopiable page 'Weight cards' from the CD-ROM.

Progress check: Visit the groups to make sure they understand what to do and that everyone is taking part.

Review
Invite the children to explain how they carried out their activities and recorded their work. Ask them to evaluate the effectiveness of their chosen recording. Discuss how they can become more accurate in estimating by learning from previous experience. Take examples of weights and record them on the board using the < and > symbols.

Lesson 3 — Oral and mental starter 53

Main teaching activities

Whole-class work: Show the capacity vocabulary from lesson 1. Discuss each word and ask the children to say them in a sentence. Sort the words according to type: descriptive, units, measuring equipment, using the vocabulary cards to help. Ask which units would be used to measure small containers such as a cup or teaspoon and then larger ones such as a bath or bucket. On the board write 1l = 1000ml and ask the children to give you other equivalences.

Use the interactive teaching resource 'Measuring jug' on the CD-ROM to demonstrate measuring volumes and capacities and ask appropriate questions. Show the children two containers of different sizes and ask: *Which holds more? Which holds least? Why do you think that? How can you check your estimate?* Establish that they would need a measuring jug. Invite some children to check the capacity of each of the containers using a measuring jug.

Group work: The children work in mixed-ability groups of four. Ask each group to tackle one of the activities on photocopiable page 'Capacity cards' from the CD-ROM.

Progress check: Visit the groups to make sure they understand what to do and that everyone is taking part.

Review
Invite the children to explain how they carried out their activities and recorded their work. Ask them to evaluate the effectiveness of their chosen recording. Discuss how they can become more accurate in estimating by learning from previous experience. Take examples of capacities and record them on the board using the < and > symbols.

Curriculum objectives
- To recognise and use symbols for pounds (£) and pence (p); combine amounts to make a particular value.
- To find different combinations of coins that equal the same amounts of money.

Success criteria
- I can recognise the coins we use.
- I can make amounts of money using different coins.

You will need
Equipment
Individual whiteboards; coins: 1p, 2p, 5p, 10p, 20p, 50p, £1, £2

Differentiation
Less confident learners
Ask the children to find change from £2.
More confident learners
Encourage the children to find change from £5 and £10.

Lesson 4 — Oral and mental starter 62

Main teaching activities

Whole-class work: Show the children a selection of coins; ask them to identify the different coins and say what each is worth. Hold up some pre-prepared price label cards and ask the children which coins they could use to make each amount. Tell the children that you have £1. Choose a volunteer to be the shopkeeper. They pick a pence price label and tell you what it is. Say: *That is the amount I want to spend. I am going to give my pound to the shopkeeper. What change does he/she need to give me?* Check answers by counting up on a number line. Ask the children which coins the shopkeeper could give you. Repeat for different price labels.

Group work: Ask the children to work in similar-ability groups of three or four. Each group needs a pile of price label cards (pence and £.p.) facedown and a container of coins including £1 and £2 coins. They take it in turns to pick a card and decide how many pounds to give the 'shopkeeper', then the group works out the change using a number line.

Progress check: Visit groups to make sure they know what to do. Ask questions such as: *If I give the shopkeeper £1 and spend 55p, how much change do I need? How do you know?*

Review

Invite a few children, particularly any you wish to assess, to show you what they did in the group activity. Ask questions such as: *How are you going to find out the change? What amount will you count on from?*

Curriculum objectives
- To solve simple problems in a practical context involving addition and subtraction of money of the same unit, including giving change.
- To recognise and use symbols for pounds (£) and pence (p); combine amounts to make a particular value.
- To find different combinations of coins that equal the same amounts of money.

Success criteria
- I can solve simple problems involving money.

You will need
Photocopiable sheets
'How much change?'

Differentiation
Less confident learners
Adapt the photocopiable sheet to show simpler amounts.
More confident learners
Adapt the photocopiable sheet so that the children are working with more complex amounts.

Lesson 5 — Oral and mental starter 62

Main teaching activities

Whole-class work: This lesson is about real-life money problems. Ask: *When do we have problems to solve that involve money?* Talk about shopping and how we might ask ourselves 'Can I afford both of those?' Set this problem: *Sadie was in the greengrocers. Her mum had given her £2 to buy 5kg of potatoes. The potatoes cost £1.40. How much change will she receive?* Recap on what the children need to do when solving a problem like this, for example: find out what the problem is asking, look for the relevant information, work out the answer and check to make sure it makes sense. Focus on counting on to find the change, demonstrating on the board. Ask a similar problem that involves adding two amounts of money before finding the change. For addition, encourage the children to use partitioning or sequencing.

Paired work: Children work in pairs on photocopiable page 'How much change?' from the CD-ROM. Once they have completed the problems, they make up their own real-life problems.

Progress check: Visit pairs who you particularly wish to assess. Ask questions such as these:
- *What is the information you need to answer this questions?*
- *How would you find the change?*

Review

Invite a few children to show what they did to find the answers. Invite others to ask their problems and the class to work out the answers. Also recap addition and subtraction strategies by asking: *Show me how you could add 47p and 29p. What about 72p and 48p? Can you find your answer in a different way?* Repeat with subtractions.

Curriculum objectives
● To add and subtract using pictorial representations, and mentally, including: two two-digit numbers and ones.

You will need
1. Check
Oral and mental starter
47 Adding 9 and 11

2. Assess
'0–100 number cards'

3. Further practice
Oral and mental starters
48 Doubling and near doubling
51 Make ten
52 Number pairs again

Photocopiable sheets
'Which strategy? (1)'

Addition

Most children should be able to use strategies for adding such as partitioning, sequencing, adding near multiples of ten and using facts.

Some children will not have made such progress and will require additional practice at partitioning and sequencing.

1. Check
47 Adding 9 and 11

After practising adding 9 and 11 with a 100 square ask the children to visualise one in their minds and ask them to add 9 to 34, 11 to 45 and so on. Observe which children are confident and which need still need a 100 square.

Ask questions such as:
- *What is 9 more than 73? How did you work that out?*
- *What is 11 more than 24? How do you know?*

2. Assess

Give each child two number cards. Ask them to add them together using the strategy they prefer and then ask them to check by adding them using a different method. Repeat for other pairs of numbers. On occasions give them cards that are near doubles and cards where one card number ends with a 9. Record the outcomes.

3. Further practice

Photocopiable page 210 'Which strategy? (1)' provides the opportunity for the children to decide which calculation method is the most appropriate for the numbers they are adding. Encourage them to check using a different method. They should work on this independently.

Curriculum objectives
● To add and subtract using concrete objects, pictorial representations, and mentally, including: a two two-digit number and ones.

You will need
1. Check
Oral and mental starter
47 Adding 9 and 11

2. Assess
'0–100 number cards'

3. Further practice
Oral and mental starters
31 Number pairs to 20
34 Bridging ten again
62 Making numbers again

Photocopiable sheets
'Which strategy? (2)'

Subtraction

Most children should be able to subtract by counting on, sequencing and subtracting multiples of ten and adjusting.

Some children will not have made such progress and will need to focus on counting on.

1. Check
47 Adding 9 and 11

After practising subtracting 9 and 11 with a 100 square ask the children to visualise one in their minds and ask them to subtract 9 from 34, 11 from 45 and so on. Observe which children are confident and which need still need a 100 square.

Ask questions such as:
- *What is 9 less than 62? How did you work that out?*
- *What is 11 less than 84? How do you know?*

2. Assess

Give each child two number cards. Ask them to subtract the smallest from the largest using the strategy they prefer and then ask them to check by subtracting using a different method. Repeat for other pairs of numbers. On occasions give them cards that end with 9. Record the outcomes.

3. Further practice

Photocopiable page 211 'Which strategy? (2)' provides the opportunity for the children to decide which calculation method is the most appropriate for the numbers they are subtracting. Encourage them to check using a different method. They should work on this independently.

Curriculum objectives
- To calculate mathematical statements for multiplication and division.

You will need
1. Check
Oral and mental starter
49 Counting in steps of different sizes

2. Assess
'0–100 number cards'; individual whiteboards

3. Further practice
Oral and mental starters
41 Spider charts

Photocopiables sheets
'Quick tables'

Multiplication and division facts

Most children should be able recall facts for the two-, three-, five- and ten-times tables.

Some children will not have made such progress and will focus on the two- and ten-times tables.

1. Check

49 Counting in steps of different sizes

Use the oral and mental starter to check which children can now quickly recall multiplication and division facts. Ask:

- *What is 2 × 4? How can you find out if you don't know?*
- *What is 30 ÷ 5? How can you find out if you don't know?*
- *How can you check that you are right?*

2. Assess

Tell the children that you are going to hold up number cards 1–9 and when you do they multiply the number shown by two and write their answer on their whiteboard. Repeat for multiplying by three, five and ten. Record the outcomes.

3. Further practice

The photocopiable sheet on page 212 is designed to assess how quickly children can recall multiplication and division facts for their two-, three-, five- and ten-times tables. Adapt this for children who you know will struggle to recall facts for the three-times table. Time them as they do this.

Curriculum objectives
- To recognise and use symbols for pounds (£) and pence (p); combine amounts to make a particular value.
- To find different combinations of coins to equal the same amounts of money.

You will need
1. Check
Oral and mental starter
51 Make ten

2. Assess
1p, 2p, 5p, 10p, 20p, 50p in a container

3. Further practice
Oral and mental starter
52 Number pairs again

Photocopiable sheets
'Making money'

Measurement: money

Most children should be able to successfully make amounts of money using a variety of coins.

Some children will not have made such progress and will need to focus on exchanging 1p coins for 10p coins.

1. Check

51 Make ten

As you work through the oral and mental starter put this into the context of money so that the children are thinking of ways to use coins to make 10p. Observe the children to assess their confidence in using different coin values and a mixture of addition and subtraction. Ask:

- *What coins could we add to 5p to make 10p? Are there any others?*
- *What coins could we take away from a 20p coin to give 10p? Are there any others?*

2. Assess

Provide a container of different coins. Ask the children to make different amounts using the coins, for example, 21p, 45p, 63p. Can they find the fewest number of coins? Can they make the amount in different ways? Record the outcomes.

3. Further practice

Adapt the oral and mental starter so that you work through it in the context of money. The photocopiable sheet asks the children to explore different ways to make given amounts of money. Encourage them to make the amounts using coins and then choose two ways to record on the sheet.

Oral and mental starters

Number and place value

49 Counting in steps of different sizes

Count in twos together, using fingers so that, when you stop part of the way through the children can tell you what the multiplication fact is and its corresponding division. For example, if you stop on 12 the multiplication fact is 2 × 6 = 12 and the division is 12 ÷ 2 = 6. Expect the children to write these on their whiteboards. Do this for counting in twos, threes, fives and tens.

50 Missing numbers

Write some missing number sentences on the board and time the children to see how many they can answer in two minutes. Expect varying results. Repeat two or three times. Using talk partners, ask them to think of as many words as they can for addition and subtraction.

51 Make ten

Write 10 on the board. Time the children for two or three minutes to see how many ways they can make ten and write them down on their whiteboards. Encourage them to use multiplication and division as well as addition and subtraction, for example, 7 + 3 = 10, 20 − 10 = 10, 5 × 2 = 10, 50 ÷ 5 = 10. Suggest that they could use more than two numbers, for example, 6 × 2 − 2.

52 Number pairs again

Swing the pendulum from side to side. As it swings one way you call out a number to 20, as it swings the other way the children call out the number that goes with it to make 20. For example, you call out 13 the children call out 7. Do this for number pairs to ten, multiples of 10 to 100 and also pairs for other numbers to 20.

54 Odd and even

Ask the children to tell you what they know about odd and even numbers. If necessary, remind them that an odd number always has one left over when it is divided by two and an even number has nothing left over. Give them various two-digit starting numbers and ask them to count on and back in ones, clapping when they say an even number and stamping when they say an odd number.

61 Double that number

Call out random numbers to 5 and ask the children to show you the double of each number with number cards. Discuss the opposite of doubling as halving and that if you double a number and then halve it you get back to the starting number. Call out even numbers to 10 for the children to halve. Repeat for doubles of numbers to 10 then 20 and their corresponding halves. Extend to numbers to 50.

62 Making numbers again

Give each child a set of number cards 1–9. Ask them to use the words to make a two-digit number and say it to their partner. On their whiteboards they write what the number is in words and then show you. Repeat this a few times. On occasions, invite five children to bring their numbers to the front of the class and the rest of the class orders them from smallest to largest. Ask them to make 235 with their cards. Next ask them to make other numbers from these cards and write them on their whiteboards. Take feedback and write these numbers on the board: 235, 253, 325, 352, 523, 532. Ask questions about them, for example, *What is 10 more than 352?... 10 less than 235?... 100 more than 253?... 100 less than 532? Which numbers are odd numbers?*

Addition and subtraction

 Adding 9 and 11

Give each child a 100 square. They place their finger on 4. Call out instructions for the children to follow that involve adding or taking away 1 and 10 and also 9 and 100, e.g. add 10, add 9, take away 1, add two lots of 10, add 11, take away 9. Once you have given five or six instructions ask the children to tell you what number they are on. Repeat several times.

48 Doubling and near doubling

Call out numbers to 20. The children double these and show their answers on their whiteboards. Repeat for multiples of 10 to 100. Next ask them to add two numbers together that are near doubles, for example 6 + 7, 15 + 16, 12 + 13. They double one of the numbers and then adjust by adding or taking away one. For example 8 + 9 (double 8, add 1 or double 9 subtract 1).

Fractions

53 Finding fractions again

Show a number card 1–40. Say: *These are the number of sweets I have. I am going to give you half. How many do I need to give you?* Ask the children to try to find half of the number of sweets. If it is an even number they write half of it on their whiteboard. If it is an odd number they draw a sad face because you won't be able to give them any sweets. Repeat for other numbers. Then do this again for quarters. Encourage them to use a halving and halving again strategy. Extend this by asking the children to find three quarters.

Name: _____   Date: _____

Which strategy? (1)

- Add these numbers together using the way you think is best.
- Check your answers by adding in a different way.

46 + 19

Show your strategy:	Show your strategy for checking:

23 + 17

Show your strategy:	Show your strategy for checking:

54 + 38

Show your strategy:	Show your strategy for checking:

25 + 26

Show your strategy:	Show your strategy for checking:

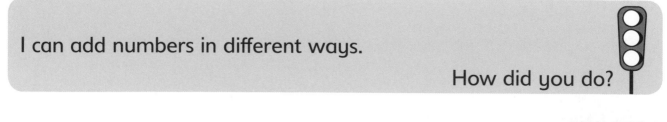

I can add numbers in different ways.

How did you do?

PHOTOCOPIABLE

Which strategy? (2)

- Subtract these numbers using the way you think is best.
- Check your answers by subtracting in a different way.

78 – 35

Show your strategy:	Show your strategy for checking:

48 – 19

Show your strategy:	Show your strategy for checking:

84 – 76

Show your strategy:	Show your strategy for checking:

59 – 37

Show your strategy:	Show your strategy for checking:

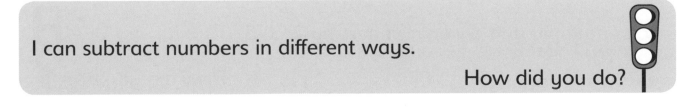

I can subtract numbers in different ways.

How did you do?

Quick tables

■ Answer these as quickly as you can.

2 × 6 = ☐   60 ÷ 5 = ☐

5 × 8 = ☐   18 ÷ 2 = ☐

10 × 6 = ☐   3 × 8 = ☐

24 ÷ 2 = ☐   3 × 4 = ☐

20 ÷ 5 = ☐   12 ÷ 3 = ☐

50 ÷ 10 = ☐   21 ÷ 3 = ☐

2 × 7 = ☐   2 × 5 = ☐

5 × 9 = ☐   5 × 7 = ☐

10 × 3 = ☐   3 × 9 = ☐

70 ÷ 10 = ☐   25 ÷ 5 = ☐

I can multiply and divide numbers by 2, 3, 5 and 10.

How did you do?

Number and place value: estimating, counting, comparing and ordering

Expected prior learning

Children should be able to:

- count forwards or backwards in steps of two, three, five and ten
- partition two-digit numbers in different ways
- round numbers to the nearest ten.

Topic	Curriculum objectives	Expected outcomes
Number and place value	**Lesson 1**	
	To identify, represent and estimate numbers using different representations, including the number line. To read and write numbers to at least 100 in numerals and in words.	Estimate quantities and count to check. Begin to write numbers to 100 in words.
	Lesson 2	
	To recognise the place value of each digit in a two-digit number (tens, ones). To identify, represent and estimate numbers using different representations, including the number line. To compare and order numbers from 0 up to 100; use <, > and = signs.	Partition numbers. Order and compare using < and >.
	Lesson 3	
	To recognise the place value of each digit in a two-digit number (tens, ones). To use place value and number facts to solve problems.	Solve problems using number facts.
	Lesson 4	
	To recognise the place value of each digit in a two-digit number (tens, ones). To use place value and number facts to solve problems.	Solve money problems using number facts.
	Lesson 5	
	To recognise the place value of each digit in a two-digit number (tens, ones). To use place value and number facts to solve problems.	Solve measurement and money problems using number facts.

Preparation

Lesson 1: collect 76 counters and put them in a container; adapt photocopiable page 'Groups of three' to suit the attainment levels of the children

Lesson 2: adapt photocopiable page 'Greater than or less than?' to suit the attainment levels of the children

You will need

Photocopiable sheets

'Groups of three'; 'Greater than or less than?'; 'What could it be?'; 'What's my answer?'; 'Solve me!'; 'Problems'

General resources

'Blank number lines'; 'Arrow cards'

Equipment

Counters; individual whiteboards; coins

Further practice

Adapt 'Blank number lines' or the interactive teaching resource 'Number line'. Set start and finish numbers within 100 and ask the children to position target numbers. Check for any misconceptions.

Oral and mental starters for week 1

See bank of starters on page 249. Oral and mental starters are also from the CD-ROM.

 Money

56 Which fraction?

57 Telling the time again

Overview of progression

During this week the children will continue to practise their counting skills by counting in steps of two, three, five and ten from and to zero. They will reinforce and continue to consolidate partitioning numbers in different ways and comparing and ordering them. They will extend and develop their understanding and knowledge of number pairs to 10, 20 and 100 to solve problems involving measurement and money.

Watch out for

Some children may have difficulty remembering number facts to ten. For those that do, give them written prompts such as number cards with the number facts to ten on. Ask them to practise using the card and to refer to it when they need to.

Creative context

Ask the children to make up a number rhyme or rap for number pairs to ten.

Vocabulary

count in twos, count in fives, count in tens, continue, **multiple of**, one-digit number, place, **place value**, predict, represents, stands for, tens digit, two-digit number, 'teens' number

Curriculum objectives

- To identify, represent and estimate numbers using different representations, including the number line.
- To read and write numbers to at least 100 in numerals and in words.

Success criteria

- I can count in threes.
- I can write numbers to 100 in words.

You will need

Photocopiable sheets

'Groups of three'

General resources

'Blank number lines'

Equipment

Individual whiteboards; counters

Differentiation

Less confident learners

Adapt photocopiable page 'Groups of three' so that there are 15 and 16 dots respectively. Give the children number lines to help them count in threes.

More confident learners

Adapt photocopiable page 'Groups of three' so that there are over 50 dots in each group.

Lesson 1

Oral and mental starter 55

Main teaching activities

Whole-class work: Show the container filled with 76 counters. *What is the best way to count these?* If necessary remind the children of previous work. Agree that counting groups of ten would be helpful. Invite them to help you to count out groups of ten counters. Part of the way through the count, ask the children to estimate how many there will be. When you have the seven groups of ten, together count in tens to 70. Group those remaining into five and count on to make 75, then add the final one. Repeat for other numbers of counters. How close were the children's estimates? Ask them to write the number in words on their whiteboards.

Are there any other ways we could group them? Establish that the children could group them in twos, threes and fives. Give pairs between 30 and 40 counters. They explore counting them in groups of two, three, five and ten. As they do this they consider which they think is the most efficient method. Invite them to explain what they think to the rest of the class.

Paired work: Distribute photocopiable page 'Groups of three' from the CD-ROM. Explain that the children need to estimate the dots and then count them by grouping them in threes and then counting in threes to find the total.

Progress check: Check the class are on the right track by asking:

- *If we need to count lots of things, how could we do this? What size of groups could we make? Are there any others?*
- *I grouped some dots into threes and I had four groups. How many dots did I have? How do you know?*

Review

Take feedback from the task. Ask the children to tell you what they could use to help them find the total dots. Aim towards counting on in threes using their fingers, such as 10 lots of 3 is 30. Link to multiplication tables, for example $3 \times 10 = 30$. Finish the lesson by discussing the grouping methods they used. Which did they think were the most efficient?

Curriculum objectives

- To recognise the place value of each digit in a two-digit number (tens, ones).
- To identify, represent and estimate numbers using different representations, including the number line.
- To compare and order numbers from 0 up to 100; use <, > and = signs.

Success criteria

- I can tell you what each digit in a number is.
- I can compare and order numbers.

You will need

Photocopiable sheets

'Greater than or less than?'

General resources

'Arrow cards'

Equipment

Individual whiteboards

Differentiation

Less confident learners

Adapt photocopiable page 'Greater than or less than?' so that the children work with numbers to 20.

More confident learners

Adapt photocopiable page 'Greater than or less than?' so that the children create three-digit numbers.

Main teaching activities

Whole-class work: Ask each child in turn to say a two-digit number. As they do everyone partitions it and writes the appropriate number sentence, such as 35 = 30 + 5. Choose some of the numbers and ask the children to order them from smallest to largest. Focus on partitioning numbers in different ways, such as 35 = 20 + 15; 10 + 25.

Write on the board 34 > ?. Ask the children to think of a number that could replace the question mark. *What does this symbol mean?* Agree it is the *greater than* symbol. Repeat for the *less than* symbol (<). Give pairs a set of arrow cards. Ask them to make a two-digit number. They read their number to a partner and write two number sentences using the > and < symbols on whiteboards. Repeat this a few times. Next ask them to make four two-digit numbers. They write them in order from smallest to largest. They then use them to make up more *greater than* and *less than* number sentences.

Independent work: Distribute photocopiable page 'Greater than or less than?' from the CD-ROM. Explain that the children need to make greater than/less than two-digit number sentences.

Progress check: Check that the children are working in the correct way. Ask questions such as:

- *Which is the larger number, 45 or 54? How do you know?*
- *How can you partition 78? Is there another way? What about another?*
- *If I partition 34 into 20 and another number, what would that number be? How do you know?*

Review

Take feedback from the task. Invite the children to share the numbers and number sentences that they made. Finish the lesson by writing partially completed number sentences, such as, 24 + ? < 13 + ?. Ask the children to suggest numbers to replace the question marks.

Curriculum objectives

- To recognise the place value of each digit in a two-digit number (tens, ones).
- To use place value and number facts to solve problems.

Success criteria

- I can tell you the number pairs to ten.

You will need

Photocopiable sheets
'What could it be?'

Equipment
Individual whiteboards

Differentiation

Less confident learners
Adapt the photocopiable sheet to concentrate addition and subtraction facts to at least ten.

More confident learners
Adapt the photocopiable sheet to facts to 10 and then multiples of 5 and 100.

Lesson 3   Oral and mental starter 55

Main teaching activities

Whole-class work: Tell the children that in this lesson they will be using addition and subtraction facts to ten and multiples of ten to 100 to solve problems. Say: *I bought a candy stick and a toffee. They cost 10p. How much was each of them?* Discuss how they should go about this and then ask them to write down all the possibilities on their whiteboards. Take feedback and systematically writing their responses on the board. Repeat for other amounts of money to 10p. Say: *I have 100 counters. Some are red and some are blue. How many red and blue do I have? I can tell you that they are in multiples of ten.* Ask how knowing number pairs to ten can help. Aim towards the fact that if they know that 7 + 3= 10, they know that 70 + 30 = 100, if 8 + 2 = 10, then 80 + 20 = 100 and so on. Explain why this is, linking 1 to 10 with 10 to 100.

Independent work: The children complete photocopiable page 'What could it be? from the CD-ROM'

Progress check: Ask questions such as:
- *If I know that 4 + 6 = 10, what else do I know?*
- *If I know that 10 − 5 = 5, what else do I know?*

Review

Go through a few examples from the children's work, then write on the board: $\square$ + $\bigcirc$ = 100 and ask: *What two numbers could go into the square and the circle? Are there any other possibilities?*

Curriculum objectives

- To recognise the place value of each digit in a two-digit number (tens, ones).
- To use place value and number facts to solve problems.

Success criteria

- I can use number pairs to ten to solve problems.

You will need

Photocopiable sheets
'What's my answer?'

Equipment
Individual whiteboards

Differentiation

Less confident learners
Adapt the photocopiable sheet to give simpler prices.

More confident learners
Adapt the photocopiable sheet to give more complex prices.

Lesson 4   Oral and mental starter 55

Main teaching activities

Whole-class work: This lesson continues using addition and subtraction facts to ten and also 20 and multiples of ten to 100 to solve problems within the context of money. Begin by practising these. Call out numbers to 20. The children write down the number that goes with them to make 20. Repeat with multiples of ten to 100. Remind them to make use of number pairs to ten, for example 2 + 8 = 10 so 20 + 80 = 100. Write 12 + 23 + 18 on the board. Ask: *How can we use this strategy to help us work this out?* Listen to their suggestions. Focus on partitioning and then adding the tens, then the 2 and 8 to make another 10 and then add the 3 to make 53. Repeat with other examples.

Independent work: Ask the children to solve the problems on photocopiable page 'What's my answer?' from the CD-ROM focusing on the strategies discussed to answer them. Model an example. Some of the questions are open-ended having more than one answer.

Progress check: Check that everyone knows what to do by inviting a child from each ability level to explain their first problem. Do the rest of the children agree with what they did and the answer?

Review

Discuss the questions that ask what someone could have bought and ask the children to tell you their different answers and how they worked them out. Ask similar questions using the price list on photocopiable page 'What's my answer?'

Curriculum objectives
● To recognise the place value of each digit in a two-digit number (tens, ones).
● To use place value and number facts to solve problems.

Success criteria
● I can solve word problems using number facts.

You will need
Photocopiable sheets
'Problems'; 'Solve me!'
Equipment
Individual whiteboards

Differentiation
Less confident learners
Adapt photocopiable page 'Solve me!' to show simpler measures and prices.
More confident learners
Adapt photocopiable page 'Solve me!' to show more complex measures and prices.

Lesson 5

Main teaching activities

Whole-class work: Tell the children that in this lesson they will be using the strategies from the previous two lessons to solve problems that involve measures and money. Discuss the mental calculation strategies for addition that they have been learning about. Recap adding using partitioning and number pairs to ten with examples such as 37 + 43, 25 + 16 + 15. Highlight the fact that they need to partition the numbers, then find any ones numbers that make ten, add these and then any other numbers if appropriate and finally recombine. Repeat with several additions, expecting the children to write their answers on their whiteboards.

Move on to subtraction. Write 36 − 24 on the board. Discuss how knowing number pairs to ten can help here. Agree that when counting on the children jump to the next multiple of ten and so need to know what to add to the existing ones number to make ten, for example 24 + 6 = 30, 30 + 6 = 36, the answer is 12. Repeat with other subtraction calculations.

Next discuss what the children need to do to solve a problem. Draw out these steps: 1) look for the question, 2) look for the information, 3) decide what to do, 4) estimate the answer, 5) work out the answer, 6) check the answer. Work through the problems on photocopiable page 'Problems' from the CD-ROM ensuring that you follow these steps and use the strategies discussed.

Independent work: Distribute photocopiable page 'Solve me!' from the CD-ROM and model an example. Encourage the children to use the strategies discussed to solve the problems.

Progress check: Invite volunteers to share examples of the problems they are solving. Does the class agree with their answers?

Review

Invite some children to explain how they solved their problems. Use this as an assessment opportunity. Question them carefully about the process and about why they chose the strategy they used. Ask how they checked their answers and encourage them to use inverses. Demonstrate this with an arrow (inversion) diagram.

Addition and subtraction: using partitioning and sequencing

Expected prior learning

Children should be able to:

- add and subtract using mental calculation strategies
- use a different method to check additions and subtractions
- use the inverse operation to check additions and subtractions.

Topic	Curriculum objectives	Expected outcomes
Addition and subtraction	**Lesson 1** To add and subtract using concrete objects, pictorial representations, and mentally, including: • a two-digit number and ones • two two-digit numbers.	Use mental calculation strategies to add and subtract: bridging ten, adding multiples, sequencing.
	Lesson 2 To add and subtract using concrete objects, pictorial representations, and mentally, including: two two-digit numbers. To recognise and use the inverse relationship between addition and subtraction and use this to check calculations and solve missing number problems.	Use mental calculation including near doubling and counting on to solve problems in the context of money.
	Lesson 3 To add and subtract using concrete objects, pictorial representations, and mentally, including: two two-digit numbers. To recognise and use the inverse relationship between addition and subtraction and use this to check calculations and solve missing number problems.	Add using the vertical (column) partitioning method. Find differences by counting on.
	Lesson 4 To add and subtract using concrete objects, pictorial representations, and mentally, including: a two-digit number and ones.	Exchanging ones for a ten in addition. Exchanging a ten for ones in subtraction.
	Lesson 5 To solve problems with addition and subtraction: • using concrete objects and pictorial representations, including those involving numbers, quantities and measures • applying their increasing knowledge of mental and written methods.	Use addition and subtraction strategies to solve simple addition and subtraction problems within the context of money.

Preparation

Lesson 1: copy photocopiable sheet 'Home we go! gameboard' and 'Target board' for groups of children

Lesson 4: copy, cut up and laminate photocopiable page 'Place value circles' in squares or circles depending on the time you have (either will work well)

Lesson 5: prepare containers of 10p and 1p coins for pairs of children

You will need

Photocopiable sheets

'How much?'; 'Shopping'; 'Exchange'; 'Column addition and subtraction template'

General resources

'Home we go! gameboard'; 'Target board'; 'Place value circles'; '0–100 number cards'

Equipment

Individual whiteboards; dice; 10p and 1p coins; counters

Further practice

'Column addition and subtraction template' can be used to give children further practice of this new method. You will need to provide children with suitable number sentences or money problems for this purpose.

Oral and mental starters for week 2

See bank of starters on pages 249 to 250. Oral and mental starters are also from the CD-ROM.

56 Which fraction?

58 Times tables

59 Addition strategies

60 Subtraction strategies

Overview of progression

During this week children will continue to develop their understanding of addition and subtraction. There will be a focus on mental calculation strategies for addition and subtraction – for example bridging ten, adding multiples of ten and adjusting, sequencing. The children will be encouraged to the strategy that they think best fits the calculation. They will also focus on adding using partitioning vertically and practically exchanging tens and ones as an introduction to the more formal written methods they are likely to encounter in Year 3.

Watch out for

Some children may find it difficult to use a variety of mental calculation strategies. These children should focus on partitioning for addition and counting on for subtraction.

Creative context

Ask the children to make up a game or scavenger hunt activity which enables them to practise the different strategies for addition and subtraction.

Vocabulary

add, addition, altogether, **bridging ten**, counting on, difference, exchange, **inverse operation**, make, more, **partitioning**, plus, subtract, sum, take away, **tens boundary**

■SCHOLASTIC

Curriculum objectives
● To add and subtract using concrete objects, pictorial representations, and mentally, including: a two-digit number and ones; two two-digit numbers.

Success criteria
● I can add using different mental calculation strategies.
● I can subtract using different mental calculation strategies.

You will need
Photocopiable sheets
'Home we go!'
General resources
'Target board'
Equipment
Individual whiteboards; counters

Differentiation
Less confident learners
Adapt the photocopiable page 'Target board' to include smaller numbers.
More confident learners
Adapt the photocopiable page 'Target board' to include larger numbers.

Lesson 1   Oral and mental starter 56

Main teaching activities

Whole-class work: Explain that this week the children will be looking at addition and subtraction. Ask: *What can you tell me about addition and subtraction?* Take feedback gathering all the important facts. In particular establish that numbers can be placed in any order for addition and the answer will be the same, for subtraction the answer will usually be different, addition and subtraction are inverse operations. Write examples of these on the board to demonstrate.

Today the children will be rehearsing mental calculation strategies. Begin with bridging ten. Check that they understand what this means: going through a tens boundary. Write 26 + 8 on the board. Ask: *What is the next tens number after 26? How many ones are needed to get to it? How can you partition eight into two numbers, one to make 30?* Write what they say as a number sentence, for example 26 + 8 = 26 + 4 + 4 = 30 + 4 = 34. Do this for subtraction: 26 − 8 = 26 − 6 − 2 = 18. Repeat with other examples. The children write their bridging methods on their whiteboards

Now write 35 + 19 on the board. Ask: *What is a good strategy to use for this?* Agree rounding 19 to 20, add this and subtract one: 35 + 20 − 1 = 54. Do this for subtraction: 35 − 20 + 1 =16. Ensure your explanations are clear. Now remind the children of sequencing: keeping the first number whole and partitioning the second. Demonstrate adding and subtracting using this example: 28 + 16 = 28 + 10 + 6 = 38 + 6 = 38 + 2 + 4 = 44; 28 − 16 = 28 − 10 − 6 = 18 − 6 = 12. Repeat with other examples.

Group work: The children work in similar attainment groups. Demonstrate how to use photocopiable pages 'Home we go! gameboard' with 'Target board', both from the CD-ROM. For each addition they use the best of the strategies discussed during the lesson.

Progress check: Visit groups to make sure that they understand how to play the game. Recap the different strategies they could use for their additions.

Review

Invite some children from each group to demonstrate which numbers they chose and to explain clearly how they worked out the calculation. Write 19 + 26 on the board and ask the children to answer this using the three strategies practised: 26 + 4 + 15; 26 + 20 − 1, 26 + 10 + 9. Ask them which strategy they thought was the best and why. Repeat for 26 − 19.

Curriculum objectives
● To add and subtract using pictorial representations, and mentally, including: two two-digit numbers.
● To recognise and use the inverse relationship between addition and subtraction.

Success criteria
● I can choose the best strategy to use for addition and subtraction.
● I can check my answers using the opposite operation.

You will need
Photocopiable sheets
'How much?'
Equipment
Individual whiteboards

Differentiation
Less confident learners
Adapt the photocopiable sheet so that children work with amounts to £10.
More confident learners
Ask children to find the differences between their chosen toys.

Lesson 2   Oral and mental starter 58

Main teaching activities

Whole-class work: Set this problem: *At the school fair, Courtney bought a drink for 37p and a cake for 35p. How much did she spend? Discuss this with your partner.* Take feedback. Agree that they need to add the amounts together. *What strategy would you use to find the total?* Encourage the strategies used in Lesson 1 and also near doubling (because 35 and 37 are close together, one can be doubled and the answer adjusted: 35 + 35 + 2). Ask the children to work out the answer in different ways. *How can we check that our answer is correct?* Agree that they can either add the numbers in a different order or use subtraction (inverse operation) and take one of the numbers away from the answer. Ask: *How much more is the drink than the biscuit? Discuss with your partner.* Agree that as the numbers are close together they could count on from 35 to 37. Discuss how they could check using addition: add the answer to the lowest number. If they get the largest number they are correct. Repeat this with similar problems.

Independent work: Distribute photocopiable page 'How much?' from the CD-ROM and demonstrate what the children need to do. Encourage them to use what they think is the best strategy for finding each total.

Progress check: Invite some children to describe their work so far. Compare their strategies with those other children suggest.

Review
Take feedback from the activity. Invite children to share some of their choices and totals. Expect them to demonstrate their methods.

Curriculum objectives
● To add and subtract using pictorial representations, and mentally, including: two two-digit numbers.
● To recognise and use the inverse relationship between addition and subtraction.

Success criteria
● I can partition and add numbers using the vertical method.
● I can check a calculation by doing the opposite operation.

You will need
Photocopiable sheets
'Shopping'
Equipment
Individual whiteboards

Differentiation
Less confident learners
Adapt the photocopiable sheet so that children work with whole pounds to £20.
More confident learners
Adapt the photocopiable sheet to show costs of toys in pounds and pence.

Lesson 3   Oral and mental starter 59

Main teaching activities

Whole-class work: Set this problem: *Sasha bought a teddy bear for £12 and a doll for £13. How much did she spend? Talk to your partner about how to work that out.* Take feedback and agree that they add to find the total. Discuss strategies, for example partitioning, sequencing, near doubling. Show them the partitioning strategy set out vertically:

```
    £13
 +  £12
    £20
     £5
    £25
```

Agree that this involves less writing than partitioning along the line and so is more efficient. Discuss checking by adding in a different order or using subtraction. *If Sasha gave the shopkeeper £30 how much change would she receive?* Agree they need to find the difference between £25 and £30. They could count on to give £5. Again, discuss how to check. Repeat with similar problems.

Independent work: Give the children photocopiable page 'Shopping' from the CD-ROM to complete. They should use the method practised in the lesson.

Progress check: Check to make sure everyone has understood what to do by asking two or three children to give an example of the toys they chose.

Review
Invite children to share the toys they bought and demonstrate their totals by partitioning vertically. They show how they found the change by counting on.

Curriculum objectives
● To add and subtract using concrete objects, pictorial representations, and mentally, including: two-digit number and ones.

Success criteria
● I can exchange ten ones for a ten when I add.
● I can exchange a ten for ones when I subtract.

You will need

General resources
'Place value circles'

Equipment
Individual whiteboards; dice

Differentiation
The children work in mixed-ability pairs during the game.

Lesson 4 · Oral and mental starter 60

Main teaching activities

Whole-class work: Ask the children if they can remember playing the 'Place-value circle game' from autumn 2, week 1. Show the circles and remind them about counting ten ones circles and exchanging them for a tens circle. Tell the children that they will play this game again with a partner. Give each pair ten tens circles and 30 ones circles. Explain: *Take it in turns to throw the dice, collect that number of ones circles. Keep doing this. Each time you collect ten, exchange them for a tens circle. The winner is the first one to get 50 or more.* Let them play until someone gets to 50 then stop everyone. Take five tens circles and say: *This time I am going to play a different game. I have 50 (five tens) and I need to take away ones to get to zero.* Ask a child to roll the dice. *How can I take that number of ones away when I only have tens circles? Talk to your partner about what I should do.* Take feedback and establish that you need to exchange a tens circle for ten ones circles. Keep demonstrating this, exchanging when you need to until you have none left.

Paired work: The children play the game with place value circles as you demonstrated.

Progress check: As this is likely to be a new concept for the children, stop a few times to make sure they understand what to do. If necessary give another demonstration. Ask questions such as: *If I have two tens circles and need to take away four ones, what should I do?*

Review

Take feedback from the game. How did the children get on? Did they understand the idea of exchanging a ten for ones? Finish the lesson by playing the game again. Split the children into two or three groups and they play against each other. Tell the children they will be doing something similar in the next lesson.

Curriculum objectives

● To solve problems with addition and subtraction: using concrete objects and pictorial representations, including those involving numbers, quantities and measures; applying their increasing knowledge of mental and written methods.

Success criteria

● I can solve word problems by exchanging.

You will need

Photocopiable sheets

'Exchange'

Equipment

10p and 1p coins

Differentiation

Adapt photocopiable page 'Exchange' so that the children are using amounts that match their attainment levels.

Main teaching activities

Whole-class work: Set this problem: *Stacey had four 10p coins. She needed to give 8p to her brother. How much will she have left? How can what we did yesterday help us work this out?* Take feedback. Agree that the children could take one of the 10p coins and exchange it for 1p coins then take eight away leaving 32p. Demonstrate this using 10p and 1p coins. Repeat with a similar problem.

Next say: *Theo had 62p. He spent 46p on a can of cola. How much did he have left?* Discuss with your partner. Show six 10p coins and two 1p coins. Take four tens away from the 60 to leave two 10p coins. *I now need to take 6p away but only have two, what should I do?* Show the two 1p coins and then the remaining 10p coins. Expect someone to tell you that you need to exchange a 10p coin for ten 1p coins. Do this and then take the six away to leave 16p. Repeat for similar problems that involve subtracting, for example, 63p and 27p, 84p and 38p. Demonstrate how to take the tens away and then exchange a 10p coin for 1p coins in order to take away the ones each time. Give the children containers of 10p and 1p coins and ask them to do what you do.

Paired work: Distribute photocopiable page 'Exchange' from the CD-ROM which gives a set of subtraction problems for the children to solve. Give each pair 10p and 1p coins. They find the solutions using the method you have been working on. When they have their answer they check by adding the answer to the amount left to see if they end up with the original amount. As this is a practical activity, the children just write their answers and draw the coins left on their sheet.

Progress check: Invite some children to describe their work so far. Are they able to take away the tens and then exchange when necessary?

Review

Take feedback from 'Exchange', inviting pairs to show how they found their answers and checked. Finish the lesson by asking the children a range of questions to assess how well they understand the concept of exchange.

Multiplication and division: partitioning and grouping

Expected prior learning

Children should be able to:

- answer multiplication calculations by counting up along a number line
- answer division calculations by grouping.

Topic	Curriculum objectives	Expected outcomes
Multiplication and division	**Lesson 1**	
	To calculate mathematical statements for multiplication and division within the multiplication tables and write them using the multiplication (×), division (÷) and equals (=) signs. To show that multiplication of two numbers can be done in any order (commutative) and division of one number by another cannot.	Double and halve single and two-digit numbers.
	Lesson 2	
	To calculate mathematical statements for multiplication and division within the multiplication tables and write them using the multiplication (×), division (÷) and equals (=) signs. To recall and use multiplication and division facts for the 2, 5 and 10 multiplication tables, including recognising odd and even numbers.	Complete missing number sentences. Use what we know about multiplying and dividing to solve calculations.
	Lesson 3	
	To calculate mathematical statements for multiplication and division within the multiplication tables and write them using the multiplication (×), division (÷) and equals (=) signs.	Multiply using partitioning.
	Lesson 4	
	To calculate mathematical statements for multiplication and division within the multiplication tables and write them using the multiplication (×), division (÷) and equals (=) signs.	Understand division as grouping. Understand that there might be a remainder when dividing.
	Lesson 5	
	To solve problems involving multiplication and division, using materials, arrays, repeated addition, mental methods, and multiplication and division facts, including problems in contexts.	Use division to solve simple problems and multiplication to check. Make up division problems.

Preparation

Lesson 1: enlarge, copy onto card and laminate photocopiable page 'Multiplication and division vocabulary'

Lesson 2: copy and cut out the cards on photocopiable page 'What we know' for groups of children

You will need

Photocopiable sheets

'Dartboard doubles game'; 'Dartboard doubles spinner'; 'Dartboard doubles gameboard'; 'What we know'; 'Multiplication'; 'Grouping problems'

General resources

'Multiplication and division vocabulary'; '0–100 number cards'; interactive activity 'Face the facts'

Equipment

Individual whiteboards; interlocking cubes; bags; counters

Further practice

Photocopiable page 'Home we go! gameboard' and interactive activity 'Face the facts', can be used to check children's understanding of 2-, 5-, and 10-times tables.

Oral and mental starters for week 3

See bank of starters on pages 167 and 249. Oral and mental starters are also on the CD-ROM.

41 Spider charts

61 Double that number

56 Which fraction?

58 Times tables

Overview of progression

During this week children will consolidate and extend their knowledge of multiplication and division. There will be a focus on doubling and halving and using known facts to work out missing number sentences. They will explore partitioning for multiplying two-digit numbers by a single digit. They will focus on grouping for division.

Watch out for

Some children may have difficulty with the concept of grouping. Give them simple number problems and practical apparatus so that they can practise taking groups of the divisor away.

Creative context

You could ask the children to make up games to practise multiplication and division.

Vocabulary

divide, divided by, equal groups of, grouping, groups of, lots of, multiple of, multiplied by, multiply, **remainder**, repeated addition, repeated subtraction, times

Curriculum objectives

Curriculum objectives
● To calculate mathematical statements for multiplication and division within the multiplication tables and write them using the multiplication (×), division (÷) and equals (=) signs.
● To show that multiplication of two numbers can be done in any order (commutative) and division for one number by another cannot.

Success criteria
● I can double two-digit numbers.
● I can halve two-digit numbers.

You will need
Photocopiable sheets
'Dartboard doubles game'; 'Dartboard doubles spinner'; 'Dartboard doubles gameboard'
General resources
'Multiplication and division vocabulary'; '0–100 number cards'
Equipment
Individual whiteboards

Differentiation
Less confident learners
Children use numbers to 20, with counting apparatus if that helps.
More confident learners
Write extra numbers on the blank cards provided such as 34, 45, 16 and 150.

Lesson 1   Oral and mental starter 61

Main teaching activities

Whole-class work: This week the children will be working on multiplication and division. Ask: *What do we mean by 'multiply' and 'divide'? What vocabulary do we use for these two operations?* Show the 'Multiplication and division vocabulary' cards from the CD-ROM as the children say the words and stick them on the board; add any words the children don't say. Group the cards into multiplying and dividing words and any that can be for both. Bring out the fact that it doesn't matter which way round you multiply the answer will be the same but that this doesn't apply to division. Also that multiplication and division are inverse operations and one can be used to check or solve the other.

Say: *Today we are thinking about doubling and halving. What do we mean by doubling? What can we do to double four?* (add 4 + 4, multiply 4 × 2) Write 4 + 4 and 4 × 2 on the board. *What do we mean by halving?* Agree that it is a number grouped into two equal amounts. Use an arrow diagram to demonstrate that halving is the inverse of doubling as they are multiplication and division.

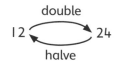

Write some numbers below 20 on the board and ask the children to draw inversion arrow diagrams on their whiteboards. Say: *How can we double 24? Talk to your partner.* Take feedback and establish that they could partition 24 into 20 and 4, double each number and recombine. Remind them that they could use their knowledge that double two is four to work out double 20. Give the children some two-digit numbers to double.

Next say: *How can we halve 48? Talk to your partner.* Agree that, again, they could partition 48 into 40 and 8, halve each number and recombine. *How could we halve 30?* Establish that they could partition 30 into 20 and 10, halve them and recombine.

Give the children some two-digit numbers, including multiples of ten, to halve.

Group work: Ask the children to play the 'Dartboard doubles game' from the CD-ROM in pairs or groups of three. Use the instructions to demonstrate.

Progress check: Visit pairs and groups to check that they are playing the game correctly.

Review

Play the oral and mental starter game 'Doubles and halves' as a class. Give a few number cards to groups of three or four. This is more effective than giving each child a card for two reasons: it gives support to any children who might be anxious and it keeps the children involved throughout the game.

Curriculum objectives
● To recall and use multiplication and division facts for the 2, 5 and 10 multiplication tables.
● To calculate mathematical statements for multiplication and division.

Success criteria
● I can use my times tables to multiply and divide.

You will need
Photocopiable sheets
'What we know'
General resources
Interactive activity 'Face the facts'
Equipment
Individual whiteboards

Differentiation
The children work in mixed-ability groups. Ensure that everyone takes an active part.

Lesson 2 — Oral and mental starter 41

Main teaching activities

Whole-class work: Explain that today's lesson is about using what we know to multiply and divide mentally. Establish that the children know the two-, five- and ten-times tables, and are beginning to know the three-times table. They know that a number times 1 is the same number and they can also double. Write these missing number sentences on the board: $1 \times \square = 7$, $\square \times 10 = 60$, $2 \times \square = 20$, $15 = 3 \times \square$, $\square \times 2 = 50$, $\square \div 2 = 20$, $5 \div \square = 5$, $80 \div \square = 8$, $\square \div 3 = 10$. Ask the children to write on their whiteboards what they think should go in each box. Discuss what information they knew that helped them to find the answers.

Group work: The children work in mixed-ability groups of four. Demonstrate one of the 'What we know' cards from the CD-ROM, then ask the children to work together in their groups to solve the calculations on the rest of the cards.

Progress check: Visit the groups to ensure that everyone is taking part and that they are discussing what they know.

Review

Go through the cards the children worked out in the activity. Ask them to tell you the answers and what they knew that helped them to find the answers. For example: *What multiplied by nine is nine? How do we know that? What is the rule that helps us? Can that help us to work out what number divided by nine gives one?*

Curriculum objectives
● To calculate mathematical statements for multiplication and division.

Success criteria
● I can multiply using partitioning.

You will need
Photocopiable sheets
'Multiplication'
Equipment
Individual whiteboards

Differentiation
Less confident learners
Adapt the photocopiable sheet so that children multiply two-digit numbers to 20 by 2 and 5.

More confident learners
Adapt the photocopiable sheet so that children multiply numbers up to 100 by 3 and 4.

Lesson 3 — Oral and mental starter 58

Main teaching activities

Whole-class work: Say: *We have been using what we know to help us multiply and divide. Today we are going to learn how to multiply when we can't use what we know.* If necessary, remind the children what they did when they doubled and halved in lesson 1. Agree that they could use partitioning.

Write 14×5 on the board. Together, partition 14 into 10 and 4 and multiply each number by 5 then recombine. Use this model to demonstrate:

Show this method as well (it links to the work they did in the previous week on addition):

```
    14
 ×   5
    50
    20
    70
```

Write some more two-digit numbers on the board for the children to practise multiplying in one of these ways. Ensure they multiply by two, three, five or ten. Let them choose the model that they prefer.

Independent work: Ask the children to complete photocopiable page 'Multiplication' from the CD-ROM.

Progress check: Ask:
● *How are you going to multiply that number?*
● *What will you partition this two-digit number into?*

Review

Invite the children to share examples of the work they did using both methods explored today. Ask them which method they preferred and why.

■SCHOLASTIC

Curriculum objectives

● To calculate mathematical statements for multiplication and division within the multiplication tables and write them using the multiplication (×), division (÷) and equals (=) signs.

Success criteria

● I can divide by grouping.
● I can tell you if there will be a remainder when I group.

You will need

Equipment

Interlocking cubes; bags; individual whiteboards; counters

Differentiation

Less confident learners

Give children 20 counters to investigate.

More confident learners

Give children 50 counters to investigate.

Lesson 4   Oral and mental starter 56

Main teaching activities

Whole-class work: Explain that today the children will focus on division. Recap the two aspects of division: grouping and sharing. Briefly explain the difference using two word problems as follows:

- *I have 15 cakes and I am going to share them equally between my three friends. How many will they each get?*
- *I have 15 cakes and I am going to put them in bags of three. How many bags do I need?*

Demonstrate sharing by involving three children to act as friends and share 15 cubes (representing cakes) between them (one for you, one for you, and so on). Next demonstrate grouping by taking groups of three cubes away from the 15 and placing them in bags. Focus on grouping for the rest of the lesson. Demonstrate grouping practically, on a number line and as arrays. Give the children 20 counters each. Ask them to group them into groups of two. When they have they write the division number sentence on their whiteboards: $20 \div 2 = 10$. Next ask them to group the 20 counters into groups of three. What do they notice? Agree that there are two left over. *What are these two left over counters called?* Agree the *remainder*. They write the number sentence $20 \div 3 = 6$ remainder 2.

Paired work: Tell the children that they will investigate finding how many groups they can take from 30 counters. They group in all the numbers 2–10 and record their results in their books with the remainder.

Progress check: Visit pairs of children. Ask questions such as:

- *How many groups of ten will I have? How do you know?*
- *If I group 30 into threes, would I have a remainder? Why not?*

Review

Take feedback from the activity. Ask the children how they could work out some of their answers without physically grouping counters, for example 30 into groups of 5. Agree that they could count in fives or use their five-times table facts.

- To solve step problems involving multiplication and division, using materials, arrays, repeated addition, mental methods and multiplication and division facts, including problems in contexts.

Success criteria
- I can solve simple problems involving multiplication and division.

You will need
Photocopiable sheets
'Grouping problems'
Equipment
Individual whiteboards

Differentiation

Less confident learners
Adapt photocopiable page 'Grouping problems' so that children focus on dividing by two, five and ten.

More confident learners
Adapt photocopiable page 'Grouping problems' so that children focus on dividing by three, four and six.

Lesson 5   Oral and mental starter 58

Main teaching activities

Whole-class work: Recap the important things to remember about multiplication and division: multiplication is repeated addition; division is repeated subtraction or grouping and also sharing; you can solve these using tables facts, number lines and arrays; they are inverse operations; it doesn't matter which way round you multiply the answer will be the same, this is not so for division because the answer is usually different. Ask the children to draw some examples of multiplying and dividing using a number line and arrays. They explain what they have done to a partner. Take feedback, inviting children to demonstrate their examples on the board.

Explain that today the children will make up and solve problems involving division. Say: *Max had 18 sandwiches. He wanted to put 3 into each bag. How many bags will he need? How will you find the answer to this problem?* Agree that they need to find out how many groups of three can be made out of 18. Ask the children to work this out using a number line and then to check by counting on in threes to 18. Ask similar problems, including those that will leave remainders.

Independent work: Distribute photocopiable page 'Grouping problems' from the CD-ROM and explain that they need to solve problems using the strategy of their choice and then to make some up of their own.

Progress check: Ask the children who you might want to assess to show you how they solved one of their problems.

Review

Invite a few children to share how they solved one of their problems. Ask the class how they could check that the answer is correct. Agree by using the inverse operation of multiplication. Invite different children to do this. Invite some to share the problems they made up and ask the class to solve them.

Fractions: finding fractions of quantities, shapes and sets of objects

Expected prior learning

Children should be able to:

- find halves, quarters and three quarters of small amounts
- be familiar with thirds.

Topic	Curriculum objectives	Expected outcomes
Fractions	**Lesson 1**	
	To recognise, find, name and write fractions ⅓, ¼, ²⁄₄ and ¾.	Find halves and quarters of shapes.
	Lesson 2	
	To recognise, find, name and write fractions ⅓, ¼, ²⁄₄ and ¾. To write simple fractions such as ½ of 6 = 3 and recognise the equivalence of ²⁄₄ and ½.	Link fractions to sharing. Find fractions of numbers including thirds.
	Lesson 3	
	To recognise, find, name and write fractions ⅓, ¼, ²⁄₄ and ¾. To write simple fractions such as ½ of 6 = 3 and recognise the equivalence of ²⁄₄ and ½.	Explore fractions of a clock face and equate the fractions to the number of minutes.
	Lesson 4	
	To recognise, find, name and write fractions ⅓, ¼, ²⁄₄ and ¾.	Find halves, quarters and thirds of numbers.
	Lesson 5	
	To recognise, find, name and write fractions ⅓, ¼, ²⁄₄ and ¾. To write simple fractions such as ½ of 6 = 3 and recognise the equivalence of ²⁄₄ and ½.	Solve simple problems involving fractions.

Preparation

Lesson 1: prepare enough pieces of square paper for four per child

Lesson 2: prepare containers of cubes for each pair of children

Lesson 3: prepare enough copies of photocopiable page 'Clock faces' two per child

Lesson 4: each group needs three pieces of A4 paper for the task

You will need

Photocopiable sheets
'Are they fractions?'; 'Fraction problems (2)'

General resources
'Clock faces'

Equipment
Square paper; scissors; glue; counters; interlocking cubes; individual whiteboards; individual clocks; paper copies of a clock face; coloured A3 paper; A4 paper; £1 coins

Further practice

Interactive activity 'Finding fractions' can be used for additional practice in finding simple fractions.

Oral and mental starters for week 4

See bank of starters on pages 249 to 250. Oral and mental starters are also from the CD-ROM.

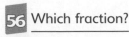

56 Which fraction?

57 Telling the time again

63 Multiplying

64 Grouping

65 More time differences

Overview of progression

During this week children will extend and consolidate their knowledge of fractions. They will recap the key ideas that they have learned so far. They will link finding fractions to sharing, and use this knowledge to find fractions of shapes and small numbers. They will explore different ways of making halves, quarters and thirds and link to time and money. They will use their understanding gained during the week to solve simple problems in the context of money.

Watch out for

Some children may still think fractions need to look the same. Give them opportunities to make halves, quarters and thirds in different ways on squared paper, for example shading these fractions in different ways on 12 squares, so that they can 'see' that is the same amount but doesn't necessarily look the same.

Creative context

You could ask the children to draw rectangles and shade halves, quarters and thirds, then they cut them up to make a collage. Can other children identify which fraction each one is?

Vocabulary

divide, equal parts, **equivalent**, four quarters, fraction, group, one half, one quarter, one whole, part, share, **third**, three quarters, two halves, two quarters

Curriculum objectives

● To recognise, find, name and write fractions ⅓, ¼, ¾ and ¾.

Success criteria

● I can recognise halves and quarters of shapes.

You will need

Photocopiable sheets

'Are they fractions?'

Equipment

Square paper, scissors

Differentiation

Less confident learners

When working on photocopiable page 'Are they fractions?' the children focus on the halves.

More confident learners

When the children have completed the photocopiable sheet ask them to draw their own shapes and find ways to show quarters.

Lesson 1   Oral and mental starter 56

Main teaching activities

Whole-class work: Ask: *Who can tell me something about a fraction?* See Summer term 1 week 4 lesson 1 for the statements that the children should be able to tell you.

Set this problem: *Sally has a rectangular shaped cake. She wants to give a quarter of it to her mum. How can she do this?* Invite the children to share their thinking. Agree that the cake needs to be divided into four equal parts and Sally's mum will need one piece out of the four. Give pairs of children several pieces of square paper. Between them they find ways of making quarters. Expect these:

They fold the paper in half and in half again to do this and draw pencil lines along the folds. Some children might make eighths and be able to tell you that Sally's mum will need two of these pieces. Ask them to make sure they have drawn the four shown above and then to cut them out to make sure they are the same size. What do they notice about the shape with the diagonal lines? Agree that they don't appear to be the same size because the triangles look different. Ask them to explore how they could check this. If they cannot tell you, demonstrate cutting the quarters in half. Each resultant shape will be the same size and therefore the same fraction, so the originals are quarters. Highlight that this shows that fractions are the same size but might look different.

Draw a selection of shapes on the board. Divide some of them into half and others into two unequal parts. The children identify those that show half.

Draw this triangle with four parts on the board:

How can we prove that these parts of the triangle are not quarters? Establish that they could cut out the pieces and see if they are the same size. *Can you think of a way that we can divide the triangle to make quarters?* Test out their ideas. Draw them on paper and invite individuals to cut out the pieces to see if they are the same size. Agree that this shows quarters:

Independent work: Distribute photocopiable page 'Are they fractions?' from the CD-ROM. Explain that the children need to cut out the shapes and find out if they have been divided into halves or quarters as appropriate.

Progress check: Ask questions such as:

- *How do you know whether the shape has been divided into halves?*
- *How do you know the shape has been divided into quarters? How many equal parts should there be?*

Review

Take feedback from the activity. Invite individuals to explain what they did and to say whether the shapes had been divided into halves and quarters or not. Finish the lesson by recapping halves and quarters in terms of size and equivalences.

Curriculum objectives
- To recognise, find, name and write fractions ⅓, ¼, ²⁄₄ and ¾.
- To write simple fractions such as ½ of 6 = 3 and recognise the equivalence of ²⁄₄ and ½.

Success criteria
- I can find thirds.
- I can explain what a third is.

You will need

Equipment

Interlocking cubes; individual whiteboards; counters

Differentiation

The children should work in mixed-ability pairs. Ensure that each child takes an active part in the activity.

Lesson 2

Oral and mental starter 57

Main teaching activities

Whole-class work: Remind the children that finding a fraction is the same as sharing which is a type of grouping which is division. To find fractions they are sharing amounts from a whole group equally into smaller groups. Give a volunteer 20 cubes and ask them to share these equally between four other volunteers. Each volunteer will have five cubes. Each volunteer will have one out of the four groups or one quarter. Ask: *How many would ²⁄₄ be? What is this the same as? What about ¾?* Write these as number sentences: ¼ of 20 = 5, ²⁄₄ of 20 = ½ of 20 = 10, ¾ of 20 = 15.

Give the children a pile of counters. Ask them to count out 18. Ask them to share these equally into three groups. *How many are in each group?* Agree six. *What fraction have you made?* Establish that they have shared the counters into three groups so each group is one third. *How many thirds make the whole amount?* (3) *How many are the same as two thirds?* (12). Write the appropriate number sentences on the board: ⅓ of 18 = 6, ⅔ of 18 = 12. Repeat with different numbers of counters that are multiples of three. Revise finding halves and quarters in the same way.

Paired work: Give the children 12 cubes. They find ½, then ¼ , ¾, ⅓ and finally ⅔. They should record their results in fractions sentences, for example, ½ of 12 = 6. They repeat this for 24 cubes and, if time, 36 cubes.

Progress check: Check that the class is following your instructions by asking questions such as:

- *How can you find ⅓ of 12?*
- *What is ⅔ of 12? How can you write this as a number sentence?*

Review

Take feedback from the task. Invite pairs to demonstrate how they found the different fractions of 12, 24 and 36 cubes. Ask volunteers to write the appropriate number sentences on the board.

Curriculum objectives

- To recognise, find, name and write fractions ⅓, ¼, 2/4 and ¾.
- To write simple fractions such as ½ of 6 = 3 and recognise the equivalence of 2/4 and ½.

Success criteria

- I can find halves, quarters and thirds of a circle.
- I can link fractions to time.

You will need

General resources

'Clock faces'

Equipment

Individual clocks; paper copies of a clock face; scissors; glue; A3 coloured paper

Differentiation

The children work in mixed-ability groups. Ensure that each child takes an active part in the activity.

Lesson 3

Oral and mental starter 63

Main teaching activities

Whole-class work: The children will need a card clock each. Ask them to find 12 o'clock. Now ask them to move the minute hand around in fractions of an hour and to tell you the new time. For example: *Move clockwise a quarter of an hour; Clockwise half an hour; Anticlockwise a quarter of an hour.* Ask them to tell you how many minutes are the same as a quarter of an hour (15), half an hour (30) and three quarters of an hour (45). Next, ask them to look carefully at their clocks and to work out what a third would be. Agree 20 minutes. Ask them to move the minute hand of their clocks around in 20 minute intervals from 12. *How many of these make a whole hour?*

Group work: The children work in mixed-ability groups of three or four. Give them several copies of photocopiable page 'Clock faces' from the CD-ROM, A3 coloured paper, scissors and glue. They make a poster to show half an hour, quarter of an hour, three quarters of an hour, third of an hour and two thirds of an hour in at least two different ways. They stick their pieces on the A3 paper and label with the fraction and the equivalent number of minutes.

Progress check: Visit the groups to make sure they are all working on this and that they are following your instructions properly.

Review

Take feedback from the task by inviting the children to share and explain their posters. Finish the lesson by recapping what each fraction looked at is – for example, a third is a whole amount shared into three equal pieces.

Curriculum objectives

- To recognise, find, name and write fractions ⅓, ¼, 2/4 and ¾.
- To write simple fractions such as ½ of 6 = 3 and recognise the equivalence of 2/4 and ½.

Success criteria

- I can find halves, quarters and thirds of numbers.

You will need

Equipment

Individual whiteboards; three pieces of A4 paper per group

Differentiation

The children should work in mixed-ability groups. Ensure that each child takes an active part in the activity.

Lesson 4

Oral and mental starter 64

Main teaching activities

Whole-class work: Recap on finding fractions of clocks from Lesson 3. Find out what the children know about halves, quarters and thirds. Focus on multiples of the denominator for this lesson. Write ½ on the board. Ask the children what types of numbers can be shared into halves to give a whole-number answer. Agree even numbers which are also numbers that are in the two-times table. Call out even numbers for the children to halve. They show their answers on their whiteboards. Repeat this for quarters. Agree that these must come in the four-times table. Ask: *What numbers can be shared into thirds?* Agree those in the three-times table. Call out some multiples of three and ask them to find a third of them.

Group work: Give the children about 10 minutes for this task. They should work in mixed-ability groups of about three or four. Give them three pieces of A4 paper. They write ½ at the top of one, ¼ at the top of the second and ⅓ at the top of the third. Together they make a list of numbers for each column and what the answer would be when they share them equally into the fractions.

Progress check: Visit the groups to make sure they are all working on this and that they are following your instructions properly.

Review

Take feedback from the activity. Ask the children to look at their lists and to tell you any of the numbers that can be divided into halves, quarters and thirds (12, 24, 36, 48 and so on).

Curriculum objectives
● To recognise, find, name and write fractions ⅓, ¼, ⅔ and ¾.
● To write simple fractions such as ½ of 6 = 3 and recognise the equivalence of ¾ and ½.

Success criteria
● I can solve simple problems involving fractions.

You will need
Photocopiable sheets
'Fraction problems (2)'
Equipment
£1 coins

Differentiation
Less confident learners
Adapt the photocopiable sheet so that the children are working with lower amounts. Provide counting apparatus to help if required.

More confident learners
Adapt the photocopiable sheet so that the children are working with more complex amounts.

Lesson 5
Oral and mental starter 65

Main teaching activities
Whole-class work: Recap on what the children have done during the week. Ensure you reinforce that the bottom number of the fraction (denominator) tells them how many to share into, fractions are equal amounts but do not necessarily look the same. Talk through the equivalences for halves and quarters and discuss thirds: *How many thirds will make a whole? Is a third bigger or smaller than half?...quarter?* Demonstrate all points on the board using the children to help you.

Set this problem: *Sue had £21. She decided to save a third of it and spend the rest on a pair of jeans. How much did she save and how much did she spend on her jeans?* Give the children a few minutes to work out how they could find the answer. Take feedback and establish that they need to find a third of £21. This will give the amount she saved. They would then take that away from £21 to find the cost of the jeans. Demonstrate this using £1 coins, sharing them equally into three groups. Ask similar problems that involve halves, quarters and thirds within the context of money.

Tell the children that they will now use their knowledge of fractions to solve problems.

Paired work: Distribute photocopiable page 'Fraction problems (2)' from the CD-ROM. Demonstrate an example of a problem that the less confident learners will be working from.

Progress check: Visit pairs to find out how they are getting on. Resolve any issues. If there are any common issues, stop the class to address these.

Review
Go through some examples of the children's problems. Write ½, ¼ and ¾ on the board. Ask the children to work with a partner to make up a problem using one of the fractions. Listen to some of the problems and as a class answer them.

Geometry: position and direction
Measurement: time

Expected prior learning

Children should be able to:

● describe movements, including quarter and half clockwise and anticlockwise turns

● tell the time to the quarter hour and draw the hands on a clock face to show these times.

Topic	Curriculum objectives	Expected outcomes
Geometry: position and direction	**Lesson 1**	
	To order and arrange combinations of mathematical objects in patterns and sequences.	Make and describe patterns.
	Lesson 2	
	To use mathematical vocabulary to describe position, direction and movement, including movement in a straight line and distinguishing between rotation as a turn and in terms of right angles for quarter, half and three-quarter turns (clockwise and anti-clockwise).	Use the appropriate vocabulary to describe movement. Find quarter and half turns on a clock.
Measurement: time	**Lesson 3**	
	To tell and write the time to five minutes, including quarter past/to the hour and draw the hands on a clock face to show these times. To know the number of minutes in an hour and the number of hours in a day.	Find o'clock, quarter past, half past and quarter to times on a clock. Begin to find times to the nearest 5 minutes.
	Lesson 4	
	To compare and sequence intervals of time. To tell and write the time to five minutes, including quarter past/to the hour and draw the hands on a clock face to show these times.	Compare and sequence times during the day. Show times to five minutes.
	Lesson 5	
	To tell and write the time to five minutes, including quarter past/to the hour and draw the hands on a clock face to show these times.	Solve problems involving time.

Preparation

Lesson 1: make collections of about four of these 3D shapes: cylinder, cone, cube, cuboid, square-based pyramid, triangular prism

Lesson 3: enlarge a copy of photocopiable page 'Up the mountain gameboard' to A3 paper

You will need

Photocopiable sheets

'Can you see the right angle?'; 'From 3D to 2D'; 'Feeding time at the zoo'

General resources

'Analogue time cards'; 'Up the mountain gameboard'; 'Race against time instructions'; 'Race against time gameboard'; 'Race against time instruction cards'; interactive teaching resource 'Clocks'

Equipment

Individual whiteboards; 3D shapes: cone, cylinder, cube, cuboid, square-based pyramid, triangular prism; Plasticine®; small clocks; A3 paper; scissors; glue

Further practice

Photocopiable sheets

'Units of time'

Oral and mental starters for week 5

See bank of starters on pages 249 to 250. Oral and mental starters are also on the CD-ROM.

55 Money

57 Telling the time again

58 Times tables

59 Addition strategies

60 Subtraction strategies

Overview of progression

During this week children will extend their knowledge of making patterns, direction and motion. They will recap their knowledge of 3D and 2D shape while making patterns using them. They will explore direction through the use of clocks. They will also extend their knowledge of time. They will find o'clock, quarter to, half past, quarter to times and times to five minute on clocks. They will also sequence times and find differences between them. They will use their understanding of time to solve problems.

> ### Watch out for
> Some children may still not be able to tell o'clock and half past times on a clock. Provide these children with clock faces and ask them to match them with different o'clock and half past times on the class clock during the day and to tell you the times they have made.

Creative context

Position, direction and motion could be included in PE activities. Encourage the children to tell the time at different times of the day, for example lunch time, home time, time when literacy starts.

Vocabulary

analogue clock/watch, **anticlockwise**, **clockwise**, digital/analogue clock/watch, half past, half turn, hands, hour, left, minute, o'clock, pattern, quarter past, quarter to, quarter turn, right, right angle, second, straight line, three-quarter turn, whole turn

Curriculum objectives

● To order and arrange combinations of mathematical objects in patterns and sequences.

Success criteria

● I can make and describe patterns.

You will need

Photocopiable sheets

'From 3D to 2D'

Equipment

Individual whiteboards; a selection of 3D shapes; Plasticine®

Differentiation

Less confident learners

Give children actual 3D and 2D shapes.

More confident learners

Ask children to try to draw a representation of a whole shape, for example, a cube rather than the square face.

Lesson 1   Oral and mental starter 55

Main teaching activities

Whole-class work: Tell the children that they are going to make patterns using 3D shapes. Give groups of children a selection of 3D shapes. Discuss the names and properties of these in terms of number of faces, edges, vertices and shapes of shapes and their lines of symmetry. Next ask them to arrange them in a pattern. Once they have done this they think of a description of their pattern to share with the class. Give each child a piece of Plasticine and ask them to make a sphere. Discuss its properties and then ask them to hold it in front of them and draw what they see on their whiteboards. Ask them to tell you what shape they drew. Agree a circle. Repeat for cube (square), cuboid (rectangle), square-based pyramid (triangle).

Independent work: The children should each make a shape and draw it, completing photocopiable page 'From 3D to 2D' from the CD-ROM. Once they have done this, they use their drawings for reference and make up a pattern using these shapes.

Progress check: Check that the children understand what a repeated pattern is and are able to make them.

Review

Show some examples of the children's work. Ask others to identify each shape and to tell everyone something about it. Ask them to identify how the patterns repeat and to say the next few that will occur if the patterns continued.

Curriculum objectives

● To use mathematical vocabulary to describe direction and movement.

Success criteria

● I can use words to describe different positions.

You will need

Photocopiable sheets

'Can you see the right angle?'

Equipment

Small clocks

Differentiation

The children work in mixed-attainment pairs. Differentiation can be through peer support.

Lesson 2   Oral and mental starter 57

Main teaching activities

Whole-class work: Revisit the vocabulary of direction and movement. Ensure all the words in the vocabulary section are covered. Ask the children to look at their clocks and to find half past five. Ask: *In which direction do the hands move?* Agree clockwise. Ask them to move the minute hand a quarter turn clockwise, show you where it is and say the new time. Explain that a quarter turn is 15 minutes. Link back to the fractions work from week 4. Repeat for different positions and directions. Repeat for half turns and equate these to 30 minutes. For each, ask for the time. Discuss right angles and ask the children to place their hands on their clocks to show different right angles, for example, between 6 and 9, 2 and 5. Make the link that a quarter turn is the same size as a right angle. Repeat for half turns and link to this being the same as two quarter turns.

Paired work: First demonstrate the task using an example similar to those on photocopiable page 'Can you see the right angle?' from the CD-ROM. Then ask the children to complete the sheet as a paired activity.

Progress check: If necessary, check that the children are clear on the instructions and recap what a right angle is.

Review

Together, point out the right angles in the classroom, for example corners of windows, books and paper. Ask: *How can we use these to check those other right angles in the classroom?* (by seeing if they fit exactly in the other right angles). Finish by recapping the vocabulary and different turns.

Curriculum objectives

● To tell and write the time to five minutes, including quarter past/to the hour and draw the hands on a clock face to show these times.
● To know the number of minutes in an hour and the number of hours in a day.

Success criteria

● I can show o'clock and half past times on a clock.
● I can show quarter past and quarter to times on a clock.
● I am beginning to show 5 minutes past times.
● I can say how many minutes there are in an hour.

You will need

General resources

'Analogue time cards'; 'Up the mountain gameboard'

Equipment

Small clocks; dice

Differentiation

This is a whole-class activity. The children should work together in mixed-ability pairs or groups to support each other.

Lesson 3

Main teaching activities

Whole-class work: Introduce the next few lessons on time by looking at the vocabulary of clock times from photocopiable page 'Analogue time cards'. Ask the children to try to give you a sentence using each word. Next, give each child a clock. Ask them to look at it and give you some facts about it. Look for answers such as: *The numbers go round from 1 to 12. Those numbers show us what the hour is. If the minute hand is on the 12, it is something o'clock. If the minute hand is on the 6, it is half past something. If the minute hand is on the 3 it is quarter past. If the minute hand is on the 9 it is quarter to. The little marks in between the numbers are minutes. There are five minutes from one number to the next.*

Focus on the last two points. Ask the children to put a finger on the 12 then move to the 1. Ask how many minutes it is. Then repeat, with a finger on 2 and so on so that the children are counting in fives from zero to 60. Use the clock as a spider chart as in the oral and mental starter 'Spider charts' on page 167. Count round in fives again and make the link that these are 5, 10, 15 and so on minutes past the hour. Tell the children that 35 minutes past the hour is also 25 minutes to the next hour. Repeat for all the minutes to times. Link 15 minutes to quarter past, 30 minutes to half past and 45 minutes to quarter to, reminding them of the work they did on this in week 4.

Ask the children to find different times that you call out, for example, 10 minutes past 3, 20 minutes past 2, quarter to 10, 40 minutes past 6 (and link to the fact that this is also 20 minutes to 7). Remind the children of the game that they played called 'Up the mountain'. Divide the class into two teams, one 'even' and one 'odd'. Call out a time, wait until everyone has found it on their clocks (the children can help each other) and then throw the dice. If an even number is thrown the even team moves up the mountain. If an odd number is thrown the odd team moves. The winning team is the one that reaches the top of the mountain first.

Review

Ask the children how this game has helped them in their learning about time. Give them a clock each and finish the session by asking them some problems, such as: *My clock says quarter past 6, but it is one hour slow. Show me what time it really is. My clock says 10 minutes past 8 but it is half an hour fast. What time is it really?*

Lesson 4

Oral and mental starter 59

Main teaching activities

Whole-class work: Invite children up to find various o'clock, quarter past, half past, quarter to and times to 5 minutes. As in lesson 3, refer to minutes past the hour and link when appropriate to the equivalent 'minutes to' time, for example, 50 minutes past 3 and 10 minutes to 4. Ask children to find specific times during the day, for example, when school starts, lunchtime, playtime, the mathematics lesson. List these times on the board. Ensure the order isn't in sequence. Ask the children to tell you the order of these times during the day. After they have, ask them to tell you different times that come between them. Together, using clocks, work out the differences between times.

Paired work: Distribute photocopiable page 'Feeding time at the zoo' from the CD-ROM. The children work in mixed-ability pairs to draw the times on the clocks, cut them out and then sequence them from earliest to latest. They stick these in order on a piece of A3 paper.

Progress check: Visit pairs to make sure that they are on task and doing what is required.

Review

Invite pairs to show their work to the class. Ask the children to work out the differences in times between different feeding times. Set them some problems that they can answer using clocks, such as: *My clock says 10 minutes past 7, but it is an hour fast. Show me the time it really is. My clock says 40 minutes past 3 (or 20 minutes to 4) but it is an hour slow. Show me the time it really is.*

Curriculum objectives
● To compare and sequence intervals during the day.
● To tell and write the time to five minutes, including quarter past/to the hour and draw the hands on a clock face to show these times.

Success criteria
● I can show o'clock and half past times on a clock.
● I can show quarter past and quarter to times on a clock.

You will need
Photocopiable sheets
'Feeding time at the zoo'
Equipment
Small clocks; A3 paper; scissors; glue

Differentiation
The children should work in mixed-ability pairs. Check that more confident learners do not dominate.

Lesson 5

Oral and mental starter 60

Main teaching activities

Whole-class work: Generate some random times using the interactive teaching resource 'Clocks' on the CD-ROM and ask the children what the times say. Then ask them to find different times on their clocks. Pose some problems similar to those in lesson 3's and 4's reviews. Choose a theme, such as Sports Day, and make up problems: *It is now 1 o'clock. The race starts in an hour and a half. What time does it start? It took Sam one hour and a half to finish his race. He started at half past two, what time did he finish?* Ask the children to use their clocks to find the answers and then demonstrate on a time number line:

Agree that he finished at 4 o'clock. *Does this sound right? How could we check?* Agree that they could count back 1½ hours from 4:00 or use a clock. Ask them to check using their clocks. Repeat with similar problems.

Group work: Tell the children that they will be playing a game. Demonstrate the 'Race against time' game. They solve the problems using a clock or number line.

Progress check: Visit groups to check that they understand what to do.

Review

Discuss the problems described on the 'Race against time instruction cards', inviting children to explain how they solved them. Ask them to talk to each other about some of the things they have learned to do with time. Take some whole class feedback.

Curriculum objectives
● To tell and write the time to five minutes, including quarter past/to the hour.

Success criteria
● I can solve problems involving time.

You will need
General resources
'Race against time instructions'; 'Race against time problem cards'; 'Race against time gameboard'; interactive teaching resource 'Clocks'
Equipment
Small clocks; individual whiteboards

Differentiation
Ask more confident learners to help those who are less confident.

Statistics: pictograms and block graphs

Expected prior learning

Children should be able to:

- answer a question by collecting and recording information in a pictogram
- present outcomes using pictograms and block graphs
- use diagrams to sort objects into groups according to given criteria.

Topic	Curriculum objectives	Expected outcomes
Statistics	**Lesson 1**	
	To interpret and construct simple pictograms, tally charts, block diagrams and simple tables.	Gather information using a tally.
	To ask and answer simple questions by counting the number of objects in each category and sorting the categories by quantity.	Make and interpret lists and tables.
	To ask and answer questions about totalling and comparing categorical data.	
	Lesson 2	
	To interpret and construct simple pictograms, tally charts, block diagrams and simple tables.	Make and interpret pictograms.
	To ask and answer simple questions by counting the number of objects in each category and sorting the categories by quantity.	
	To ask and answer questions about totalling and comparing categorical data.	
	Lesson 3	
	To interpret and construct simple pictograms, tally charts, block diagrams and simple tables.	Make and interpret pictograms.
	To ask and answer simple questions by counting the number of objects in each category and sorting the categories by quantity.	
	To ask and answer questions about totalling and comparing categorical data.	
	Lesson 4	
	To interpret and construct simple pictograms, tally charts, block diagrams and simple tables.	Make and interpret block graphs.
	To ask and answer simple questions by counting the number of objects in each category and sorting the categories by quantity.	
	To ask and answer questions about totalling and comparing categorical data.	
	Lesson 5	
	To interpret and construct simple pictograms, tally charts, block diagrams and simple tables.	Make and interpret block graphs.
	To ask and answer simple questions by counting the number of objects in each category and sorting the categories by quantity.	
	To ask and answer questions about totalling and comparing categorical data.	

Preparation

Lesson 1: enlarge and copy onto card photocopiable page 'Organising data vocabulary cards' and cut out

Lesson 2: prepare a sheet of A1 paper with the axes of a pictogram

Lesson 3: prepare sheets of A3 paper, one for each pair of children

Lesson 4: prepare a sheet of A1 paper with the axes of a block chart

Lesson 5: prepare sheets of A3 paper, one for each pair of children

You will need

Photocopiable sheets

'Table information'; 'Which colour?'; 'Sports block graph'

General resources

'Organising data vocabulary cards'

Equipment

Individual whiteboards; sticky notes; A1 paper (plain or squared); dice; A3 paper (plain or squared)

Further practice

Provide further opportunities for understanding and interpreting data presented in pictograms using photocopiable sheets 'Favourite colours'.

Oral and mental starters for week 6

See bank of starters on pages 249 to 250. Oral and mental starters are also from the CD-ROM.

 Multiplying

 Grouping

66 Days and months

65 More time differences

Overview of progression

During this week children will extend their understanding of handling data. They will do this by being given problems to solve. They will be encouraged to evaluate the different methods of presenting information with regard to their suitability in each case. They will explore, collect information, represent and analyse lists, tables, pictograms and block charts.

> ### Watch out for
> Some children may find it difficult collecting, recording and interpreting information using pictograms. This is one of the early stages in data handling so it is important that the children are able to do this. Provide opportunities to practise in other areas of mathematics and, when appropriate, in other curriculum areas.

Creative context

Look for opportunities to make lists, tables, pictograms and block graphs in science and other topic work.

Vocabulary

block graph, count, label, list, most/least common/popular, pictogram, set, sort, represent, table

Curriculum objectives
- To interpret and construct.
- To ask and answer simple questions by counting the number of objects in each category and sorting the categories by quantity.
- To ask and answer questions about totalling and comparing categorical data.

Success criteria
- I can make lists and tables.
- I can tell you information from lists and tables.

You will need

Photocopiable sheets
'Table information'

General resources
'Organising data vocabulary cards'

Equipment
Individual whiteboards

Differentiation

Less confident learners
Ask children to work on one set of information. Provide them with a blank table.

More confident learners
Children work on all the sets of information, making three tables in all.

Lesson 1   Oral and mental starter 63

Main teaching activities

Whole-class work: Remind the children of the work they did on organising and using data so far this year. Ask: *Tell me what we mean by 'data' and 'organising and using data'? What words can you think of about this topic?* Write any words that they say on the board and use the cards from photocopiable page 'Organising data vocabulary cards' to prompt when necessary. Discuss the meanings of these words. Ask who remembers the ways of organising data: counting, tallying, sorting, voting and making graphs, such as block graphs and pictograms. Recap that these are ways we can represent, group or list information and they save us having to write lots of words. They also help us to see information clearly and easily. Focus on lists and tables. As a class, make up some categories for lists, for example, food, shapes, colours, and ask the children to think of examples to go in each. During their paired activity they will focus on tables.

Paired work: The children work in pairs. Give each pair a copy of photocopiable page 'Table information' from the CD-ROM. Discuss the example. There are an additional three sets of information. The children should choose two to put into two tables and then make up questions about them for the rest of the class to answer during the Review.

Progress check: As the children are working on the activity visit pairs and ask questions such as:
- *How are you going to make your table?*
- *What questions could you ask about this table?*

Review

Pairs choose the best two questions they have compiled to ask the rest of the class.

Curriculum objectives
- To interpret and construct simple pictograms.
- To ask and answer simple questions by counting the number of objects in each category and sorting the categories by quantity.
- To ask and answer questions about totalling and comparing categorical data.

Success criteria
- I can tell you information from a pictogram.

You will need
Photocopiable sheets
'Which colour?'
Equipment
A1 plain or squared paper

Differentiation
Make sure that less confident children have the opportunity to take part and more confident learners don't dominate.

Lesson 2 — Oral and mental starter 64

Main teaching activities

Whole-class work: This is a whole class lesson; the associated group work will take place in the next lesson. Explain to the children that the focus today will be on pictograms. Remind them of the school caretaker's problem 'Which colour?' (Spring 2, week 6). Say that today they are going to solve another problem using a pictogram: *Ivan Apple owns a fruit shop. He wants to find out which are the most popular fruits.* Give the children some time to talk to a friend and discuss their favourite fruit. Make a tally of their choices on the board. Draw a skeleton pictogram on a sheet of A1 paper. Say: *Each smiley face represents one child. How many faces do we need to draw for apples?* Focus on one fruit at a time and invite some children to draw smiley faces onto the skeleton pictogram according to the tally results. Repeat for the other fruits. Ask the children what labels are needed and add these. Together make up a title for the pictogram. If there is time you could ask the children to make a copy of this on paper.

Review

Analyse the class pictogram with the children, asking them to tell you as many facts about it as possible. Say: *Ivan Apple wants to order four different fruits.* Together come to a conclusion about which fruits he should order.

Curriculum objectives
- To interpret and construct simple pictograms.
- To ask and answer simple questions by counting the number of objects in each category.
- To ask and answer questions about totalling and comparing categorical data.

Success criteria
- I can make a pictogram.
- I can tell you information from a pictogram.

You will need
Equipment
A3 paper; dice

Differentiation
Less confident learners
Provide a skeleton pictogram for children to use.
More confident learners
Ask children to generate numbers by multiplying the dice numbers together.

Lesson 3 — Oral and mental starter 66

Main teaching activities

Whole-class work: Discuss and review the pictogram work the class did in lesson 2. Explain that today the children will be making up their own pictogram based on a similar problem.

Paired work: The children work in similar-ability pairs. They need to imagine that Ivor Potato owns a vegetable shop and needs to find out what vegetables to order. Together, generate a list of eight vegetables. The children make up the numbers 'voted' by throwing two dice and finding the total. They should then make up a pictogram to show the information. Remind them to add labels and a title. Once they have completed their pictogram they should make up statements from it to share during the Review.

Progress check: Spend a few minutes with pairs of children as they work and ask questions such as:
- *What is a pictogram? Explain this in a different way?*
- *How many symbols will you need for potatoes? How do you know?*

Review

Invite the children to show their pictograms and share their information statements. Assess their work and how confident they are in talking about it.

Curriculum objectives
● To interpret and construct simple block diagrams.
● To ask and answer simple questions by counting the number of objects in each category and sorting the categories by quantity.
● To ask and answer questions about totalling and comparing categorical data.
Success criteria
● I can find information from a block graph.

You will need
Photocopiable sheets
'Sports block graph'
Equipment
Sticky notes; A1 paper

Differentiation
Check that the less confident learners have the opportunity to take part and that the more confident learners don't dominate.

Curriculum objectives
● To interpret and construct simple charts, block diagrams.
● To ask and answer simple questions by counting the number of objects in each category and sorting the categories by quantity.
● To ask and answer questions about totalling and comparing categorical data.
Success criteria
● I can make a block graph.
● I can find out information from a block graph.

You will need
Equipment
Block graph from lesson 4; A3 squared paper; dice

Differentiation
Less confident learners
Provide a skeleton graph for this group to use.
More confident learners
Children total three dice and extend their vertical axis to 18.

Lesson 4 — Oral and mental starter 65

Main teaching activities

Whole-class work: As in lessons 2 and 3, the whole-class work will take up this lesson and the group work will take place in the next lesson. Explain that the children are now going to look at block graphs. Show photocopiable page 'Sports block graph' from the CD-ROM. Ask the children to tell you as much as they can about it. Encourage them to state all the possible facts. Give them each a sticky note and ask them to draw a picture of their chosen sport. While they are doing this, write the sport names and appropriate numbers (for the vertical axis) on sticky notes and draw a skeleton graph on A1 paper stuck to the board.

Gather the class together. Show them your labels and numbers. Invite children to stick them onto your skeleton graph. Encourage them to explain why they have put them in those places. Do the other children agree? Now invite everyone to come to the front in small groups and add their picture to the correct column, starting from the horizontal axis. Remember to keep the graph for the next lesson. Say: *We are going to make our own block graph to show our favourite animals.* Collect about six examples of animals that the children like. Ask them to choose their favourite one from the list.

Review

Discuss what the graph shows and ask questions (particularly of the *How many more/less...* type). Encourage the children to ask each other similar questions, perhaps after talking to a friend and making up a question together. Finally ask: *Which is the most popular animal for this class?*

Lesson 5 — Oral and mental starter 65

Main teaching activities

Whole-class work: Show the class the block graph from lesson 4. Ask questions about it and invite children to make up statements. Say: *Today you are going to make you own block graph. You need to help Anne Emu, the pet shop owner, decide what to order for her pet shop.*

Paired work: Model what the children need to do using A3 squared paper. Say: *In your group, you need to choose six animals that would make good pets. You need to finish a skeleton graph like the one we used yesterday by adding labels like this* (label the axes and fill with some animals and numbers up to 12). *Make up the numbers for your totals by throwing two dice and adding them. Draw blocks of the right height for each animal – so if you make five, colour in five squares above that animal.*

Progress check: During the activity visit pairs of children to check that they understand what they need to do.

Review

Ask each pair to join with another pair, share their graphs and say four facts that their graph shows. Invite pairs to share their graphs and facts with the class. Let the more confident pairs ask the class a few of their questions. Recap this unit of work by asking questions such as: *Why are lists, tables, pictograms and block graphs useful for showing information? What is the difference between a list and a table? What is the same? What does a pictogram look like? What about a block graph?*

Curriculum objectives
• To solve problems with addition and subtraction.

You will need
1. Check
Oral and mental starters

59 Addition strategies

60 Subtraction strategies

2. Assess
'0–100 number cards'

3. Further practice
Oral and mental starters

47 Adding 9 and 11

51 Make ten

61 Double that number

Photocopiable sheets
'Which strategy would you use?'

Mental calculation strategies

Most children should be able to use addition and subtraction strategies such as sequencing, bridging ten, adding 9 and 11 by adding/subtracting ten and adjusting and using facts.

Some children will not have made such progress and will require additional practice at sequencing.

1. Check

59 Addition strategies

60 Subtraction strategies

As you do the oral and mental starters observe which children are confident at using a variety of mental calculation strategies and which would benefit from focusing on one (such as sequencing). Ask:

- *What is 9 more than 64? How did you work that out?*
- *How would you add 15 and 16?*
- *How would you subtract 8 from 24?*

2. Assess

Give each child two number cards. Ask them to add them together using the strategy they prefer and then ask them to check by adding them using a different method. Next ask them to subtract the smaller number from the larger one and check using a different method. Repeat for other pairs of numbers. Record the outcomes.

3. Further practice

Photocopiable page 251 provides the opportunity for the children to decide which calculation method is the most appropriate.

Curriculum objectives
• To tell and write the time to five minutes, including quarter past/to the hour and draw the hands on a clock face to show these times.

1. Check
Oral and mental starter

65 More time differences

2. Assess
Small clocks

3. Further practice
Oral and mental starters

57 Telling the time again

66 Days and months

Photocopiable sheets
'Telling the time (2)'

Telling the time

Most children should be able to tell o'clock, quarter past, half past and quarter to times.

Some will be able to tell the time to five minutes. Other children will need to focus on o'clock and half past times.

1. Check

65 More time differences

As you carry out the oral and mental starter, observe which children are confident and can draw their own number lines to find time differences and which need to use pre-drawn ones or clocks. Ask:

- *What is the time difference between 4 o'clock and half past 5? How did you work that out?*
- *What is two and a half hours after 10 o'clock in the morning? How do you know?*

2. Assess

Give each child a small clock. Call out some times for them to find. Ensure you call out a mixture of o'clock, quarter past, half past and quarter to times and also five minute times, such as 25 past 6. Finally ask them if they can remember another way to say 40 minutes to 3 (20 to 4). Record the outcomes.

3. Further practice

Photocopiable page 252 'Telling the time (2)' provides the opportunity for the children to show you how well they can draw times on a clock. Encourage them to check using a different method. They should work on this independently.

Curriculum objectives
• To recognise, find, name and write fractions ⅓, ¼, ⅔ and ¾.
• To write simple fraction and recognise the equivalence of ¾ and ½.

You will need
1. Check
Oral and mental starter
56 Which fraction?

2. Assess
Counters; individual whiteboards

3. Further practice
Oral and mental starters
53 Finding fractions again

Photocopiable sheets
'Fractions of numbers'

Curriculum objectives
• To solve problems involving multiplication and division.

You will need
1. Check
Oral and mental starter
63 Multiplying
64 Grouping

2. Assess
'0–100 number cards'; individual whiteboards

3. Further practice
Oral and mental starters
58 Times tables

Photocopiable sheets
'Multiplying and dividing'

Finding halves, quarters and thirds

Most children should be able to find halves, quarters and thirds.

Some children will not have made such progress and will need to focus on finding halves and quarters.

1. Check
56 Which fraction?

Use the oral mental starter to check which children can count in halves and quarters and find fractions of small numbers. Ask:
- If I am counting in halves, which number comes after 3?
- What is a quarter of 16? How did you work that out?
- What is three quarters of 16? How could you use your knowledge of a quarter to work that out?

2. Assess

Give each child a pile of counters. Ask them to count out 12. They then find half and write the answer on their whiteboards. Next they find a quarter, then three quarters and finally a third. Repeat this for 24. Record the outcomes.

3. Further practice

Photocopiable page 253 'Fractions of numbers' is designed as an activity to assess how confidently children can find fractions of numbers. Provide counters for them to use if they wish. They should do this activity independently.

Solving problems

Most children should be able to successfully solve multiplication problems using partitioning and grouping.

Some children will not have made such progress and will need to focus on repeated addition for multiplication and use practical apparatus for grouping.

1. Check
63 Multiplying
64 Grouping

As you work through these activities observe the children to assess their confidence in multiplying using partitioning and grouping by counting on in multiples of the divisor using their fingers. Ask:
- How can we multiply 23 by 2? Is there another way?
- How many groups of 5 can I take out of 30? How do you know?

2. Assess

Show the children a number card between 1 and 50. Ask them to multiply it by five by partitioning and multiplying each number and then recombining. Repeat this for other number cards and numbers to multiply by. Next show a number card between 1 and 30 and ask the children to find out how many groups of five they can make and, if appropriate, what the remainder will be. Record the outcomes.

3. Further practice

Photocopiable page 254 'Multiplying and dividing' assesses the children's ability to solve problems involving these two operations.

Oral and mental starters

Measurement

55 Money

Have available a selection of coins, from 1p to £2. Show each coin in turn and ask the children to write on their whiteboard how many 1p coins they are worth, e.g. show a 20p coin, the children write 20. Then call out different numbers of each coin, for example, three 5p coins. The children write down how many 1p coins are the same as the number you call out. Next mix the coins and show, for example, a 10p coin and a 20p coin. The children write 30p.

57 Telling the time again

Give each child a small clock. Call out times for the children to find. These should be o'clock, quarter past, half past and quarter to times initially. Recap that there are 5 minutes from one hour number to the next. Ask the children to count round the clock in fives pointing at each hour number as they do. Begin at 12 with zero. Then ask them to find: 5 past 3, 20 past 7 and so on.

Fractions

56 Which fraction?

As you swing the pendulum from side to side, ask the children to count in halves from zero to ten and back. Repeat for quarters from zero to ten. Call out numbers for the children to halve and then quarter. Ask them to find three quarters of small numbers such as 4, 8, 12 and 16.

Multiplication and division

58 Times tables

Use the photocopiable sheets 'Spider charts for multiplying' and 'Spider charts for multiplying and dividing by 5' from the CD-ROM to practise the two-, five- and ten-times tables. Focus on each one in turn. Point to different numbers randomly. As you do the children call out the answers. Time them for two minutes. How many times can they go round the chart? Draw a spider chart for the three-times table on the board and repeat.

63 Multiplying

Call out some two-digit numbers below 50, or write them on the board. Ask the children to multiply them by two then five and ten. They should partition the numbers into tens and ones, multiply each number and then recombine.

64 Grouping

Write some numbers to 20 on the board. Ask the children to group them in twos, threes, fives and tens. Let them count on in multiples using their fingers. They write down how many groups there are and if appropriate any remainder, for example: *How many groups of three are there in 15? How many groups of five are there in 12?*

Addition and subtraction

59 Addition strategies

Tell the children that they will add numbers using mental calculation strategies. Write some two-digit additions on the board, for example 25 + 15, 36 + 19, 32 + 33. Point to them one at a time. Give the children about 30 seconds to find the answer. They should aim to use the most appropriate strategy, for example, finding numbers that total ten, bridging ten, sequencing, adding a multiple of ten and adjusting, near doubling. Invite children to explain their strategies.

60 Subtraction strategies

Tell the children that they will subtract numbers using mental calculation strategies. Write some two-digit subtractions on the board, for example: 36 − 19, 32 − 28, 67 − 23. Point to them one at a time. Give the children about 30 seconds to find the answer. They should aim to use the most appropriate strategy, for example sequencing, subtracting a multiple of ten and adjusting, counting on. Invite children to explain their strategies.

Measurement

65 More time differences

Ask the children to use a number line to find time differences, for example, 3 o'clock to half past 6. Focus on o'clock, quarter past, half past and quarter to times initially. Next ask them to work out how many minutes between such times as 5 past 4 and 25 past 4. You could put these into problem scenarios such as: *Sultan went for a run. He started his run at 5 past 2, he finished at 50 minutes past 2. For how long did he run?*

66 Days and months

Begin by reciting both the days of the week and months of the year in order. Give clues for days and months, for example the day after Tuesday, the month before June. The children put their hands up as soon as they know which you are looking for.

Name: _____   Date: _____

Which strategy would you use?

■ Add and then subtract these numbers together using the way you think is best.

57 + 11

> Show your strategy:

57 – 11

> Show your strategy:

43 + 27

> Show your strategy:

43 – 27

> Show your strategy:

45 + 25

> Show your strategy:

45 – 25

> Show your strategy:

41 + 39

> Show your strategy:

41 – 39

> Show your strategy:

I can decide which strategy to use when I add.

How did you do?

Telling the time (2)

■ Draw the times on these clocks.

1. 5 o'clock

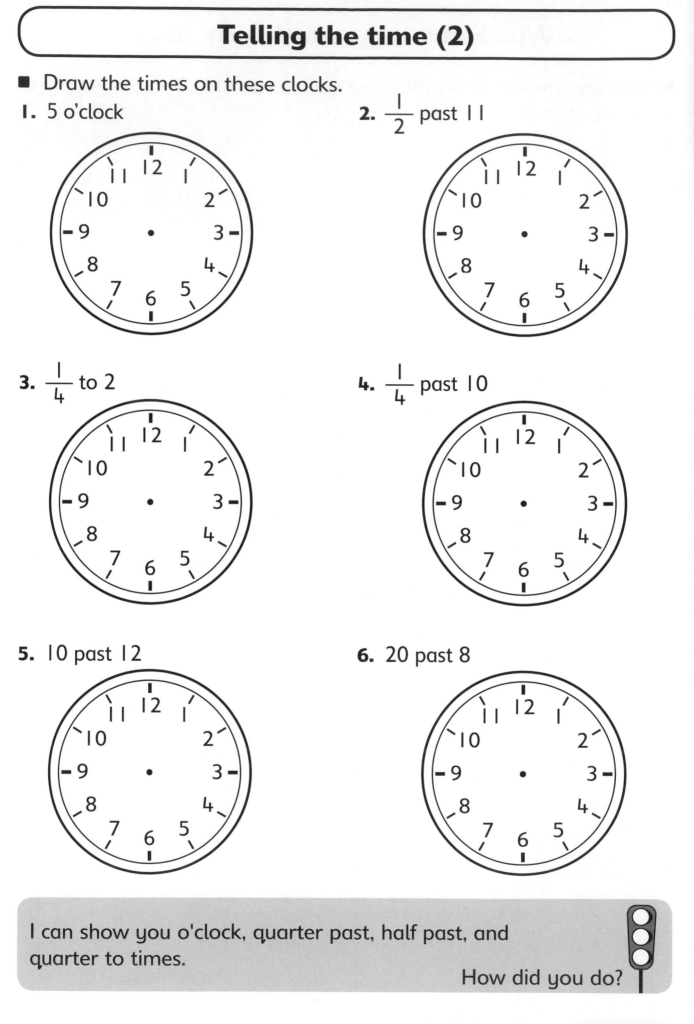

2. $\frac{1}{2}$ past 11

3. $\frac{1}{4}$ to 2

4. $\frac{1}{4}$ past 10

5. 10 past 12

6. 20 past 8

I can show you o'clock, quarter past, half past, and quarter to times.

How did you do?

Fractions of numbers

- Find the fractions of the numbers.

$\dfrac{1}{2}$ of 14

$\dfrac{1}{4}$ of 24

$\dfrac{1}{4}$ of 16

$\dfrac{3}{4}$ of 12

$\dfrac{3}{4}$ of 20

$\dfrac{1}{3}$ of 24

$\dfrac{1}{3}$ of 21

$\dfrac{1}{2}$ of 40

$\dfrac{1}{2}$ of 18

$\dfrac{3}{4}$ of 28

I can find $\dfrac{1}{2}$, $\dfrac{1}{4}$, $\dfrac{3}{4}$ of 2-digit numbers.

How did you do?

Multiplying and dividing

1. Naomi had 3 boxes. In each box were 4 books. How many books did she have?	
2. Ruth baked 5 batches of 13 buns. How many buns did she bake altogether?	
3. Ivor the pet shop owner had 24 fish. He put them in bowls. There were 3 goldfish in a bowl. How many bowls did he have?	
4. Mrs Swede had 40 potatoes. She put them in bags. There were 10 potatoes in each bag. How many bags of potatoes did she have?	
5. Mrs Swede had 40 potatoes. She put them in bags. There were 10 potatoes in each bag. How many bags of potatoes did she have?	

I can solve multiplication and division problems.

How did you do?

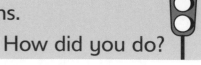

Year 2 vocabulary list

Number and place value

count in twos, count in fives, count in tens, continue, **multiple of,** nearest ten, one-digit number, place, **place value**, predict, represents, round, sequence, stands for, tens digit, two-digit number, 'teens' number

Addition and subtraction

add, addition, altogether, **bridging ten**, counting on, difference, exchange, find the difference, how many left, how many more, **inverse operation**, make, minus, more, partition, **partitioning,** plus, subtract, subtraction, sum, take away, **tens boundary**, total

Multiplication and division

array, column, divide, divided by, equal groups of, grouping, groups of, lots of, **multiple of,** multiplied by, multiply, **remainder**, repeated addition, repeated, subtraction, row, times

Fractions

divide, equal parts, **equivalent,** four quarters, fraction, group, one half, one quarter, one whole, part, share, **third,** three quarters, two halves, two quarters

Measurement

always, analogue clock/watch, capacity, Celsuis, Centigrade, centimetre, day, degrees, digital clock/watch, empty, fortnight, full, gram, half past, hands, heavy, hour, kilogram, length, light, litre, long, mass, measure, measuring jug, metre, millilitre, minute, month, months of the year: January, February, March, April, May, June, July, August, September, October, November, December, never, o'clock, often, quarter past, quarter to, second, sometimes, short, **temperature**, **thermometer**, timer, today, tomorrow, twice, usually, once, volume, week, weekend, weigh, year, yesterday

Geometry: properties of shapes

angle, apex. circle, cone, corner, cube, cuboid, curve, cylinder, edge, face, hexagon, octagon, pentagon, pyramid, quadrilateral, rectangle, side, sphere, square, symmetry, triangle, **triangular prism, vertex,** vertices

Geometry: position and direction

apart, **anticlockwise**, beside, between, centre, **clockwise**, corner, direction, edge, half turn, journey, left, middle, next to, opposite, over, pattern, position, quarter turn, right, right angle, straight line, whole turn

Data

block graph, count, label, list, most/least common/popular, pictogram, sort, set, represent, table

Year 2 equipment list

Number and place value

£1.50p, 20p, 10p, 5p, 2p and 1p coins, 100g and 50g weights, A2 paper, balance, scales, bead string, Blu-Tack®, counters, counting stick, dice, elastic bands, individual whiteboards, interlocking cubes, partitioning cards, pendulum, small string, bags or similar, straws

Addition and subtraction

10p and 1p coins, A2 paper, base 10 equipment, counters, counting apparatus, dice, individual whiteboards, interlocking cubes, straws, sugar paper

Multiplication and division

bags, coins, counters, counting apparatus, counting stick, cuboids, individual whiteboards, interlocking cubes, nine pairs of socks, playing cards, plastic bags (or similar), sugar paper, teddy bears, toy cars

Fractions

£1.50p, 10p and 1p coins, A3 paper (plain and coloured), A4 paper in two different colours, apples, card, chocolate bar with 2×4 sections, counters, glue, individual clocks, individual whiteboards, interlocking cubes, knife, paper copies of a clock face, paper with large squares, Plasticine®, sandwich, scissors, strips of paper 3cm wide

Measurement

5kg bag of potatoes, 1kg bag of sugar, 1p, 2p, 5p, 10p, 20p, 50p, £1 and £2 coins, ½l, 1l and 2l bottles of water, 30cm rulers, 1 kg, 100g and 50g weights, A3 paper, bucket, bucket balance, class clock, containers, cup, dial scales, glue, kitchen weighing scales, litre bottles, measuring jugs, metre stick, modelling material in red, green, orange and yellow, packet of crisps, pictures of different types of scales, measuring jug, saucepan, scissors, small clocks, sticky tape, water

Geometry: properties of shape

3D shapes: spheres, cones, cylinders, cubes, cuboids, square-based pyramids, triangular prism, 3D objects, classroom objects that are shaped like a: sphere, cone, cylinder, cube, A4 paper, A3 paper, card, counters, feely bag, glue, individual whiteboards, Plasticine®, scissors, sticky tape, string

Geometry: position and direction

class analogue clock, coloured pencils, counters, counting toys, dice, floor robot, individual whiteboards, individual small clocks, sugar paper, toy car

Statistics

A1 paper (plain or squared), A3 paper (plain or squared), coloured marker pens, counters, counting toys (such as bears), dice, individual whiteboards, interlocking cubes (white, pink, yellow and brown), large pieces of sugar paper, sticky notes